CAMBRIDGE
CHECKPOINTS
2016 – 18

HSC Legal Studies

- Practice questions arranged by topic
- Past examination questions up to 2014
- Suggested responses included
- Study cards for revision

Paul Milgate

CAMBRIDGE
UNIVERSITY PRESS

477 Williamstown Road, Port Melbourne, VIC 3207, Australia

Cambridge University Press is part of the University of Cambridge.

It furthers the University's mission by disseminating knowledge in the pursuit of education, learning and research at the highest international levels of excellence.

www.cambridge.edu.au
Information on this title: www.cambridge.org/9781107561908

© Paul Milgate 2015

Cover image © Shutterstock.com/Jovan Mandic

First published 2015

Printed in Australia by Ligare Pty Ltd

A Cataloguing-in-Publication entry is available from the catalogue of the National Library of Australia at www.nla.gov.au

ISBN 978-1-107-56190-8 Paperback

Additional resources for this publication at www.cambridge.edu.au/hsccheckpoints

Table of contents

Introduction

Congratulations on choosing to continue with Legal Studies as a part of your pattern of study in the Higher School Certificate.

The rights that people enjoy within democratic societies can at times become eroded when governments and citizens become apathetic about their freedoms and liberties. Legal Studies will allow you to explore the power vested in our democratic institutions and wielded by our elected leaders. It explores issues that are fundamental to our way of life. It will challenge the way you see the world.

Legal Studies will give you the confidence to engage with the world with a more open mind, a healthy cynicism and a willingness to participate in the social and political world in which we live.

As you negotiate the coursework you will derive your information from many sources, including statutes of Parliament, judgements handed down by the courts and reports and discussions of law and society in the media and on the internet. In the following pages, you will find useful advice on how to best use these sources.

Checkpoints follows the structure of the HSC course and the format of the new HSC that began in 2011. It is divided into three core areas of study:
• Section I: Crime
• Section II: Crime and Human Rights
• Section III: Options

Checkpoints provides past HSC questions (adapted to the new HSC), and similar questions with worked solutions. The answers, especially to the extended response questions, are not definitive but a suggested response to what has been asked.

Good luck!

Paul Milgate

How to use this book

As mentioned earlier, this book does not provide definitive responses especially to extended response questions. It offers suggested answers that should help orientate you to the type of content that may be used for particular questions. This text should not be a replacement for your own class notes or study notes that you have prepared. You should be looking to add to the suggestions in this text for a more comprehensive overview and critical analysis of the questions asked.

Rote-learning some of these responses to past questions is ill advised. Better candidates respond to the question asked of them during the exam and attempt to analyse the issues presented in each question, particularly the extended response. It should also be noted that Checkpoints is designed to help prepare you for the HSC exam and not other forms of assessment.

As the new HSC was examined in 2011, this text has drawn on past official Board of Studies questions from previous HSC exams. The multiple-choice Crime questions are not official, as Crime has not been examined in this style of objective question before.

NB: This book does not provide content or suggested examination answers for Options Indigenous Peoples or Shelter.

QuizMe App

The Cambridge QuizMe App, compatible with all internet-enabled devices, is available at www.cambridge.edu.au/hsccheckpointsapp. It features quizzes that are an extra revision tool for use throughout the year and are a fun add-on to your study experience.

Understanding the HSC Legal Studies syllabus

The syllabus for Legal Studies – Higher School Certificate is divided into four main objectives, three relating to your knowledge and understanding of the law and a fourth relating to your skills in investigating, analysing and communicating legal issues. There are a total of seven desirable outcomes for students that correspond to these objectives. The objectives and outcomes for the Higher School Certificate course are listed in the table at the end of this section.

The **themes and challenges** of the syllabus appear at the top of each beginning page for every topic. The themes and challenges represent the 'spirit' of the new syllabus and cannot be ignored. While they are to be incorporated into every topic you learn about, your teacher should also make specific reference to them by way of an overview as to how the material covered in each topic applies to each one. At the end of each topic you should be able to explicitly respond to these. It also should be noted that the themes and challenges may be used as questions, especially in the extended response questions.

The **outcomes** are presented as broad statements designed to measure your understanding in relation to the knowledge and skills objectives of the course. These outcomes will appear in the outline/task description of your HSC assessment tasks and are reflected in the marking criteria against which you will be assessed.

Outcomes P1 to P7 aim to develop your **knowledge and understanding** of the nature, dimensions and operation of the Australian legal system, in both a national and international context. You will also develop your knowledge and understanding of the Australian legal system's ability to deliver just and fair outcomes for individuals and society and you will have to make a judgement – using evidence based on the ability of the legal system to do so.

The **directive terms** such as evaluate, assess, explain and describe are some of the words that appear in the listed outcomes in bold-type (see the 'Glossary of key words' at www.boardofstudies.nsw.edu.au/syllabus_hsc/glossary_keywords.html).

Outcomes P8 to P10 are intended for you to demonstrate your ability to research and decide what is most useful and important, and your ability to communicate this information in a logical and coherent manner. It is important throughout the HSC course that your teacher critiques (gives you feedback on) your ability to communicate your ideas, and whether you are developing your ability to analyse and make judgements on how well the legal system is addressing a particular area of law and on legal information and issues.

Preparing for the HSC external examination

Sitting your HSC exams can be a nerve-wracking experience. Exams are designed to assess what you have learned, not what you can remember. This is an important thing to keep in mind when you are studying. Your teacher or an examiner will be looking for evidence that you can draw on what you know to develop and sustain an argument and reasoned point-of-view. This is why cramming the night or morning before a test or exam is never a sound strategy for success.

The revision tips and strategies outlined in this section will help you to develop a solid revision plan before a test or exam. Below are some additional and practical tips to help you deal with nerves and make the most of the exam experience.
- It's natural and normal to feel nervous before a test or exam. This is not necessarily an indication that you are poorly prepared or don't know enough. You want to do well and succeed – that's usually why nerves set in. The more prepared you feel, the easier it will be to conquer your anxiety.
- Make sure you know what is involved in the exam:
  - Where is it being held?
  - What time does it start?
  - How many questions will you have to answer?
  - How much time do you have to complete the exam?

These points are covered in detail in the next section – Format of the HSC Legal Studies external examination.
- Eat well and make sure that you get enough sleep. Drink plenty of water too – dehydration makes you tired and reduces concentration.
- Make sure that you have everything you need (e.g. pens, pencils etc.).
- Bring a watch so that you know how to allocate your time effectively.
- Read over the test or exam paper carefully. Look at the marks that are available for each question. Once you are permitted to pick up a pen/pencil, make a note of any

difficult elements and note down your initial thoughts on how you might address them.
- Use the information provided in the paper – there are often clues about the best way to answer the questions.
- Pace yourself and give yourself enough time to answer all questions to the best of your ability.
- Write as neatly as you can, as marking untidy writing is difficult and the teacher/examiner may miss something important.
- Try to allow 10 minutes at the end of the test/exam to read through what you have written and correct any obvious errors.
- Stay positive and don't panic!

Format of the HSC external examination

The HSC Legal Studies examination will consist of a written paper worth a combined total of 100 marks. The length of the paper is 3 hours working time and 5 minutes reading time. It is important you use the reading time well. Read the multiple-choice questions and scan the short answer and essay questions in Sections II and III. Make an initial choice as to which questions you may answer in Section III. Decide how you will use the reading time before you enter the examination room.

Section I: Core – Crime and Human Rights   20 marks
Section I of the exam will be made up of objective response (i.e. multiple-choice) questions. There will be objective response questions to the value of 20 marks:
- Questions to the value of 15 marks will be drawn from Crime.
- Questions to the value of 5 marks will be drawn from Human Rights.
Some of these questions may be based on, or refer to, stimulus materials.

NB: Suggested time to spend on this section is 20 minutes.

Section II: Core – Crime and Human Rights   30 marks
Section II of the exam is divided into two parts, Part A and Part B.

Part A: Human Rights   15 marks
- Part A contains short answer questions to the value of 15 marks.
- The questions may be in parts. There will be 3–4 items in total.
Some of these questions may be based on, or refer to, stimulus materials.

Part B: Crime   15 marks
- Part B contains one extended response question to the value of 15 marks.
- The expected length of response is around 4 examination writing booklet pages (approximately 600 words).
The question may be based on, or refer to, stimulus materials.

NB: Suggested time to spend on this section is 60 minutes.

Section III: Options   50 marks
Section III of the exam will contain seven extended response questions, one for each Option.

- You will need to answer 2 questions, each from a different Option.
- Each of the questions will have 2 alternatives (i.e. a OR b). You are only required to answer 1 alternative per question.
- Each question is worth 25 marks.
- The expected length of each response is around 8 examination writing booklet pages (approximately 1000 words).

NB: Suggested time to spend on this section is 100 minutes.

Different types of exam questions

Multiple-choice
It is usually a good idea to do the multiple-choice first. These items may stimulate your mind and get you ready to attack the more difficult parts of the question. This may not suit everyone.

The multiple-choice questions will be derived from part I and part II of the HSC course, Human Rights and Crime. Try the following approaches when answering the multiple-choice questions:

- Read the stem carefully and try to answer the question before you look at the alternatives.
- Read all the alternative answers carefully and try to eliminate the one or two that are obviously incorrect.
- If it looks as though more than one answer is correct, this may be the case. You have to find the answer that is the most correct.
- Carefully analyse the directive terms, phrases or concepts of the questions. What is being asked?
- Don't waste time on difficult questions. Leave them and come back to them.
- Spend a maximum of 1 minute per question.
- If all else fails – 'guesstimate'. Do not leave a question blank – 'None of the above' is usually a poor guess, and 'All of the above' is usually a good guess.

Short answer
The short answer questions will be worth 30 marks will also be derived from part I and part II of the HSC course, **Human Rights** and **Crime**. **Part A** of this section will be based on the Human Rights topic and totals 15 marks in the form of short answer questions.

A guide to maximising your marks in this section is to remember that you only need to write 2 lines for every 1 mark allocated. Use the space allocated in your answer booklet. There may be a lot of scope to go into great detail here but resist the urge. Again, answer the question succinctly and move on. The number of questions and the mark allocated to them will vary from year to year depending on the examination committee. Questions that have a mark range of 5 or more will more than likely ask for some degree of analysis but given the space provided, again, this has to be succinct.

NB: Remember you will need to have studied and prepared a contemporary human rights issue.

Part B of Section II will be ONE 15-mark extended response question that may or may not refer to stimulus from the **Crime** topic. Page 40 of the syllabus suggests that this response should be around 600 words. You may go over this, keeping in mind your timing for other parts of the question, but the key to success is threefold. Do I have a good recall of the course work, can I relate this directly to the question being asked, and lastly, can I sustain my analysis of the issues embedded in the question?

Options
At the beginning of Section III there will be 4 'dot-points' that state guidelines on which your response to each question in this section will be marked. These are:
- Demonstrate knowledge and understanding relevant to the question.
- Communicate using relevant legal terminology and concepts.
- Illustrate your answer with relevant examples such as legislation, cases, media reports and treaties.
- Present a sustained, logical and cohesive response.

Again, time should be allocated to planning your answer in terms of the points you wish to make. Organise these into a logical sequence.

The 2 questions that you will have a choice of completing will ask you to carry out higher order tasks such as evaluate the effectiveness, assess the place of the law, discuss, apply, etc.

Page 40 of the syllabus recommends that the length of this response should be around 1000 words. Again, you may write more but the advice given on answering the Crime extended response applies here as well.

Glossary of key words

Syllabus outcomes, objectives, performance bands and examination questions have key words that state what students are expected to be able to do. A glossary of key words has been developed to help provide a common language and consistent meaning in the Higher School Certificate documents. Using this glossary will help students and teachers understand what is expected in responses to examinations and assessment tasks. To view these key words go to:
www.boardofstudies.nsw.edu.au/syllabus_hsc/glossary_keywords.html. It should be noted that recent past examinations have diverged from the directive terms but ultimately you will need to assess, evaluate and critique the law to respond to higher order questions.

Section I: Core – Crime and Human Rights

Chapter 1

Crime

Summary of key points

The nature of crime

A crime can be defined as any conduct which violates the rights of the community at large, punishable by a recognised criminal sanction upon proof of guilt in a criminal proceeding initiated and presented by officers of the Crown or its agencies (Marantelli, S, Tikotin, C. *The Australian Legal Dictionary*). Put another way, a crime is an act or omission of duty that results in harm to society, which is punishable by the state (Hawthorn, R, Champion, J., *Problems of the Criminal Justice System*).

What constitutes a crime in one society may vary in another society because all crimes are a reflection of the 'public morality' at the time. As the values of a society shift and evolve, so does the criminal law. The same reason is applied to why punishments for similar offences vary from culture to culture.

In attempting to investigate, prosecute and punish criminal offences, the state attempts to balance the tension between the rights of the community and those of individuals, as is evident in sections two to four of the topic outline on pages 16–19 of the syllabus.

In order for a crime to be committed, there must be present two fundamental elements. These are:

- The physical act of committing a criminal offence. This is called the *actus reus* (a Latin term meaning **guilty act**). Another aspect of the guilty act that must be established is **causation.** Apart from establishing that the act occurred, the prosecution must also show that there is a link between the act and the crime. The act must be **at least the substantial cause of the crime**.
- The mental element, namely the guilty mind of the offender or the intention to commit a crime. This is called the *mens rea* (a Latin term meaning **guilty mind**).

Some crimes (due to the reason that they are regulatory offences) do not require the mental element of *mens rea* in order for the state to prove they have been committed. These are called **strict liability** offences. The logic behind this is that if the state had to prove a mental element to these crimes, the criminal justice system would grind to a halt.

Crimes can also be defined by the nature of the act committed and the mental aspect required to be present at the commission of the crime.

Some of these categories are:
- Offences against the person
- Offences against the sovereign
- Economic offences
- Drug offences

- Driving offences
- Public order offences
- Preliminary crimes.

All of the crimes listed are also categorised according to the seriousness of the offence. These are referred to as **summary** or **indictable** offences.

- **Indictable offences:** These are concerned with the more serious offences. Here the accused is first charged in the local court. If a *prima facie* case exists (if there is sufficient evidence to warrant a case), then a trial takes place before a judge and jury. Some examples are breaking and entering, and murder.
- **Summary offences:** These are less serious offences. They are tried directly by a magistrate of the local court and include minor theft and vandalism as well as matters under the *Summary Offences Act 1988* (NSW). Some of the offences outlined in the Act include minor theft or drink driving offences.

The law will distinguish between the various roles a person may play before, during and after the commission of a crime. These are referred to as:

- **Principal in the first degree** – refers to the person who actually carries out the crime. An example would be a person holding a gun and threatening the attendant in an armed robbery.
- **Principal in the second degree** – refers to a person who assists in the commission of a crime. They are present during the actual crime but are not the main participant. Usually referred to as an accessory.
- **Accessory before the fact** – refers to a person who helps other people commit a crime by planning or preparing for the criminal act. They are not present at the time the criminal act is committed.
- **Accessory after the fact** – refers to a person who helps criminals after they have committed a crime but is not present during the commission of it, nor aware of it beforehand.

There are many reasons as to why some people do not comply with the law and find themselves committing a crime. Some of the main reasons are the differential association theory, economic factors, political factors and self-interest.

One of the main problems in many jurisdictions is that not enough resources are targeted at preventing crime. Crime prevention strategies generally fall into two categories:

- **Situational prevention:** This applies to two different sets of schools – urban planning/architectural design and focused prevention. This aims to change the environment in which crimes may be committed.
- **Social prevention:** This focuses on values and discipline systems that influence whether people commit crimes. It is possible to generalise as to which people may be more at risk of committing crimes and thereby support them to act within the boundaries of the community.

The criminal investigation process

The reporting of crime will usually put into motion the machinery of the criminal justice system. Nearly all crimes are reported by the general public. If it is serious enough or if the resources available warrant it, the police will investigate a reported crime.

The police have a number of powers to carry out the investigation of a crime. Most of the NSW Police powers are found in the *Law Enforcement (Powers and Responsibilities) Act 2002* (NSW) (LEPAR). There is other legislation that outlines additional powers generally in respect to search and seizure.

The main powers that the police have are those around charge and arrest, use of warrants, use of electronic surveillance, and collection of DNA evidence for the interrogation and detention of suspects.

At a federal level, the Australian Federal Police also have similar powers to carry out investigations involving Commonwealth matters. Over the last 20 years there has been a general increase in the powers at the disposal of the police. Anti-terrorism legislation at a state and federal level has seen some erosion of individual rights for the benefit of the community. Being able to hold for a prolonged period of time without charges is one worrying development.

The issues to be critiqued in this section of work are whether or not the balance of police powers against the rights of an accused person is well weighted. The above powers should be assessed in this light.

The criminal trial process

The adversary system of trial involves adversaries, the prosecution and the defence doing battle in the courtroom. Each party presents their side of the case before an independent third party, who then decides the outcome of the case.

In essence, the features of the system include a contest between two adversaries, with each side being responsible for their case, the independence of the judge and jury, the conduct of the contest according to strict legal rules, the finality of the judge's decision unless subject to appeal and the presumption that all are equal before the court.

The jurisdiction of the criminal courts will depend on the seriousness of the offence. Minor matters are heard in the local court; more serious matters such as aggravated assault will be heard in the District Court and the most serious crimes such as murder are heard in the Supreme Court. All courts, except the local court, have appellate jurisdiction to hear appeals from lower courts. The highest of these in NSW is the NSW Court of Criminal Appeal. Criminal matters may also end up in the High Court of Australia on appeal.

The adversary system has specialised people who work in the courts, representing the state or the accused. In the lower courts magistrates preside whereas from the District Court up a judge hears matters. Lawyers, who can be either barristers or solicitors, will represent the defendant or the Director of Public Prosecutions.

Before a matter is commenced, the accused must enter a plea of guilty or not guilty.

Plea bargaining is sometimes mentioned as a solution to trying to resolve the lengthy delays that are evident in the criminal trial process. This generally can occur in three ways.
- If the accused is facing several charges in relation to the same crime, the court may drop some charges if the defendant pleads guilty to some of the remaining charges. This is called **charge bargaining**. This may also occur when the accused agrees to assist the police in other matters under investigation.

- The charge may be reduced to a lesser one if the accused pleads guilty. For example, murder might be reduced to manslaughter.
- In some courts a **sentence indication hearing** may be held, in which a judge will indicate the kind of sentence the accused might expect if they plead guilty.

There is no implied right to legal representation, although the High Court in *Dietrich v The Queen 1992* provides for a limited right in serious indictable offences. Accused who cannot afford a lawyer may be eligible for legal aid if they pass a means test. The merit test is not applied in criminal matters. Most people in the community would fail the means test.

In criminal trials, the burden of proof is on the state and the standard of proof is 'beyond a reasonable doubt'. There are also strict rules about the presentation of evidence and its admissibility outlined under the *Evidence Act*. All evidence is able to be tested during cross examination where both sides can question witnesses about the evidence they have put before the court.

At times the accused will argue a defence to the charges against them. **Defences** are used by an accused to reduce or admonish their criminal liability. It must be in the form of a pleading recognised by law. The consequences of a successful defence vary. There are a range of defences open to the defendant but they are categorised into two main types:
- **Complete or absolute defence** – a justification that excuses the defendant's action and results in an acquittal. An example is self-defence.
- **Partial or qualified defence** – an excuse for the defendant's action that might result in a reduction in the charge and/or punishment. An example is provocation to a murder charge.

A **jury** is a panel of citizens selected off the electoral role. After having heard the evidence before them and having the judge sum up the facts of the case and the law, the jury decides the guilt or innocence of an accused person in an indictable criminal matter. NSW until recently had unanimous verdicts, that is, 12 out of 12 jurors agreeing on the verdict. The *Jury Amendment (Verdicts) Act 2006* (NSW) amended the *Jury Act 1997* (NSW) to allow for majority verdicts of 11:1 or 10:1 after a reasonable time for deliberation has passed (being not less than eight hours) and where the court is satisfied that it is unlikely the jury will reach a unanimous verdict.

Sentencing and punishment
There are a number of statutory and judicial guidelines that judges are bound to follow when passing sentence. Some of these are explained below.

The *Crimes Act 1900* (NSW) and other statutes set out maximum sentences for certain crimes, and judges are not permitted to exceed the maximum sentence. However, judges can impose a sentence less than the maximum due to the factors discussed above. Generally, the Crimes Act allows judges a wide degree of discretion to find a suitable sentence depending on the circumstances of each matter before them.

However, Parliament can and does limit judicial discretion through legislation that imposes certain restrictions on the sentences handed down. Some critics argue this is an erosion of the rule of law and a blurring of the lines of the separation of powers. Some of these Acts are as follows.

The *Crimes Sentencing Procedure Act 1999* (NSW) contains the provisions for sentencing first established under the *Sentencing Act 1989* (NSW), also called the 'Truth in Sentencing Act'. This was the first in a series of legislations to restrict the discretion of the judiciary in sentencing by providing that:

- A prisoner may not be released on parole until they have served three quarters of the total sentence. This increased prison time spent.
- Any sentence of six months or less is fixed with no parole.
- If a judge sentences someone to life imprisonment it will mean that they will never be released except in exceptional circumstances.
- **Remissions** may be granted, taking time off the original sentence for good behaviour. Prisoners can also receive extra time in prison for misbehaviour.

The *Criminal Procedures Amendment Act 1986* (NSW) was amended in 1998 to enable the NSW Attorney General to ask the court and the judge to give a **guideline sentence** for a certain criminal offence. This means that the sentence a judge gives in a particular case is the sentence that would be given for all similar offences.

The *Crimes (Sentencing Procedures) Amendment (Standard Minimum Sentencing) Act 2002* (NSW) was passed to ensure tougher sentences for very serious offences such as murder, gang rape, aggravated robbery, etc. The Act provides for mandatory minimum sentences for these offences, e.g. 15 years' imprisonment for gang rape. This Act has removed judges' discretion to make sentencing decisions for these offences.

The *Crimes (Sentencing Procedure) Amendment Act 2007* (NSW) has added standard non-parole periods of 25 years for a number of offences, such as murder of a victim under 18 years of age.

The purposes of punishment are traditionally represented by the following:

- **Deterrence** is designed so that the punishment handed down will deter the offender and/or the general public from committing such a crime again. There are two types of deterrence: general and specific.
- **Rehabilitation** aims to change the behaviour of the offender to that which society deems acceptable. It focuses on the future behaviour of convicted individuals and is highly beneficial to the individual and society as a whole.
- **Retribution** is the legal principle that functions upon the old Hebrew rule 'an eye for an eye'. Retribution is the idea that an offender should suffer a punishment that corresponds with their culpability; exact retribution is where the punishment is the direct equivalent of the crime committed.
- **Incapacitation** is the most direct way of protecting society from criminals. The aim is to protect society by imprisoning (in a prison or through home detention) an offender so that they are unable to commit further offences (apart from those committed inside prison).
- **Re-integrative shaming** encourages offenders to confront their offences and experience shame due to the harm they have brought about for others. Examples can include youth justice conferences and circle sentencing for Indigenous offenders.

When sentencing, the magistrate or judge will obviously consider the traditional objectives or purposes of punishment as outlined above. In addition to this the judge will also consider the **circumstances of the offence** and **the circumstances of the offender**.

The judge will also consider if there are any **aggravating** or **mitigating circumstances** surrounding the commission of the crime.

Victim Impact Statements (VISs) can be made by the victim or the victim's family. Proponents of VISs argue that they provide an important opportunity for family members to express their anger and grief in a public forum and that it can be a confronting experience for perpetrators of violence, acting on the principle of deterrence in sentencing theory.

Once a sentence is handed down, the defence and the prosecution may appeal the sentence. The defence may appeal the harshness of the sentence and the prosecution may appeal the leniency of the sentence.

The types of penalties that a magistrate or judge may hand down are varied. Some punishments are suitable for particular types of offences and all vary in the manner in which they help achieve the purposes of punishment.

Fines are usually ordered for minor summary offences; however, regardless of an upper limit, fines can discriminate against poorer individuals, whose ability to pay is significantly less than someone of a higher economic standing.

Good Behaviour Bonds are granted when an offender agrees to be on good behaviour for a specified time and may have to comply with certain conditions. Good behaviour bonds usually last for no more than three years. Failure to comply results in the offender being liable for further punishment such as a fine or a jail sentence.

A **probation order** requires an offender to keep good behaviour, stay in contact with the probation officer and commit no new offences.

Community Service Orders (or CSOs) require the offender to perform unpaid community work in his or her leisure time. A CSO specifies the number of hours the offender needs to perform, but there is a statutory maximum of 500.

Home detention is a relatively new form of punishment which requires offenders to wear a bracelet or anklet which must be attached to a phone line when the supervising officer rings or sends a signal. If the bracelet or anklet is not attached, the supervising officer visits the offender's home to ensure the offender has not breached the conditions of his or her home detention.

A **Community Correction Order** replaced periodic detention. It combines a more intensive form of community supervision with participation in community or educational programs. A CCO would be a term of imprisonment ordered to be served in the community subject to compliance with a number of conditions such as a curfew or residential requirement, participation in rehabilitation or educational programs, performance of community work and such other requirements as the individual would require. As such it could involve aspects of home detention and Community Service Orders as they applied previously.

When the state believes that a person has acquired assets through the proceeds of crime it will confiscate these unless that person can prove how those assets were acquired. This is called **forfeiture of assets** and is provided for under the *Criminal Assets Recovery Act*

1990 (NSW). In 2010 the NSW Government reversed the onus of proof onto the person suspected of acquiring the assets through the proceeds of crime.

The harshest punishment an Australian court can hand down is **imprisonment.** Prisons in Australia are classified so as to separate the most violent criminals from the remaining prison population and to make sure the most dangerous criminals are kept in the most secure prisons.

A **diversionary program** is a court program set up to divert certain offenders away from more traditional criminal processes in the hope that they can be rehabilitated and encouraged not to reoffend. The programs are only available for particular offences or types of offenders.

Recent developments in the law have introduced **alternative forms** of sentencing, targeting particular types of offenders. Like diversionary programs, they attempt to combat some of the issues associated with recidivism and more traditional forms of sentencing. They include:

- **Circle sentencing**, a new method of deciding punishment for Indigenous offenders. It has proven to be effective, in that fewer offenders are reoffending. The **circle** consists of elders, victims, the prosecutor and a magistrate. Circle sentencing is seen by Indigenous offenders as being more legitimate because the penalties imposed by the circle are **not** perceived as **'white man's law'**, but rather as condemnation of their behaviour by their own community.
- **Restorative justice**, another alternative to traditional sentencing methods that involves bringing together the offender and the victim of the offence. It offers the chance for the offender to take responsibility for their actions and the impact they have had on others, while giving victims a voice and an opportunity to confront the offender and work out a way to repair the damage done.

After an offender has been sentenced to a custodial punishment, there are particular **post-sentencing** matters that must be addressed. These include a **security classification**, whether the offender needs or requests **protective custody** and **parole.**

Developments over the last 10 years have expanded post-sentencing considerations to include **preventative detention** and **continuing detention**. This is possibly the harshest form of sentence. It is also the most controversial. **Preventative detention** involves imprisonment of a person for some type of future harm that they 'may' commit. The person is detained in custody without actually having committed or being found guilty of any offence. The purpose may be incapacitation of a person considered to constitute a significant threat to community safety, or rehabilitation of the offender. **Continuing detention** involves keeping the offender in prison after they have served their sentence because they are considered a risk to the community.

There are both state and federal databases of sexual offenders who have been convicted of certain sexual offences. The Australian National Child Offenders Register (ANCOR) and the NSW Child Protection Registry are web-based systems designed to assist police with the registering and case management of adults who commit sexual offences against children. As established under the *Child Protection (Offenders Registration) Act 2000* (NSW), persons convicted of a nominated violent or sexual offence against a child are required to register at the local police station within 28 days of sentencing or release from custody, or after being found guilty of a registered offence in another jurisdiction.

Young offenders

The *Children's (Criminal Proceedings) Act 1987* (NSW) clearly outlines the **age of criminal responsibility**. It states, 'It shall be conclusively presumed that no child who is under the age of 10 years can be guilty of an offence'. This is the same in all criminal jurisdictions.

Children are classified as 'vulnerable persons' under the *Law Enforcement (Powers and Responsibilities) Act 2002* (LEPAR). As such, when it comes to the rights of children being arrested or questioned, the Act differentiates between them and adults.

Children must have an **'interview friend'** present when they are questioned by police and like adults they must be **cautioned** about what they may say. Arrest should be used as a last resort, not as a method to further the investigation. It is also recommended that children be held no longer than two hours while they are being questioned.

Once a child is under arrest, the police (after a period of interrogation) may wish to take fingerprints, photographs or palm prints of the child. If the child is under 14 years, an officer of or above the rank of Sergeant has to apply to the Children's Court to decide if this is necessary.

If a matter against a child or young person is not proved, then the court must give notice to the parents/guardians of the accused so that they can request the court to have any fingerprints, photographs or palm prints destroyed.

The Children's Court will only hear less serious offences by children and any committal proceedings involving children alleged to have committed a serious offence.

When courts sentence children they differentiate these cases from adult ones. In the case of *R v GDP* (1991) 53A Crim R 112, the court of Criminal Appeal held that sentencing principles for children are different to those for adults. In this case, had the offender been an adult then the objectives of retribution and general deterrence would have pointed to a prison term of some length. It went on to say that with an offender this young, rehabilitation must be a primary consideration.

The exception to this is when the court considers the child to have engaged in **'grave adult behaviour'**. In this situation the courts will make little allowance for the defendant's age when, as mentioned above, the offender conducts themselves like an adult, there is a serious pattern of offending and the offender is close to the legal age of adulthood.

Under section 33A of the *Children's (Criminal Proceedings) Act 1987* (NSW) the Children's Court, upon a finding of guilt, can:
- dismiss the charge, or dismiss with a caution
- adjourn the matter from a finding of guilt for up to 12 months to assess the individual's prospects in respect to rehabilitation
- release on a bond not exceeding two years
- impose a fine not exceeding the maximum prescribed for the offence, or $1000, whichever is less
- release on probation not exceeding two years
- impose a community service order of up to 250 hours and of only up to a 100 hours if the person is under 16

- release on a condition that the young person complies with a youth justice conference outcome plan determined at a conference held under the Young Offenders Act
- impose a control order in a detention centre for a period no longer than two years.

In NSW the primary diversionary method **(alternatives to court)** used by the courts with respect to juvenile offenders is provided for by the *Young Offenders Act 1997 (NSW)*. The Young Offenders Act became operational in NSW in 1998. Its aim is to provide diversionary measures for young offenders as alternatives to court appearances. The Act only applies to summary offences and those indictable offences that can be dealt with summarily.

Under the Act, children and young offenders who have committed an offence covered in the Act may proceed through a three-tiered system of diversionary processes – **warnings**, **cautions** and **youth justice conferences**.

International crime
International crime can be said to be any act or omission that has international consequences on nation states, their citizens and international law. There are two broad categories of international crime and these are **crimes against the international community** and **transnational crimes**.

Crimes against the international community are in breach of natural law by the very nature of the types of acts committed on groups of people in various communities throughout the world. The violence perpetrated by crimes against the international community is, as James Catano said, 'the gravest conceivable crimes', and therefore they require international attention. Examples of crimes against the international community follow.

- **Genocide** involves acts that have the intention of destroying 'all or part of a national ethnic, racial or religious group'. According to article six of the Rome Statute, genocide can take the following forms. It can be perpetrated in a number of ways including outright murder, inflicting conditions to bring about the loss of life, methods to prevent births and the systematic rape of women to dilute the ethnicity of a group. It can also involve the destruction of cultural identity through policies of assimilation, or the imposition of a language or religion upon a group. Genocide can also be implemented through the transferring of children from one group to another 'preferred' one.
- **Crimes against humanity** consist of knowledge of a sanctioned widespread or systematic attack against any civilian population.
- **War crimes** are constituted by a breach of the rules of conflict as outlined by the Geneva Conventions and any other customary rules of conflict that exist. War crimes can include things such as the unnecessary destruction of towns, villages and or other infrastructure without any military importance; murder; and rape.

Transnational crimes are crimes that cross international borders. Traversing international borders is an essential requirement for the commission of these crimes. Transnational crimes can also be crimes committed in one country that may have significant negative implications for other countries. Some transnational crimes have been around for centuries, whereas others are relatively new due to the rapid development of communications technology that has made the world interconnected.

The main ways in which the international community deals with international crimes follow.

- **Extradition** is the process of the legal surrender of a fugitive to the jurisdiction of another state, country or government for trial. It is used in situations where an offender is not residing in the state or country where they have been accused, or convicted, of a criminal offence. A judicial officer in the state or country where the criminal is found sends the criminal to the state or country in which they carried out the offence so that the offender can be dealt with.
- **The International Criminal Court (ICC)** can try people under the Rome Statute for committing crimes against the international community.
- **Interpol** and the cooperation of policing agencies around the world are used especially in the case of transnational crimes.

Limitations in dealing with international crime

The ease with which some transnational crimes are committed, coupled with the sophisticated measures taken to avoid detection, highlight some of the problematic areas of enforcing the law in this area. Authorities around the world are having to combat identity fraud, internet crime, paedophilia rings, and the trafficking and smuggling of people and contraband, to name some. Technology is a two-edged sword in that the reliance and convenience that the world enjoys is a 'Trojan horse' within our communities.

The effectiveness of the international community in dealing with crimes of genocide and crimes against humanity is mixed. Obviously a permanent court such as the ICC is powerful symbolically. It sends the message that despotic leaders can no longer hide behind the immunity of their own sovereignty and commit despicable acts against their own citizens.

Sample multiple-choice questions

Question 1
Of the following statements, which best defines what the nature of crime is?
(A) An act or omission that harms society
(B) An act or omission that harms society and the people in it
(C) An act or omission that harms society and is punishable by the state
(D) An act or omission that harms society in the context of the public morality of the time

[1 mark]

Question 2
The physical element of a crime refers to which of the following?
(A) The ratio feature
(B) The mental and physical elements combined
(C) The *mens rea*
(D) The *actus reus* which includes causation

[1 mark]

Question 3
The difference between an indictable offence and a summary offence is best reflected by which of the following statements?
(A) Indictable offences usually involve juries whereas summary offences are matters only heard on appeal.
(B) Summary offences must be committed first, followed by a more serious/indictable offence.
(C) Indictable offences are serious matters, whereas summary offences are minor matters.

(D) Summary matters are heard in the District Court, whereas indictable offences are heard in the Supreme Court.

[1 mark]

Question 4

The difference between voluntary manslaughter and involuntary manslaughter is most accurately reflected in which of the following?

(A) Voluntary manslaughter involves killing with intent with mitigating circumstances, whereas involuntary manslaughter involves killing without intent but with some recklessness.

(B) Voluntary manslaughter involves killing with intent, whereas involuntary manslaughter involves killing without intent.

(C) Voluntary manslaughter involves the accused admitting their guilt, whereas involuntary manslaughter involves the accused denying their guilt.

(D) Voluntary manslaughter involves the *mens rea*, whereas involuntary manslaughter involves the *actus reus*.

[1 mark]

Question 5

One well-recognised crime prevention strategy is situational prevention. Which of the following is a feature of this?

(A) Security and environmental prevention strategies

(B) Demographic prevention strategies

(C) Alternative dispute resolution methods

(D) Situational conflict resolution

[1 mark]

Question 6

When applying for a search warrant, the police must give substantial reasons or evidence to the magistrate to justify the use of the warrant. Once obtained the warrant must contain which of the following information?

(A) The reason why the premises are being searched and what articles are being searched for

(B) The reason the premises are being searched

(C) The items being searched for and the people suspected of possessing the items

(D) The items being searched for and the date the warrant is valid until

[1 mark]

Question 7

Which of the following statements best reflects correct police procedures?

(A) The police must accompany the person to the police station.

(B) A person does not have to go to a police station unless they are under arrest.

(C) The police are able to question suspects.

(D) The police can interrogate a suspect until they have enough evidence to lay a charge.

[1 mark]

Question 8

The *Anti-Terrorism Act (No. 2) 2005* (Cth) has been criticised for which of the following reasons?

(A) It has failed to detect any terrorist networks in Australia.

(B) It has increased police powers in respect of electronic surveillance.

(C) It allows the police to detain a suspect for an indefinite period without being charged with an offence.

(D) All of the above

[1 mark]

Question 9

A known offender is not released after his sentence has been served.
What type of detention is this?
(A) Home
(B) Periodic
(C) Weekend
(D) Continued

[BOS 2012]   [1 mark]

Question 10

Which of the following statements is correct in reference to the burden and standard of proof in criminal matters?
(A) The burden of proof is on the plaintiff and the standard of proof is 'beyond a reasonable doubt'.
(B) The burden of proof is on the state and the standard of proof is 'on the balance of probabilities'.
(C) The burden of proof is on the victim and the standard of proof is 'beyond a reasonable doubt'.
(D) The burden of proof is on the state and the standard of proof is 'beyond a reasonable doubt'.

[1 mark]

Question 11

Which of the following would be a complete defence to a crime?
(A) Substantial impairment of responsibility, provocation, self-defence and insanity
(B) Insanity, self-defence, automatism and honest mistake
(C) Substantial impairment of responsibility, provocation and insanity
(D) Provocation, self-defence and honest mistake

[1 mark]

Question 12

Of the following statements, which of the following is the most accurate in respect to unanimous verdicts in NSW?
(A) Majority verdicts are allowed where it is unlikely the jury will reach a unanimous verdict after a certain period of time.
(B) Unanimous verdicts are to be used for all serious indictable offences.
(C) Unanimous verdicts are no longer used in NSW.
(D) Majority verdicts not unanimous verdicts can be used when a juror dies or gets ill in the middle of a trial.

[1 mark]

Question 13

Which of the following statements is true in respect to the discretion of the judiciary when sentencing a guilty person?
(A) Judges have wide-ranging powers of discretion.
(B) Judges can only consider past criminal behaviour.
(C) The NSW Parliament has increasingly eroded the discretion of judges.
(D) The NSW Parliament can overrule a sentence passed down by a judge.

[1 mark]

Question 14

Which of the following statements is correct in respect to guilty pleas?
(A) There is no trial.
(B) The accused is immediately sentenced.

(C) The state presents its evidence to the court.
(D) The accused may get a reduction on their sentence.

[1 mark]

Question 15
When a judge is deciding the punishment of an offender, which of the following represents the main objectives they may be trying to achieve?
(A) Rehabilitation, retribution, reintegration into the community and incapacitation
(B) Retribution, rehabilitation, deterrence and incapacitation
(C) Retribution, rehabilitation, capital punishment and incapacitation
(D) Rehabilitation, retribution, behaviour modification and incapacitation

[1 mark]

Question 16
An accused is considered innocent until proven guilty. Which of the following best reflects this principle?
(A) Bail
(B) Remand
(C) Suspended sentence
(D) No conviction recorded
[BOS 2012]

[1 mark]

Question 17
What is the purpose of a committal hearing?
(A) To charge the accused
(B) To establish the state's case
(C) To enter into charge negotiation
(D) To empanel a jury from the electoral roll
[BOS 2012]

[1 mark]

Question 18
Which of the following most accurately reflects the main considerations in respect to post-sentencing?
(A) Protective custody, parole, security reclassification, continued detention, deportation and sexual offenders registration
(B) Protective custody, parole, security classification, continued detention, deportation and sexual offenders registration
(C) Protective custody, parole, security classification, continued detention and sexual offenders registration
(D) Protective custody, parole, security classification, retrospective detention, deportation and sexual offenders registration

[1 mark]

Question 19
Prior to handing down a sentence a judge will take into account factors that will influence the sentence given. Which of the following is NOT one of these factors?
(A) Mitigating factors
(B) Aggravating factors
(C) Nature of the offence and the offender
(D) Parole considerations

[1 mark]

Question 20
Which of the following most accurately defines the concept of *doli incapax*?
(A) The age when children can leave home
(B) The age of criminal liability
(C) The legal age for children to enter the workplace
(D) The age at which children are incapable of appearing in court
[1 mark]

Question 21
Which of the following best describes what an 'interview friend' is?
(A) A youth police liaison person designated to sit through the interview of a suspected juvenile offender
(B) A friend nominated by the accused designated to sit through the interview of a suspected juvenile offender
(C) A parent, guardian or lawyer designated to sit through the interview of a suspected juvenile offender
(D) All of the above
[1 mark]

Question 22
Which court hears serious indictable offences committed by young offenders?
(A) The Supreme court
(B) The Children's Court
(C) The court with original jurisdiction for the particular crime committed
(D) The local court
[1 mark]

Question 23
Under the *Children's (Criminal Proceedings) Act 1987* (NSW), which of the following guidelines in regards to sentencing are accurate?
(A) Detention should be used as a last resort.
(B) Detention should not be used because young offenders have a greater chance of rehabilitation.
(C) From the ages of 10 to 14 detention cannot be used.
(D) It is possible to hand down heavier sentences than those given to adults because studies have revealed 'deterrence' is more effective with young offenders.
[1 mark]

Question 24
Which of the following describes the main legal response to dealing with crimes involving mass atrocities?
(A) ICJ
(B) The United Nations
(C) The International Court of Arbitration
(D) ICC
[1 mark]

Question 25
Of the following statements, select the one that correctly explains the difference between genocide and crimes against humanity.
(A) Crimes against humanity are committed in a war context, whereas genocide is not.
(B) Crimes against humanity are not committed in a war context, whereas genocide is.

(C) Crimes against humanity do not have to be committed within the context of an armed conflict (though they may be), whereas genocide cannot be committed within the context of an armed conflict.

(D) Both are committed within the context of an armed conflict.

[1 mark]

Question 26

Which of the following statements correctly identifies the standard of proof needed to secure a conviction in genocide cases?

(A) Beyond a reasonable doubt

(B) On the balance of probabilities

(C) The standard used in the country where the crimes where committed

(D) Complementary proof

[1 mark]

Question 27

The *International Criminal Court Act 2002* (Cth) and the *International Criminal Court (Consequential Amendments) Act 2002* (Cth) are examples of:

(A) Ratification of the Rome statute

(B) Legislation that confers jurisdiction of crimes of mass atrocities committed in Australia over to the ICC

(C) Legislation that confers jurisdiction of crimes of mass atrocities committed in Australia over to the United Nations

(D) Legislation that allows Australian citizens to work for the ICC

[1 mark]

Question 28

Of the following explanations for the growth of transnational crime, which is the most accurate?

(A) Poverty, demand for illegal goods and technological advancements

(B) Poverty, demand for illegal goods, greed and technological advancements

(C) Demand for illegal goods, greed and technological advancements

(D) Poverty, greed and technological advancements

[1 mark]

Question 29

A regional response introduced to combat transnational crime is identified by which of the following?

(A) The European Union Transnational Crime Unit

(B) The Pacific Transnational Crime Network (PTCN)

(C) APEC

(D) All of the above

[1 mark]

Question 30

Before the federal government releases an accused person to be extradited to another country with which there are extradition arrangements, it must satisfied of particular concerns. Which of the following is NOT a criterion that must be met?

(A) The accused will receive a fair trial.

(B) The evidence is irrefutable.

(C) There is a 'prima facie' case.

(D) The offence is a crime in that country.

[1 mark]

Question 31
What is the use of surveillance cameras in public places an example of?
(A) Retribution
(B) Restorative justice
(C) Social crime prevention
(D) Situational crime prevention
[BOS 2011]   [1 mark]

Question 32
Who decides a question of law in a criminal case in the NSW Supreme Court?
(A) The jury
(B) The judge
(C) The defence
(D) The prosecutor
[BOS 2011]   [1 mark]

Question 33
What is the aim of a diversionary program?
(A) Imprisonment
(B) Incapacitation
(C) Rehabilitation
(D) Retribution
[BOS 2011]   [1 mark]

Use the following information to answer Questions 34–37.

18-year-old Alex and 19-year-old Dale planned to rob a bank. The next day Alex drove the car and waited for Dale to rob the bank. Dale robbed the bank and they both drove away. 12-year-old Shane was waiting at their house to assist them.

Question 34
What best describes the role played by Shane?
(A) Accessory after the fact
(B) Accessory before the fact
(C) Principal in the first degree
(D) Principal in the second degree
[BOS 2011]   [1 mark]

Question 35
What category of crime has Alex committed?
(A) Driving
(B) Property
(C) Public order
(D) White collar
[BOS 2011]   [1 mark]

Question 36
Which of the following best describes what Dale committed?
(A) Both attempted robbery and robbery
(B) Both conspiracy to rob and robbery
(C) Conspiracy to rob
(D) Robbery
[BOS 2011]   [1 mark]

Question 37
What is the most likely manner in which Alex's and Shane's cases will be dealt with in the criminal justice system?
(A) They will be heard together.
(B) They will be heard in open court.
(C) They will be heard in different courts.
(D) They will be heard by a judge and jury.
[BOS 2011]   [1 mark]

Question 38
What is the first step in a criminal trial process for murder?
(A) A jury is empanelled.
(B) An arrest warrant is issued.
(C) A committal hearing is held.
(D) The offender is charged by police.
[BOS 2011]   [1 mark]

Question 39
A police officer issues a caution instead of an on-the-spot fine to a person whose car is illegally parked.
What is the police officer's action an example of?
(A) Discretion
(B) Corruption
(C) A breach of criminal law
(D) A breach of the rule of law
[BOS 2011]   [1 mark]

Question 40
Which of the following may be an aggravating factor when sentencing in a criminal trial?
(A) The offender not being aware of the consequences of their actions
(B) The offender not planning the crime
(C) The age of the offender
(D) The age of the victim
[BOS 2011]   [1 mark]

Question 41
Which of the following is a feature of victim impact statements in NSW?
(A) They are required by the court.
(B) They are presented at sentencing.
(C) They are used in determining guilt.
(D) They are part of the prosecution case.
[BOS 2011]   [1 mark]

Question 42
Which of the following is best characterised as transnational crime?
(A) Murder
(B) Torture
(C) Sexual assault
(D) People smuggling
[BOS 2011]   [1 mark]

Question 43
Police allege a driver was speeding in a school zone.
What do the police have to prove if the matter goes to court?
(A) The driver was speeding.
(B) The driver intended to speed.
(C) The driver knew it was a school zone.
(D) The driver knew the school zone speed limit.
[BOS 2011]   [1 mark]

Question 44
Lou is suspected by the police of having stolen a car.
Which of the following is a legal power that the police have when they approach Lou?
(A) To arrest Lou
(B) To fingerprint Lou
(C) To require Lou to answer questions
(D) To require Lou to go the police station
[BOS 2011]   [1 mark]

Question 45
Which of the following has the jurisdiction to prosecute genocide?
(A) The Human Rights Council
(B) The International Criminal Court
(C) The International Court of Justice
(D) The United Nations Security Council
[BOS 2011]   [1 mark]

Use the following information to answer Questions 46–48.

25-year-old Jordan and 23-year-old Darcy stole cigarettes from a shop. As they were leaving the shop, Jordan and Darcy forced 18-year-old Ariel to hide the cigarettes under her shirt. They were then apprehended by police, taken to the local police station and charged.

Question 46
To what legal right are Jordan, Darcy and Ariel entitled while being questioned at the police station?
(A) The right to remain silent
(B) The right to apply for bail
(C) The right to make a phone call
(D) The right to be questioned together
[BOS 2012]   [1 mark]

Question 47
Which court has original jurisdiction to hear these charges?
(A) Drug Court
(B) Local Court
(C) District Court
(D) Supreme Court
[BOS 2012]   [1 mark]

Question 48
Which of the following would be the most appropriate defence for Ariel to claim?
(A) Automatism
(B) Consent
(C) Duress
(D) Provocation
[BOS 2012]   [1 mark]

Use the following information to answer Questions 49–51.

Kim and Ashley, both 14 years of age, buy spray paint cans from the local hardware store. While on the train home they take the spray paint cans out of their bags. They are spotted by two police offers who approach and question them. They take the spray paint cans from them. Kim and Ashley go voluntarily with the officers to the police station.

Question 49
Which of the following actions by the police would NOT be permitted by law?
(A) Approaching Kim and Ashley on the train
(B) Seizing the spray paint cans from Kim and Ashley
(C) Insisting Kim and Ashley go to the police station
(D) Asking Kim and Ashley a series of questions on the train
[BOS 2012]   [1 mark]

Question 50
What is the first duty of the police once Kim and Ashley arrive at the police station?
(A) To take a record of interview
(B) To photograph and fingerprint them
(C) To contact their parents or guardians
(D) To formally charge them with an offence
[BOS 2012]   [1 mark]

Question 51
Why could Kim and Ashley be charged with a strict liability offence?
(A) They had purchased the spray paint cans
(B) They had the intention to use the spray paint cans
(C) They had no proof of purchase for the spray paint cans
(D) They had possession of the spray paint cans on the train
[BOS 2012]   [1 mark]

Chapter 2

Human Rights

Summary of key points

The definition of human rights
Human rights are entitlements that all people hold. They are not granted or bestowed upon people but are grounded in the basic dignity and equality of each person. They are based on 'natural law', which is considered to emanate from a higher authority such as religious thinking and reasoning.

Human rights, therefore, have three fundamental features. They are:
- Inherent – a person possesses them the moment they are born
- Inalienable – governments may deny people access to their human rights but they cannot be taken away
- Universal – they apply to all people regardless of race, age, ethnicity, gender, etc.

Human rights can be categorised as **individual** or **collective** human rights. **Individual human rights** are rights possessed by all people in their own right. **Collective human rights** are those that belong to a distinct group of people and are exercised on behalf of that community.

A further way to categorise human rights is the following:
- First generation human rights – civil and political (individual)
- Second generation human rights – economic, social and cultural (individual)
- Third generation human rights – self-determination, peace, environmental (collective).

Developing recognition of human rights
It should also be noted that various cultures around the world have different views on the place of human rights within their societies. Most western societies take an individual-rights-based approach that emphasises liberty, freedom and equality. Other communities, including those that can be found in the Islamic world and some Asian nations, may take a more duty-based approach, emphasising the community over the individual. As such, consensus on the nature of human rights has continued to develop, spring boarding from the Universal Declaration of Human Rights (UDHR) of 1948. Such different views on the place of human rights from various nations have meant differences in the manner in which they are implemented.

The modern-day understanding of human rights has developed in stages. The abolition of slavery and the collective power of trade unionism (labour rights) with the onset of the industrial revolution were significant. Further development of individual rights such as the link of education to a person's standard of living and the right to have a say in who has governance over you (suffrage) were also seen as important developments. It was also reasoned that groups of people could possess human rights collectively, and the fight for self-determination by some cultures or ethnic groups has been prominent, especially post-World War II. More than ever, the nature of global environmental problems besetting the world, and the recognition that problems emanating from one country can affect a group of people in another country, reaffirms the importance of these rights being recognised as collectively important. Finally, the understanding that people collectively have a right to peace has evolved from the collateral damage and destruction that armed conflicts have wrought on civilian populations caught up in civil and international wars.

Formal statements of human rights

Therefore, major developments in human rights have come from formal statements made through the United Nations. The UDHR, agreed to in 1948, was proposed as a declaration – a **soft international law** that conferred only moral obligations. At this time, most nations of the world signed the Declaration, as they were only bound morally to act. This, while criticised in some quarters, was an effective development because in the ensuing decades the Declaration gathered moral momentum. Eventually, the 1960s saw the signing of the 'twin treaties' (**hard international law**) that formed the blueprint for understanding the nature of human rights into the future. These were the:

- International Covenant on Civil and Political Rights
- International Covenant on Economic, Social and Cultural Rights.

The contribution these documents have made to the development of human rights have been significant. They have had an educative effect on the international community, have sent a benchmark to the standards and have encouraged the development of numerous human rights NGOs which have promoted the protection of human rights around the world.

Promoting and enforcing human rights
State sovereignty and the role of legal and non-legal institutions and agencies

The foundation of the modern nation has at its base the concept of sovereignty – the state's control over its own affairs, without interference from other nation states. This was reaffirmed by the UDHR, but it is acknowledged that state sovereignty can promote human rights or be an impediment to them. Throughout the HSC course there are many examples of this. The driving influence to determine this is economic and political will. In other words, if it is in a state's political or economic interest to take a course of action it will do so whether or not this will promote human rights or impede them. At times, however, some countries are unable to meet their international obligations in respect to human rights due to the internal circumstances. For example, extreme poverty and civil war are just two scenarios where human rights may not rate highly as priorities. Section three of this topic asks the student to investigate a human rights issue and to evaluate the effectiveness of the legal and non-legal response to the issue. A starting point for all of these should be a discussion on state sovereignty.

The United Nations, intergovernmental organisations, international courts and independent statutory authorities have played an integral role in promoting and enforcing human rights, as examples throughout the course should have illustrated. However, with the nature of state sovereignty, it has many times fallen on non-government organisations, such as Amnesty International and the international media, to highlight human rights abuses and put pressure on nations to conform to their international obligations.

The incorporation of human rights into domestic law

The incorporation of human rights into Australian domestic law can be said to be eclectic. The Australian Constitution has a few limited human rights entrenched within it. These include Section 116 – Freedom from an imposed state religion, and Section 80 – The right to a trial by jury (for a federal offence). The founding fathers who drafted the original document did not believe an American-style 'Bill of Rights' was necessary as they believed that under the Westminster system of government there already were enough checks and balances on state power. Inserting a Bill of Rights within the constitution seems unlikely under Section 128, given the unsuccessful history of referenda in Australia.

Therefore, most human rights within Australia are found in statute; anti-discrimination legislation is one example. Laws can be amended or repealed or new ones that can either strengthen human rights or weaken them can be introduced. This can be regarded as a strength or weakness depending on how one looks at it. The introduction of a 'Statutory' Bill of Rights is also problematic given the political divide on such an issue.

The courts and other tribunals protect human rights when necessary, through the doctrine of precedent. An example of this is the limited right to legal representation created in *Dietrich v The Queen*. This approach can be effective at times but it is sporadic and haphazard if one is looking to the courts to ensure our rights are safeguarded. It should be noted though that the courts will look to our international human rights treaty obligations and may incorporate these into their decision, as seen in the Teoh case.

In addition, non-government organisations and the media can spur governments into action, or they can be ignored. The strength of these non-government responses is best examined through case studies.

The arguments for and against a Charter of Rights (which can be called a Bill of Rights) will be examined in class and centred on the debate of whether Australia would be better off with or without one. It could be said that essentially human rights in Australia are well protected for most of the people most of the time. But there have been, and will continue to be, some glaring problems within the legal system as highlighted by some high-profile cases such as the Cornelia Rau case. Also, aspects of the federal anti-terrorism legislation, such as holding suspects without charge, breach fundamental human rights. Human rights abuses are happening in Australia now and are likely to continue to occur.

A contemporary issue that illustrates the promotion and/or enforcement of human rights
There are many to choose from on the list provided in the 2011 syllabus on page 21. You will need to address the legal response from an international and domestic level. In addition to this, the role of non-legal means of responding to the issue must also be addressed and the strengths and weaknesses of this approach must also be evaluated. There are examples provided in the solutions to past HSC questions in Chapter 10 that will give you an insight into how to go about this.

Sample multiple-choice questions

Question 1
Australia is negotiating to send people seeking asylum in Australia arriving by boat to Malaysia. Malaysia in return can send up to 4 times as many people identified as refugees in their country to Australia. It has been argued that this will breach the Convention on Refugees as Australia may be sending asylum seekers to a country that administers corporal punishment and has not signed the convention. Which of the following statements most accurately reflects why Australia can ignore this criticism?

(A) Australia is a sovereign nation
(B) Australia does not have a bilateral treaty with Malaysia
(C) Australia is not a signatory to the Convention on Refugees
(D) The High Court of Australia does have jurisdiction in this area

[1 mark]

Question 2
Which of the following is the most effective means of protecting human rights under the Australian legal system?
(A) Charter of Rights
(B) Statute law
(C) Trade unionism
(D) Common law

[1 mark]

Question 3
When are breaches of individual human rights in Australia best protected by international treaties?
(A) When the High Court hands down a precedent
(B) When the federal government commits itself to upholding its treaty obligations
(C) When the International Court of Justice gives a judgement on a matter involving a breach of an individual's human rights within Australia
(D) When the federal government ratifies treaties into domestic legislation

[1 mark]

Question 4
In relation to domestic and international rights, which of the following statements is true?
(A) Domestic rights are complementary to international rights
(B) Domestic rights only apply to citizens of a country
(C) International rights give some degree of legal protection
(D) International rights can only be enforced through armed conflict

[1 mark]

Question 5
Which of the following is not an example of a non-legal measure that can be used in addressing human rights issues?
(A) The media
(B) Non-government organisations
(C) The Human Rights and Equal Opportunity Commission
(D) Political persuasion

[1 mark]

Question 6
Which of the following is an example of collective human rights?
(A) The right to vote
(B) The right to join a trade union
(C) The right to peace
(D) The right to housing

[1 mark]

Question 7
What is the main aim of the International Covenant on Civil and Political Rights?
(A) To protect the educational needs of people
(B) To protect the cultural wellbeing of people

(C) To protect people in regards to their basic needs
(D) To protect people from arbitrary use of power by governments
[BOS 2012]   [1 mark]

Question 8
Which of the following would be a feature of a statutory Charter of Rights in Australia?
(A) It would be able to be adapted to changing values.
(B) It could be changed by the House of Representatives.
(C) It could be changed by citizens through a referendum.
(D) It would be incorporated into the Australian Constitution.   · [1 mark]
[BOS 2013]

Question 9
Which of the following rights is NOT an example of a collective right?
(A) Economic
(B) Environmental
(C) Peace
(D) Self-determination
[BOS 2009]   [1 mark]

Question 10
Kim has been arrested for shoplifting. In court he exercises his right to remain silent. Which type of right is he exercising?
(A) Civil
(B) Legal
(C) Human
(D) Constitutional
[BOS 2009]   [1 mark]

Question 11
A national government bans all forms of public protest by an environmental group. What is being denied by the government?
(A) Civil and political rights
(B) The right to self-determination
(C) Environmental and peace rights
(D) Economic, social and cultural rights
[BOS 2011]   [1 mark]

Question 12
Which of the following human rights is expressly recognised in the Australian Constitution?
(A) Freedom of religion
(B) Freedom of assembly
(C) The right to marry
(D) The right to education
[BOS 2011]   [1 mark]

Question 13
Which of the following is NOT a feature of human rights?
(A) They are inherent.
(B) They are universal.

(C) They are enforceable.
(D) They are inalienable.
[BOS 2011]

[1 mark]

Question 14
The Australian Government has ratified an international human rights treaty. What is the practical effect of this?
(A) It grants human rights to Australian citizens.
(B) It makes breaches of human rights punishable in Australia.
(C) It enables the Australian Government to enact human rights legislation.
(D) It makes breaches of human rights punishable by international tribunals.
[BOS 2011]

[1 mark]

Question 15
The Australian Governing body for Netball in Australia has passed a rule banning women who are pregnant from competing in the professional competition. This was ruled by a court to be a breach of human rights. What rights have been infringed?
(A) Social and Cultural
(B) Economic
(C) Civil and political
(D) Gender

[1 mark]

Question 16
The separation of powers in the Australian Constitution establishes the independence between
(A) barristers, judges and juries.
(B) local, district and supreme courts.
(C) judiciary, legislature and executive.
(D) local, state and federal governments.
[BOS 2012]

[1 mark]

Question 17
Which of the following is an example of an intergovernmental organisation?
(A) Amnesty International
(B) Human Rights Watch
(C) Human Rights Council
(D) International Committee of the Red Cross
[BOS 2012]

[1 mark]

Section II: Core – Crime and Human Rights

Chapter 3

Part A: Human Rights

Sample short answer questions

Question 1
Describe how a domestic law has been used in response to an international human rights issue.

[3 marks]

Question 2
What are 'individual human rights'? Describe, using an example.

[2 marks]

Question 3
What are 'collective human rights'? Describe using an example.

[2 marks]

Question 4
Describe how effective legal measures have been in addressing a human rights issue.

[6 marks]

Question 5
Explain how a particular human right is recognised and protected by international law.

[2 marks]

Question 6
With regards to the protection of human rights, how effective are international and domestic legal measures?

[6 marks]

Question 7
Outline the meaning of self-determination.

[2 marks]

Question 8
Discuss the notion that a 'Charter of Rights' is required in Australia.

[6 marks]

Question 9
Explain how domestic AND/OR international legal measures have been used in response to ONE contemporary human rights struggle.
[BOS 2009]

[6 marks]

Question 10
Identify TWO non-government organisations that promote human rights.
[BOS 2011]   [2 marks]

Question 11
Define the right to self-determination.
[BOS 2011]   [2 marks]

Question 12
Outline how ONE human right has been legally recognised.
[BOS 2011]   [5 marks]

Question 13
With reference to ONE contemporary human rights issue, explain the role of state
sovereignty in enforcing human rights.
[BOS 2011]   [6 marks]

Question 14
What impact does state sovereignty have on the protection of human rights?
                                                                                                [3 marks]

Chapter 4

Part B: Crime

Sample extended response questions

> In your answer you will be assessed on how well you:
> - demonstrate knowledge and understanding of legal issues relevant to the question
> - communicate using relevant legal terminology and concepts
> - refer to relevant examples such as legislation, cases, media, international instruments and documents
> - present a sustained, logical and cohesive response.

Question 1
Assess the extent to which the criminal law reflects the moral and ethical standards of the community.

[15 marks]

Question 2
Assess the effectiveness of the legal system in dealing with international crime.

[15 marks]

Question 3
Evaluate the purpose and effectiveness of possible penalties a judge could consider before sentencing an offender.

[15 marks]

Question 4
Assess the role of law reform in the criminal justice system.

[15 marks]

Question 5
Evaluate the implications of plea bargaining in terms of justice for the accused, the victim, the community and the efficiency of the court system.

[15 marks]

Question 6
Explain the tension between community interests and individual rights and freedoms within the criminal justice system.
[BOS 2011]

[15 marks]

Question 7
Explain the role of discretion in the criminal justice system.

[15 marks]

Question 8
Brad and Jamal, both aged 13, rob a 24/7 convenience store. They use fake guns and during the robbery they push over the store attendant who hits his head and is seriously injured. Both are found guilty of a number of offences and are sentenced to a juvenile detention centre for a period of two years. At the time of sentencing it was revealed that both boys had come from dysfunctional homes where there had been no limits placed on their behaviour for a number of years.

With reference to the above scenario and your own knowledge, assess the effectiveness of the criminal justice system when dealing with young offenders.

[15 marks]

Question 9
Evaluate the extent to which criminal penalties are a reflection of public morality.

[15 marks]

Question 10
Evaluate the effectiveness of the criminal law in encouraging compliance and reducing non-compliance.

[15 marks]

Question 11
To what extent are courts the only means of achieving justice within the criminal justice system?
[BOS 2012]

[15 marks]

Section III: Options

Chapter 5

Option 1 – Consumer Law

The nature of consumer law

The need for consumer law

The nature of the commercial world has continued to evolve since the time of the industrial revolution when there was no need for consumers to have a lot of expertise when making consumer purchases. *Caveat emptor* ('let the buyer beware') was the way in which the marketplace was regulated. It was the consumers' responsibility to ensure the purchases they made were fit for the purpose intended.

In a *laissez-faire* economy there was no emphasis on government intervention in the buying and selling process that occurred in the marketplace. The market itself was seen to regulate matters between buyers and sellers. Eventually governments began to pass laws to put in place protections for consumers as the marketplace developed and became more complex.

The definition of a consumer

A consumer is a person who buys or uses goods or services that are offered for sale in the marketplace within an economy. In many cases the consumer can decide how they will use their scarce resources (money) in satisfying their needs and wants. In law, a person is considered to be a consumer when they purchase goods or services for their own personal use. **Consumer sovereignty** refers to the power of the consumer's choice, which ultimately determines what will be produced for the marketplace. If a good or service doesn't sell, then it will cease to be offered or made.

Objective of consumer laws

The objective of consumer laws is to regulate the relationship between consumers, manufacturers and the government – both state and federal. The bulk of consumer law can be found in the common law – for example, the law of contract or in numerous pieces of state and federal legislation.

The law in respect to consumers is primarily intended to protect consumers from unsafe products and misleading and deceptive behaviour, and to ensure that particularly vulnerable or disadvantaged consumers are also considered.

Contracts

A contract can be either a verbal or written agreement. The law at times demands that some contracts must be in writing and that these contracts have implied terms in them. This is discussed later. **A contract is a legally binding agreement between two or more parties.**

In order for a contract to exist there are specific elements that must be present. There must be an **intention to create legal relations** and this will be evident if there is an **offer and acceptance** of specific terms. The **terms** of a contract set out what each party's obligations are to the other parties and what each party will expect to get out of the contract. A court will examine if there was an offer and an acceptance and if the terms of the contract were clear. **Consideration** (both parties must get some benefit from the contract) will also be looked at. In addition to these, the parties to the contract must have **legal capacity** to enter into the contract from the outset.

The **terms** of the contract can either be **express** (terms spoken or written into the arrangement that the parties have agreed to), or **implied** (the terms exist no matter what; for example, if a consumer purchases a product they can expect that the product is fit for the purpose intended). **Exclusion clauses** can also be included in a contract, where one party limits its responsibility in particular situations. For example, insurance companies may not cover damage to a house by floods.

Some contracts are unjust in that they are unconscionable (unfair) to one of the parties. The **common law** may provide relief and rescind a contract if a party to the contract has been put in an unjust position.

The following cases provide examples where the courts have provided remedies for parties that were subject to unfair or unjust contracts.
- A contract must be fairly negotiated without any undue influence – *Johnson v Buttress* (1936) 56 CLR 113.
- A contract must be entered in the absence of duress or coercion – *Hawker Pacific Pty Ltd v Helicopter Charter Pty Ltd* (1991) 22 NSWLR 298.
- A product purchased must be of merchantable quality – *Australian Knitting Mills Ltd v Grant* (1933) 50 CLR 387.
- A product must match its advertised description – *Beale v Taylor* (1967) 1 WLR 1193.
- Manufacturers/suppliers cannot engage in deceptive or misleading marketing behaviour – *Qanstruct Pty Ltd v Bongiorno Ltd* (1993) 113 ALR 667.

There are also statutory protections for consumers. Some of the main legislation includes the *Sale of Goods Act 1923* (NSW), the *Trade Practices Act 1974* (Cth) renamed the **Competition and Consumer Act 2010 (Cth)**, and the *Fair Trading Act 1987* (NSW). These Acts imply conditions into contracts, and prohibit misleading and deceptive behaviour, unconscionable behaviour and selling defective or dangerous products. The *Contracts Review Act 1980* (NSW) allows the court to grant relief for unjust contracts.

The reason for various state and federal legislation is that under Section 51 of the Australian Constitution, only the federal government has power to makes laws in respect to corporations, and therefore any unincorporated businesses come under state laws.

The role of negligence in consumer law
If a good or service is provided to consumers that causes injury, loss, damage or death then it is said that the provider has been negligent in law. This means that they have failed to provide a proper standard of care and therefore have failed in their duty of care

to the consumer. There are the following protections and avenues of redress for consumers who find themselves in this situation. They can:

- Bring an action under the *Competition and Consumer Act 2010* (Cth)
- Bring an action for breach of contract, if the supplier or manufacturer has expressly or impliedly promised that the goods are free of defect
- Commence an action for the tort of negligence in the state courts.

Regulation of marketing and advertising

Laws protecting consumers from deceptive advertising and marketing practices are provided for in the *Competition and Consumer Act 2010* (Cth) and in the *Fair Trading Act 1987* (NSW). *The Competition and Consumer Act 2010* (Cth) also makes provision regarding the making of false representations.

The *Competition and Consumer Act 2010* (Cth) and the *Fair Trading Act 1987* (NSW) also make provision for:

- Vulnerable consumers against unscrupulous suppliers who use their greater bargaining power to obtain an advantage
- Enticing consumers to buy their products by offering gifts, prizes or other free items with the intention of not providing the advertised gift
- Bait and switch tactics, where consumers are lured into the premises with the lure of a very good discount or deal (that does not exist) only to be switched to a more expensive product once in the store.

The *Competition and Consumer Act 2010* (Cth) also makes it illegal to engage in referral selling, sending unsolicited or unordered goods to consumers and the use of coercion, force or harassment in obtaining a sale.

Cooling off periods are also in place to allow consumers to make up their minds about the purchase of a service or good away from the high-pressure sales environment. Most cooling off periods are for five days.

Non-statutory controls on advertising generally come in the form of industry self-regulation. This is where particular industries voluntarily regulate themselves to ensure certain standards are met in relation to advertising. The **Advertising Standards Bureau (ASB)** and the **Advertising Claims Board** are two examples.

To operate in certain industries a business must be licensed, registered or must be certified. This is known as **occupational licensing** and aims to ensure certain businesses operating in particular industries meet minimum standards or qualifications or ethical practices required to meet the needs of consumers in their respective field.

Consumer redress and remedies
Awareness and self-help
This is the most effective and efficient way of dealing with consumer issues. Self-knowledge can ensure consumers are more discriminating and therefore avoid situations that require some form of redress. Resolving the issue at the place where it began saves personal and community resources being invested. Some consumer problems are not able to be resolved without some form of intervention and there are state and federal organisations to assist with this.

There are a number of **state government organisations** that provide education, advice, investigative procedures and in some cases mediation and adjudicating mechanisms. The **Office of Fair Trading** in NSW is such an organisation. It also is the place where small businesses register an owner or their organisations.

Federal government organisations include the **Australian Competition and Consumer Commission (ACCC)**. The ACCC is an independent statutory body that administers *The Competition and Consumer Act 2010* (Cth) and other Commonwealth Acts. Its role is to promote competition and fair trade in the marketplace.

The **Australian Securities and Investments Commission (ASIC)** is an independent statutory body that regulates Australia's corporate, market and financial services sectors and ensures that Australia's financial markets are fair and transparent.

In addition to government organisations, **industry groups** also provide mechanisms to resolve consumer issues. Some industry organisations are **customer focused** and may provide training for staff and develop their own systems for handling complaints. These can be an effective way of building positive customer relationships and ensuring greater resource efficiency by reducing consumer-related problems.

Some industries have developed their own style of industry **ombudsman.** This office acts on behalf of the whole industry and consumer complaints can be dealt with at this level. Examples include the **Banking Ombudsman** and the **Energy and Water Ombudsman NSW**.

There are particular **courts and tribunals** that adjudicate consumer conflict. The *Consumer, Trader and Tenancy Tribunal Act 2001* (NSW) established the Consumer, Trader and Tenancy Tribunal. The Act outlines the operation of the tribunal. The role of this tribunal is to resolve disputes between a number of players who ultimately are involved in consumer relationships. Some of these are tenants, landlords, traders and consumers. Like most tribunals they are usually cheaper and timelier in resolving disputes especially.

The last place to hear a consumer complaint is the **courts**. If attempts to resolve matters through self-help and a tribunal resolution are not appropriate then action can commence in the courts. Some of the more complex consumer complaints can be resolved through the system of precedent where the law is affirmed or changed and developed. This is a more expensive and time-consuming avenue of redress.

Non-government organisations exist to represent the interests of consumers by raising concerns with governments, educating the public about specific issues or supporting consumers in advocacy matters. Some examples of consumer non-government organisations include Choice, Consumer Credit Legal Centre (NSW) Incorporated and Consumers' Federation of Australia.

The **media** is another important non-legal measure to raise awareness of consumer problems within society. All media is biased to some extent but it can provide an invaluable service in putting pressure on governments and informing consumers of recent developments that may put consumers at risk financially or physically.

There are many types of **remedies** that consumers may wish to access when resolving a consumer problem. The court may order the payment of damages, issue court orders to rescind or modify contracts, or order that the contract be performed. They may also issue an injunction that orders a person/body to do something or to refrain from doing something.

Alternative dispute resolution (ADR) may also be used to mediate and conciliate a consumer problem. Community Justice Centres exist throughout NSW to provide this type of service.

As a result of the legal and non-legal mechanisms in place to promote and resolve consumer issues, the society as a whole benefits. Some of the ways this occurs is through safer products on the market, a reduction in the number of consumer complaints due to greater awareness and more honest and ethical practices by business owners.

Contemporary issues concerning consumers

Credit – Our modern society depends on personal and corporate credit for it to function. There are many forms of credit, but ultimately this is where a person, group or corporation obtains goods and services in the present, to be paid for at a later date. The Commonwealth has received powers from the state in respect to consumer credit under the *Trade Practices Amendment (Australian Consumer Law) Act 2009* (Cth). This has standardised laws regulating consumer credit for providers and users. The Uniform Consumer Credit Code (UCCC) has also ensured that all laws relating to all forms of consumer lending and to all credit providers are uniform in all jurisdictions in Australia.

There are a number of **non-legal measures** in place to assist in addressing concerns around the provision of consumer credit. Some of these include the NSW Office of Fair Trading, community Justice Centres and Financial Ombudsman.

The level of personal debt in Australia is now a cause for major concern and the standardisation of consumer credit contracts, assessing an individual's ability to repay a loan, and the other obligations of credit providers are positive developments.

Product certification – this is a process to ensure that all goods sold meet certain standards in respect to quality and performance. Products sold in Australia have to meet industry standards, communicate effectively how the product is to be used and continue to improve safety standards over time.

Mandatory product standards – these can be in the form of mandatory safety standards or mandatory information standards. Once a product has been certified in Australia it may display certain logos or symbols to communicate to the consumer that the product has been endorsed to a particular standard, for example **Standards Australia**.

Marketing innovations – marketing is the process where the business entity makes the consumer aware of its product or services. With the advent of technological advancement, marketing has become sophisticated and at times quite invasive. Some invasive methods of marketing include spam, offers of unrealistic deals over the internet and phone calls from call centres. Illegal practices such as internet fraud and phishing are also of concern.

Technology – technology has broadened the consumer marketplace to a global phenomenon, allowing unscrupulous traders to escape national jurisdictions. Once consumers and businesses engage in online transactions outside of Australia they forgo the consumer protection afforded to them by state and federal laws. Therefore, the types of redress they may receive will depend on the existence of international treaties or details of the online provider that may assist in the freezing of assets or the pursuing of court orders in other national jurisdictions. The current legislative provisions within Australia are inadequate to protect Australian consumers from the majority of problems they encounter in the global marketplace due to the advancement of technology and the growth of the internet.

Sample examination questions

Question 1
To what extent are the moral and ethical standards of the community at the centre of the law in relation to consumers?
[25 marks]

Question 2
Describe how agencies of reform meet the needs of consumers, and under what conditions these needs arise.
[25 marks]

Question 3
'In order to achieve justice, it is necessary to have compliance with the law.'
In the context of consumers, discuss this in relation to compliance and non-compliance.
[25 marks]

Question 4
Assess the place of law in resolving conflict and encouraging cooperation in regulating marketing and advertising, and other aspects of consumer law.
[25 marks]

Question 5
How effective are the legal and non-legal methods available for consumer redress?
[BOS 2009]
[25 marks]

Question 6
Explain how and why the concept of the consumer in the law has changed over time.
[BOS 2009]
[25 marks]

Question 7
Why are there different legal protections for consumers and manufacturers/suppliers?
[BOS 2010]
[25 marks]

Question 8
How effective is government regulation in achieving justice for consumers?
[BOS 2011]
[25 marks]

Question 9
Why has justice for consumers been hard to achieve?
[BOS 2011]
[25 marks]

Chapter 6

Option 2 – Global Environmental Protection

The nature of global environmental protection

Environmental laws are now designed to take a more holistic view of components, causes and effects. There are a variety of definitions of what is meant by global environmental protection. The definition of 'environment' in Section 528 of the *Environment Protection and Biodiversity Conservation Act 1999* (Cth) clearly illustrates the evolution of what constitutes the environment. It states that the environment comprises ecosystems made up of natural and physical resources. It is also made up of locations, places and areas, some of which have heritage values, and all of which have social, economic and cultural features. Protection of the environment involves the law regulating the competing interests that exist in respect of use and management of the built and physical environment.

The **development of global environmental protection** has been a feature of the last 20 years. Many environmental issues reach beyond a domestic jurisdiction solution. Domestic legislation of industrialised nations in the 1970s, including Australia, focused on pollution prevention and control. Much of Australian state and federal legislation relating to the environment falls into two general categories – environmental impact and pollution control.

The 1970s and 1980s also saw a number of **international conferences** and **multilateral treaties** on the environment in response to global threats, especially highly visible ones such as marine pollution. Other examples include **The UN Conference on the Human Environment**, which was held in 1972 in Stockholm, Sweden, and was the first major conference to address broadly defined environmental issues. It was motivated primarily by concern about regional pollution that crossed national boundaries, particularly acid rain in northern Europe. Subsequent conferences following on from Stockholm have included the **1992 UN Conference on Environment and Development (UNCED)** in Rio de Janeiro, Brazil (the 'Rio Conference') and the **2002 World Summit on Sustainable Development** in Johannesburg, South Africa (the 'Johannesburg Summit').

In some countries, a treaty that the nation has signed and ratified automatically becomes part of the domestic law of that country, and its citizens are bound by it. In many others, including Australia, a treaty does not have a direct effect unless and until it is incorporated into domestic law by the enactment of a statute. There are many domestic statutes that implement and reflect Australia's international treaty obligations.

This development of international conferences is a reflection of the increased **need for global environmental protection**. One of the reasons for this is the greater environmental impact of increased consumption and development.

Nations must **cooperate** if there is to be a comprehensive response to the need for global environmental protection. While the environmental issues faced by different geographic and cultural communities are complex and individual, global environmental problems are sweeping and just as grave.

For example, the situation concerning the overexploitation of the world's fishing stocks illustrates this. By the early 1990s, 13 of the world's 17 global fisheries were in serious decline. This represents a threat not only to the maintenance of a valuable food source and the livelihood of the fishing industry and those who depend on it, but to the network of ocean ecosystems. A decision by a group of countries to limit fishing in a certain fish breeding ground would have a negligible effect if even one country continued to exploit that area.

Another international agreement, a meeting of the **Convention on the Conservation of Migratory Species of Wild Animals** (CMS) in February 2010, resulted in 113 countries agreeing to the inclusion of seven species of migratory shark on a 'threatened' list, and prohibition of their fishing. Another means of halting the commercial trade in certain fish is to have them listed as endangered under the UN Convention on International Trade in Endangered Species of Wild Fauna and Flora (1975) (CITES). It may be the case that measures such as 'plans of implementation' need to be supplemented by additional agreements, and with binding, enforceable prohibitions.

Central to the need for global environmental protection is the idea of **Ecologically Sustainable Development (ESD)**. The **Brundtland Report** commissioned in 1987 defined sustainable development as 'development that meets the needs of the present without compromising the ability of future generations to meet their own needs'. It aims to meet the needs of society today, including the alleviation of poverty, while managing natural resources, energy and waste in ways that can continue into the future without destroying the environment or endangering human health.

The keys to ecologically sustainable development are four important elements. These are as follows:
- **Biodiversity** is the variation of life forms within an ecosystem, a biome, or the planet. (An ecosystem is the set of relationships among the plants, animals, micro-organisms and habitats in a small area, and a biome is a regional, much larger group of ecosystems in a wide geographic area.) Biodiversity is important because diverse ecosystems are better able to withstand and recover from disasters and they are more sustainable in the long term because of the wide variety of interdependence that exists within such ecosystems.
- **Intergenerational equity**, or 'equity between generations', is the idea that ecosystems and the environment in general should not be passed on in any worse condition from one generation to the next. Therefore, decision-makers need to consider intergenerational equity when determining how each society is going to meet its needs year to year.
- **Intragenerational equity**, in contrast to intergenerational equity, refers to fair and just treatment of groups of people within a generation. It is accomplished through policies that endeavour to raise the standard of living of disadvantaged peoples and nations, and ensure that the management and use of the environment does not exploit them. The extent to which the developed world consumes the resources of the planet is clearly unjust. If China and India were able to give all their citizens the same standard of living as people in the west have, then the world would go into meltdown. Some fundamental shifts will be required if intragenerational equity is to

be addressed, while at the same time also working towards intergenerational equity as outlined.

- The **precautionary principle** states that if an action is suspected of causing long-term harm, even if there isn't a scientific consensus about that action, then the action should not be done. This is particularly relevant for dealing with ecological issues, as it has proven difficult to convince the developed world to work towards ecologically sustainable living. Some sceptics argue that the scientific research is not conclusive enough. The problem is that by the time the science has firmed up, it may be too late to stop dangerous ecological degradation.

Responses to global environmental protection

National **sovereignty** is the implicit recognition under international law that a nation has authority over its citizens and territory, and can govern as it sees fit. The tension between a consistent global approach to environmental protection and national sovereignty is apparent. At times what is best for the environment is not considered the best option for a country.

Generally, nations will consent to behave in a particular way if it is in their best interests to do so, and 'best interests' have often been equated with innovation, economic growth and corporate profitability. Australia's initial refusal to ratify the Kyoto Protocol on greenhouse gas emissions and Japan's refusal to stop whaling pursued for 'scientific purposes' are illustrations of national sovereignty in action.

It is the implementation of various international agreements and how vigorously they are acted upon that will determine their effectiveness in providing global environmental protection. Hence, the ultimate effectiveness of global environmental protection will need nation states to put their own economic and political interest secondary to the global environmental problems facing the planet.

The **United Nations** was established in 1945 with international peace and security as its main objective, along with the aims of developing friendly relations among nations, promoting human rights, and facilitating social and economic progress. Over time, however, its aims and functions have evolved to keep pace with changing global conditions. In its early years, global environmental protection was of little significance, but now it is one of the dominant aspects of UN affairs.

Several programs and specialised agencies have been established by the UN to deal with environmental issues. Some of these include the **Food and Agriculture Organization of the UN** and the **United Nations Development Programme (UNDP)**. The UN also established the **United Nations Environment Programme (UNEP)** in 1972, following the UN Conference on the Human Environment ('Stockholm Conference'). It is a 'programme' (i.e. a subsidiary body of the General Assembly), and its stated aim is to provide leadership and encourage partnership in caring for the environment by inspiring, informing, and enabling nations and peoples to improve their quality of life without compromising that of future generations.

In addition to the above, the UN also created the **Intergovernmental Panel on Climate Change (IPCC),** which is involved in reviewing and assessing the most recent scientific information from around the world relating to climate change. It does not itself conduct scientific research. Reviews are conducted by scientists from every part of the world, working on a voluntary basis. The IPCC strives for a complete survey and assessment of current information, and its reports reflect different viewpoints within the scientific community.

The **United Nations Educational, Scientific and Cultural Organisation (UNESCO)** is a specialised agency of the UN, founded in 1945. Its primary function is to promote international dialogue and cooperation in the fields of science, communication, education and culture. Its two highest priorities are Africa and gender equality, but it also focuses on promoting sustainable development and biodiversity along with overcoming poverty and preserving cultural heritage. Its Natural Sciences Sector has a particularly direct role in fostering environmentally sustainable development.

Over the last 30 years there have been an increasing number of **international instruments** that have been concerned with global environmental protection. There are two types – **declarations** (considered **soft international law** as they put only moral obligations on nation states) and **treaties/conventions** (considered **hard international law** as they put legal obligations on the nation states that sign them).

A **protocol** is a negotiated instrument that supplements a treaty or agreement, containing specific actions to be taken to fulfil the terms of the treaty, or provisions that modify the original treaty. For example, the Montreal Protocol is an addition to the Vienna Convention for the Protection of the Ozone Layer (1985), and, as noted above, the Kyoto Protocol is an addition to the UN Framework Convention on Climate Change. The Cartagena Protocol on Biosafety, which came into force in 2002, is a supplement to the Biodiversity Convention. The protocol seeks to protect biodiversity from potential risks posed by technological modifications to living organisms by governing their movement from one country to another. It contains a procedure for nations to obtain the information necessary to make informed decisions as to the importation of genetically modified organisms, and contains several provisions referring to the precautionary principle.

Some examples of international instruments concerning global environmental protection include:
- UN Convention on International Trade in Endangered Species of Wild Fauna and Flora (CITES), 1975. Considered hard law aimed to ensure that international trade in wild animals and plants, and products made from them, does not threaten their survival.
- Convention on Wetlands of International Importance (the Ramsar Convention), 1971. Considered hard law. Provides the framework for national action and international cooperation for the conservation and wise use of wetlands and their resources.
- Vienna Convention for the Protection of the Ozone Layer, 1988. It has no legally binding targets for reduction of substances that deplete the ozone layer (notably chlorofluorocarbons). Its aim is to protect human health and the environment from adverse effects resulting from human activities that alter the ozone layer.
- Montreal Protocol on Substances that Deplete the Ozone Layer, 1989. Considered hard law. It sets out a mandatory timetable for the phasing out of ozone-depleting substances.
- UN Convention on Biological Diversity, 1993. Considered hard law. It is concerned with the conservation of biological diversity, the sustainable use of its components, and the fair and equitable sharing of the benefits from the use of genetic resources.

- Agenda 21, 1992. Considered soft law. Sets out a plan to achieve a sustainable balance between consumption, population and Earth's capacity.
- Rio Declaration on Environment and Development, 1992. Considered soft law. It provides the principles guiding sustainable development; it defines humans' responsibilities to safeguard the common environment, as well as the rights of the people to be involved in the development of their economies.
- UN Framework Convention on Climate Change, 1994. It has no legally binding targets or enforcement mechanisms. Its goal is to stabilise atmospheric concentrations of greenhouse gases at a level that would prevent harm to the climate system.
- Kyoto Protocol, 1997. Considered hard law. It set binding targets for 37 industrialised countries and the European Community for reducing their greenhouse gas emissions by an average of 5%.
- Copenhagen Accord 2009. Considered soft law. It was intended to establish an ambitious global climate agreement starting in 2012 when the Kyoto Protocol expires, but it set no binding targets. It recognises that global temperature rises must be kept below 2°C, but no specifics are included.

Prior to the establishment of the United Nations, and thus the **International Court of Justice (ICJ)**, there was practically no court or tribunal in place to settle environmental conflicts between nation states, since few issues had arisen. Only nation states can be parties to a case before the ICJ. It has the power to decide a case only where the parties to a dispute have consented to its jurisdiction, either by special agreement of the parties (where it is specifically provided for in a treaty), or where the state parties to the Statute of the ICJ recognise its jurisdiction as compulsory in relation to any other state. Where the parties have consented, it is rare for a decision of the court not to be implemented. However, a state can raise 'preliminary objections' to the court's jurisdiction, or refuse to appear before the court because it totally rejects the court's jurisdiction. This limits the effectiveness of this judicial body.

Since the establishment of the ICJ in 1945, a range of environmental cases have been heard. An example is the **nuclear test cases (1974–75) involving Australia and New Zealand against France**, which was testing nuclear devices in French Polynesia. The cases did not proceed to the merits stage, as the ICJ decided that once France stated that it was ceasing the atmospheric tests of its own accord, the cases no longer had any object. Later, France commenced underground nuclear testing.

One problem with the ICJ's role in settling global environmental disputes is that its jurisdiction depends on whether two or more states have consented to be bound by it. This seriously constrains its jurisdiction, given that corporations are responsible for a vast number of the environmental problems today.

Some NGOs and academics believe a more effective solution lies with the formulation of an International Environmental Court that follows the International Criminal Court model. It could be permitted to settle disputes between private and public parties, if the issues are global in their magnitude; to mediate and arbitrate; and to institute investigations. Such a court could readily apply ESD principles, and could provide a high level of consistency by utilising experts in relevant fields to determine complex scientific issues. It could also be compulsory, rather than requiring consent to its jurisdiction.

Prior to 1972, international instruments promoting environmental protection were predominantly reactionary. They addressed discrete areas of environmental protection as the need arose. Early international law in this area was ad hoc and generally regional in its approach. The development of **conferences** ensured greater collaboration and coordination, especially on the different viewpoints held by various nation states on global environmental issues. A number of conferences have been held, focusing on specific issues. These often relate to a particular treaty or convention. **'Meetings of the parties'** to a framework convention are generally held at intervals to continue negotiations for specific, legally binding commitments from the state parties. For example, the Conference of the Parties to the UN Framework Convention on Climate Change of 1992 meets every year; the 1997 Conference of the Parties in Kyoto, Japan gave rise to the Kyoto Protocol.

In addition to the international framework for global environmental protection mentioned earlier, there are a number of **intergovernmental organisations** that have reference to regional environmental issues. The **European Union (EU)** has developed an Environment Section whose function is implementing environmental policies for the 25 nation states now comprising the EU; this also includes an EU Sustainable Development Strategy that took effect in 2006.

The **Organisation for Economic Co-operation and Development (OECD)** has a primary focus on the economic growth, employment and living standards of its member nations, but it too has recognised the need for the environment to be taken into account. The OECD has introduced environment performance reviews in conjunction with its usual economic reviews of member countries.

Governments are political in nature and often their perspectives on an issue are influenced by factors such as business and industrial interests. In response to growing environmental awareness over the last four decades, various **non-government organisations (NGOs)** have put pressure on governments to take into account environmental considerations. NGOs use a combination of action and advocacy to advance their agendas. Some operate nationally (within a single nation state) and others are international. Significant examples of environmental NGOs are Greenpeace, the World Wide Fund for Nature and Friends of the Earth.

The **media** is one of the most powerful forces on the planet. It has the potential not merely to shape popular opinion, but to determine it. In Australia, the power of the media in environmental matters was highlighted in the Franklin Dam protest movements of the early 1980s, which culminated in the case *Commonwealth v Tasmania (1983)* 158 CLR 1. The Wilderness Society and the Australian Conservation Foundation joined forces to mount a well-organised effort to use the media to present their version of the situation. They were spectacularly successful. The media around the world has also been responsible for communicating aspects of the scientific research on climate change.

Australia's federal structure provides constitutional constraints when attempting to effectively deal with national and global environmental issues. Under the Australian Constitution, the power to legislate on environment issues can only be considered a **residual power**. It is not one of the enumerated powers of the Federal Parliament, and therefore it falls to the states. Like the rest of the world, Australia was unaware of the consequences of exploiting the environment until relatively recently. Constitutional change via a referendum would seem to be necessary if the Commonwealth is to adequately deal with the issues facing Australia.

The main federal environmental law is the *Environment Protection and Biodiversity Conservation Act 1999* (Cth) ('EPBC Act'). It provides the legal framework for the protection and management of nationally and internationally important animals, plants, ecosystems and places defined in the Act as matters of national environmental significance.

Contemporary issues concerning global environmental protection

The global nature of environmental issues has seen the emergence of key issues around the aspect of global protection. One of these is **the role of the law in relation to global threats to the environment**. In the area of environmental law, the aim of preventing, mitigating and/or remedying damage that human activities have caused to the environment has been a major challenge. To achieve these aims, the law must also encourage cooperation and resolve conflicts between parties whose interests are affected.

At an international level, treaties and protocols set out the rules with respect to environmental protection. The International Court of Justice is the pre-eminent body for resolving disputes between nation states. **Soft law** such as declarations and action plans can also play a role in prompting national government action and influencing the behaviour of corporations and other agents.

Nation states ultimately decide the extent to which they will meet international obligations contained in international instruments and this is generally driven by economic and political will. However, international instruments can be educative and can influence the mindset of governments around the world and at times countries like Australia can ratify treaties into domestic legislation. The 2010 election campaign saw both sides of politics back away from an emissions trading scheme to put a price on carbon because the electorate was volatile on the issue.

A fundamental issue facing the world today is **the conflict between the increasing demand for resources and global environmental protection**. A non-renewable resource is a naturally occurring resource that cannot be produced, re-grown, regenerated, or reused on a scale comparable with its rate of consumption. Non-renewable resources are generally considered finite because their consumption rate far exceeds the rate that nature can replenish them; examples include coal, uranium, petroleum and natural gas. Renewable resources are those that can regenerate themselves via natural or human management processes, meaning they can be replenished for future generations – for example, timber, fish, solar energy and wind power. If a resource such as fish or timber is over-harvested it will not have the opportunity to reproduce at a rate that is sufficient to ensure that it can last indefinitely.

There is obviously a strong link between resource usage and sustainability. Resources are the fundamental component of the economic system in both industry and agriculture. The legal system has in recent times intervened in the resource markets to provide a more equitable outcome. The paradox is that the use of resources generates revenue, which provides wealth and raises living standards, but if the resources are non-renewable, they will not be available to future generations. The problems for future generations will be compounded by the 'side effects' of resource use, such as global warming, species extinction and pollution.

The 'ecological footprint' and 'The Story of Stuff' highlight the global use of resources and clearly illustrate the inequities in resource consumption between nations. Redressing this imbalance to provide justice for nation states and society creates numerous dilemmas. Nation states have their own expectations of what they hope to achieve and are averse to external standards imposed by the international community. The need to resolve the conflict between resource use and global environmental protection is at the core of sustainable development. The legal system must take into account an enormous range of competing interests (including developers, financial institutions, NGOs, governments, corporations, and future generations in both rich and poor countries) and somehow balance their competing rights.

Australia's response to international initiatives for global environmental protection has been mixed due to the restriction placed on it by the Constitution that primarily makes environmental protection a residual power. Having said this, there are numerous examples where Australian governments have ratified international instruments within Australia. Some examples include the *Environment Protection and Biodiversity Conservation Act 1999* (Cth) from CITES, 1976; the Biodiversity Convention, 1993; and the *Ozone Protection and Synthetic Greenhouse Gas Management Act 1989* (Cth) from the Montreal Protocol, 1989.

Lastly, there are considerable **barriers to achieving an international response to global environmental protection**, which were plain for the entire world to see at Copenhagen in 2009.

A cohesive, coordinated, global and holistic approach based on environmentally sustainable development is the most effective way to achieve global environmental protection. Such a large-scale international response is the ideal, but what is attainable is a different matter. A number of barriers limit a coordinated international response and the most obvious one is sovereignty. A nation's own unique circumstances can make it very reluctant to comply with international initiatives. The United Nations is in the difficult position of having to respect national sovereignty – as mandated by its own Charter – while serving as the means of achieving international cooperation.

Environmental processes and natural phenomena are different from political and other social events; they are arguably more difficult to deal with in the process of negotiation and compromise that constitutes policy-making. Environmental policy-makers must have at least some understanding of the science supporting the instruments they propose to enact, and must be able to resolve various tensions between the ethical and political implications of the precautionary principle.

The UN is large and labyrinthine, and there is some lack of coordination between the General Assembly and the other organs and agencies, and between the separate development funds and programmes. All these may be factors in international bodies' difficulty influencing national laws and policies. In addition to this, international law can struggle to get a high level of compliance.

Furthermore, the treaty-making process is time-consuming. Ratification by the parties requires persuasion at the domestic level, as governments attempt to create support for the treaty and consensus among their citizens.

Sample examination questions

Question 1
Assess the extent to which the legal system has responded to the impact of changing values and ethical standards on environmental protection.

[25 marks]

Question 2
Describe how agencies of reform meet the need for law reform in global environmental protection, and under what conditions these needs arise.

[25 marks]

Question 3
'In order to achieve justice, it is necessary to have compliance with the law.'
In the context of protection of the global environment, discuss this in relation to compliance and non-compliance.

[25 marks]

Question 4
Assess the place of law in resolving conflict and encouraging cooperation through the implementation of international agreements and other aspects of global environmental protection.

[25 marks]

Question 5
Assess the role of international tribunals in protecting the environment.

[25 marks]

Question 6
Evaluate the ability of the law to protect the environment within Australia and internationally.

[25 marks]

Question 7
To what extent have international law and environmental conferences enhanced protection of the global environment? [25 marks]

Question 8
Discuss whether the nation state limits the effectiveness of the law in protecting the global environment.
[BOS 2009] [25 marks]

Question 9
Why is there a need for an international legal response to global environmental protection?
[BOS 2011] [25 marks]

Question 10
How effective is the law in responding to conflict between the demand for resources and global environmental protection?
[BOS 2011] [25 marks]

Question 11
To what extent does the achievement of global environmental protection depend upon the level of cooperation between nation states?
[BOS 2012]   [25 marks]

Chapter 7

Option 3 – Family Law

The nature of family law

The definition of the family has continued to evolve over the last 50 years. As such, the law has responded to protect the rights and enforce the responsibilities of family members in these changing family arrangements.

Since Federation, family law has always faced constitutional constraints as a result of Section 51(xxi) mentioning the words 'marriage and divorce'. The *Marriage Act 1961* (Cth) established the legal requirements of a valid marriage, which to this day is the union of a man and a woman entered into voluntarily to the exclusion of all others for life. Other legal requirements for a marriage include:
- Marriageable age – the age of 18, except in exceptional and unusual circumstances
- Prohibited degrees of relationship – cannot marry anyone in a direct line of family relationship
- Notice of marriage.

The *Family Law Act 1975* (Cth) sets out the legal duties and obligations that a marriage creates. The principal aim of the Family Law Act was to reform the law governing the dissolution of a marriage.

In the past any other matters pertaining to family law, such as wills, adoption, child protection, etc. have been dealt with by the states. These matters are still regulated under state jurisdiction, except for dissolution matters involving de facto couples, which, since 2009, have been heard federally by the Family Law Court.

There are varied family relationships recognised by the law and these are a product of changing social conditions and moral viewpoints.

Alternative family arrangements
- Relationships within **Aboriginal and Torres Strait Islander (ATSI)** communities are bound by traditions and enforced through customary law. Children may be betrothed at an early age and parents or elders generally arrange marriages. Typically, ATSI customary law marriages do not conform to the requirements of a valid marriage under the *Marriage Act 1961* (Cth). These ATSI marriages are generally not legally recorded, nor are they registered with the relevant authorities. The law, therefore, does not formally recognise ATSI customary law marriages as having any legal standing. These relationships are recognised from state to state as de facto arrangements and are governed in the same way. For example, in NSW this recognition would be in the form of the *Property Relationships Act 1984* (NSW).
- **Single parent families** receive the same protection that other people do under discrimination legislation at federal and state levels. Having said this, single parent families face many social issues in accessing legal advice, pursuing their rights in court and obtaining adequate legal protection. Their right to receive maintenance is governed by the *Child Support (Assessment) Act 1989* (Cth).

- A **blended family** is created when a parent remarries. When a parent and his or her children from a former marriage or relationship live with another parent and children in similar circumstances, it is considered to be a blended family. The family includes the stepmother or stepfather and stepchildren. A step-parent is not responsible for the maintenance or support of a partner's child; the financial obligations towards a child remain with the child's parents. However, a court may make an order requiring a step-parent to pay financial support if satisfied that the step-parent has a duty to maintain the child (*Family Law Act 1975* (Cth) (FLA)). A step-parent may also become financially responsible for his or her partner's children if the family has existed for a long time and the natural parent is dead or cannot be found.
- A **de facto relationship** is defined in Section 4AA of the *Family Law Act 1975* (Cth) as one in which the partners are not legally married to each other, neither is the parent, child, descendant or sibling of the other, and they have a relationship as a couple living together on a genuine domestic basis. It is also defined under the *Property Relationships Act 1984* (NSW). The definition of a de facto relationship includes same-sex couples. The definition of 'de facto' in this Act also applies to persons making an application for family provision under the *Succession Act 2008* (NSW), and to entitlements of the de facto partners of individuals who died intestate, under the laws amended by the *Succession Amendment (Intestacy) Act 2009* (NSW). In other words, same-sex partners have the same entitlements under those laws as if they were married. For all intents and purposes there is very little difference between de facto couples and married couples since the passing of the *Family Law Amendment (De Facto Financial Matters and Other Measures) Act 2009*.
- A **polygamous marriage** refers to a relationship that is formed when an individual marries more than one person. While some cultures and religions permit polygamous marriages overseas, polygamous marriages are not legal in Australia. However, under Section 6 of the *Family Law Act 1975* (Cth), a polygamous marriage that was entered into overseas is deemed to be a marriage for the purpose of children's matters, property settlements and other court proceedings under the Family Law Act.

Legal rights and obligations of parents and children
Parental responsibility is shared equally in law under the *Family Law Reform Act 1995* (Cth), which made significant amendments to the *Family Law Act 1975* (Cth) with respect to children. Further amendments were made by the *Family Law Amendment (Shared Parental Responsibility) Act 2006* (Cth), which gave further emphasis to the child's right to meaningful family relationships and care, rather than either parent's 'right' to have the child live with him or her.

All parents have responsibility for their children and in addition they have certain rights to raise their children in the best manner they see fit. These are outlined as follows:
- In NSW it is compulsory for a child to attend an educational facility from the age of six until the minimum school-leaving age, which is 17 years or the completion of Year 10. Changes to the *Education Act 1900* (NSW) in 2009 now require every young person who has completed Year 10 to be in some form of education, training or employment until he or she reaches the age of 17.
- Parents have the right to **discipline** their child by using physical force in order to correct their child's behaviour, but the physical force must be 'reasonable, having regard to the age, health, maturity or other characteristics of the child, the nature of the alleged misbehaviour or other circumstance'.

- **Medical or dental treatment** of young persons aged 16 to 17 requires the consent of the young person. These requirements are contained in the *Minors (Property and Contracts) Act 1970* (NSW) Section 49. If the parents refuse medical or dental treatment (for instance, on religious grounds), a court can authorise the treatment.

Adoption
Adoption is the process of transferring parental rights and responsibilities from the biological parents to the adoptive parents. The aim of adoption law is to ensure that the best and most appropriate parents are found for the child. The needs of the adults are secondary to the needs of the child. Adoption re-creates the legal relationship between the child and his or her parents. Adoption is a state responsibility. In NSW, adoption is governed by the *Adoption Act 2000* (NSW).

Responses to problems in family relationships

Divorce
Divorce is regulated by the *Family Law Act 1975,* (Cth) the *Family Law Reform Act 1995* (Cth) and the *Family Law Amendment (Shared Parental Responsibility) Act 2006* (Cth). Divorce in Australia is treated with a no-fault approach, with the only grounds for divorce being the 'irretrievable breakdown' of the relationship. Couples must separate for 12 months (including a three-month 'kiss and make up' period) and are only free to remarry when a 'decree absolute' is issued. It is possible for couples to fulfil the separation period while living 'separate under the one roof'.

Legal consequences of separation
Matters pertaining to **children** must be resolved before a 'decree absolute' is issued. Separating parents must come to an agreement about a 'parenting plan' which will identify a number of 'parenting orders' pertaining to the children. These orders will identify the primary and secondary carer, who the children are to spend time with and any other relevant issues that need to be resolved. A major issue recently has been the court's attempt to ensure that parenting orders are complied with. Matters pertaining to the payment of child maintenance are also a matter to be resolved. This is calculated according to the formula based on how much is earned, the number of children and time spent with each parent.

Property must also be divided up. There is no set rule for property division and 'non-financial' contributions to family property are recognised. Superannuation is now included as a part of a property settlement. Child maintenance can also be included as a lump sum in a property settlement as well.

Dealing with domestic violence
The law has continued to evolve in its approach to domestic violence. Historically it was considered as a matter between husband and wife and, prior to 'rape in marriage' laws introduced in 1983, the victims (predominately women) were given little protection under the law. The law of assault under the Crimes Act failed to give victims immediate protection. Domestic violence amendments since the early 1980s introduced **Apprehended Domestic Violence Orders (ADVOs)**. To give an ADVO the court must be convinced on the 'balance of probabilities' that the violence is occurring. Amendments over the next 20 years saw the introduction of interim orders and making 'stalking and intimidation' an offence.

The *Crimes (Domestic and Personal Violence) Act 2007* (NSW) was passed, as it was believed domestic violence warranted a standalone Act, not a series of amendments to the Crimes Act.

ADVOs bring the violence out into the open, but essentially if an offender wants to breach an order they will. When a person is placed under an ADVO, they have not yet committed a crime. If a person breaches an ADVO, then they have committed a crime. Domestic violence offenders or those in breach of an ADVO may have their bail application denied. Section 9A of the *Bail Act 1978* (NSW) excludes domestic violence offenders from an automatic presumption in favour of bail. The *Firearms Act 1989* (NSW) was amended to allow police when called to a domestic dispute to be able to search for and seize any firearms found on the premises. The police are also able to seize firearms and other weapons when an ADVO is issued.

The role of courts and dispute resolution

Family dispute resolution is defined by Section 10F of the *Family Law Act 1975* (Cth) as a non-judicial process in which an independent practitioner helps people affected by a separation or divorce to resolve some of their disputes with each other. The spirit of the Act is for disputes to be mediated and for separating couples to arrive at their own agreements.

The introduction of **Family Relationship Centres** has seen a number of couples take up the offer of free initial counselling sessions (couples together for less than two years). The Family Court and the Federal Magistrates' Court (the Family Law Courts) can refer disputing parties to an extensive range of counselling services for both adults and children, and can also order separating couples to attend dispute resolution. Although individuals are required to pay for these services, some associated costs may be subsidised by the government depending on the financial circumstances of the individual parties. A majority of couples file their own agreement once it has been vetted by the registrar of the court. Matters pertaining to children must be resolved before a divorce is finalised.

Approximately 5% of matters are heard adversarially in court. In the instance where couples cannot agree, the court will make orders for them.

Prior to the establishment of the **Family Court** in 1975, the various state courts would hear matters relating to divorce. The Family Court is a specialised court – that is, outside the judicial hierarchy – and it hears matters relating to separation, divorce and other disputes related to marriage. Its jurisdiction is limited to those areas controlled by the *Family Law Act 1975* (Cth), which include property and financial matters, maintenance and parenting arrangements.

In late 1999 the **Federal Magistrates' Court** was established to relieve some of the case load of the Federal Court and the Family Court, and to reduce the cost and time required to deal with some federal matters.

The **Children's Court** hears cases relating to the care and protection of children under the *Children and Young Persons (Care and Protection) Act 1998* (NSW). Such cases are usually brought by Community Services, the division of the NSW Department of Human Services whose responsibility is keeping children and young people safe from harm and supporting the families of children and young people.

There are a number of **non-government organisations** that provide support for families and individuals who may be struggling with personal relationships and other family issues. Many of the better known organisations are operated by various religious groups such as the Salvation Army, or by churches, such as Centacare (www.centacare.org.au) and Anglicare (www.anglicare.org.au). Other groups include the Smith Family and Relationships Australia.

Contemporary issues concerning family law

Recognition of same-sex relationships
The *Property (Relationships) Act 1984* (NSW) recognised same-sex couples in the same way that de facto couples were recognised. Previously, they had no access to the law as their relationships were not recognised. The *Property (Relationships) Amendment Act 1999* (NSW) removed further discrimination arising from several laws at a state level. The federal government also removed any discriminatory pieces of law for same-sex couples at federal level and improved access to the law with the *Family Law Amendment (De Facto Financial Matters and Other Measures) Act 2009* (Cth) in matters where relationships are in the process of dissolving. Same-sex couples now have the same rights as married couples for all intents and purposes. They are not, however, recognised under the *Marriage Act 1961* (Cth) but the law has also changed in the area of access to adoption by same-sex couples. The *Adoption Amendment (Same Sex Couples) Act* allows same-sex couples living in a de facto or registered relationship to adopt jointly, as well as to adopt their partner's children (step-child adoption).

The changing nature of parental responsibility
Since the passing of the Family Law Act, which embedded the principal of the 'best interests' of the child, the law has continued to develop the rights of children in family disputes and to ensure parents meet their responsibility. The *Family Law Reform Act 1995* (Cth) changed the essential terminology around the guardianship of children and further developed the concept of parenting plans. It promoted the right of children to be able to spend as much time with each parent as is practicably possible and to be safe from violent family environments. This was taken further with the *Family Law Amendment (Shared Parental Responsibility) Act 2006* (Cth).

Surrogacy and birth technologies
The legal status of children born as a result of birth technology methods is covered by the *Status of Children Act 1996* (NSW). All women (regardless if they are single, married or in a relationship with another person) are permitted **access** to IVF treatment in New South Wales under the *Assisted Reproductive Technology Act 2007* (NSW). The *Miscellaneous Acts Amendment (Same Sex Relationships) Act 2008* (NSW) recognises co-mothers as legal parents of children born through donor insemination and provides birth certificates allowing both mums to be recognised.

Commercial surrogacy is outlawed in Australia but altruistic surrogacy is permitted under the *Surrogacy Act 2010* (NSW). The birth mother is always the legal mother in surrogacy, including when birth technologies are used. The Act provides for the automatic presumption of paternity for all children but male donors in IVF and surrogacy procedures are not included in this presumption. The Act also stipulates that a parentage application must be supported by an independent counsellor's report to assure the order is in the best interests of the child. The Act does not impose conditions about the gender of the parents. Commercial surrogacy, advertising surrogacy arrangements and also going overseas to enter into a surrogacy arrangement are illegal under the *Surrogacy Act 2010* (NSW).

Child protection
At a state level the *Children and Young Persons (Care and Protection) Act 1998* (NSW) provides for mandatory reporting to Community Services NSW (formally referred to as DOCS) of children considered to be **'at risk'** of harm. Community Services NSW (CSN) can apply to the Children's Court for a range of orders to ensure the safety of the child reported to them. The NSW Ombudsman's annual report of **'reviewable deaths of children'** in NSW each year highlights cases of children known to CSN who have died as a result of abuse or neglect. The NSW Government has increased resources and a review in 2009 by Justice Wood has recommended (adopted) a need to streamline reporting so that only more serious cases are referred on and others are dealt with at a more localised level, e.g. at schools, etc.

Child protection issues are dealt with at a federal level when couples are separating through the Family Court. Orders can also be made through the court to ensure the protection of children considered at risk.

Sample examination questions

Question 1
Evaluate how the law responds to changing values in the community with respect to Australian families.   [25 marks]

Question 2
Describe legal remedies available to family members when they have legal issues relating to family. How easy or difficult is it to access these remedies? Discuss.
[25 marks]

Question 3
In the context of family law, discuss the effectiveness of the legal remedies in obtaining justice for family members.
[25 marks]

Question 4
'In order to achieve justice, it is necessary to have compliance with the law.'
In the context of family law, discuss this in relation to compliance and non-compliance.
[25 marks]

Question 5
Assess the ability of the law in resolving conflict and encouraging cooperation during divorce and other aspects of family law.
[25 marks]

Question 6
How effective is the court system in dealing with issues affecting family members?
[BOS 2009]   [25 marks]

Question 7

Compare and contrast the legal consequences and responsibilities of marriage with those of ONE alternative family arrangement.
[BOS 2009]   [25 marks]

Question 8

Assess whether changes to family law are an improvement on previous law.
[BOS 2010]   [25 marks]

Question 9

To what extent have changing values in the community improved the legal rights of parents and children?
[BOS 2011]   [25 marks]

Question 10

Evaluate the effectiveness of the law in achieving justice for parties involved in relationship breakdown.
[BOS 2011]   [25 marks]

Question 11

To what extent does the law adequately protect family members in relation to birth technologies and surrogacy?
[BOS 2012]   [25 marks]

Chapter 8

Option 4 – Workplace

The nature of workplace law

There has been gradual development of the nature of the workplace over many centuries from the rigid system of feudalism to the master/servant relationship in the early 19th century. The most dramatic of changes occurred during the Industrial Revolution, which transformed societies from primarily agrarian to industrialised. Because the pace of change was rapid, there were many upheavals in the way people lived and how and where they worked.

Machines began to replace skilled labour in many industries and as a result employers were able to exploit workers, especially in cities where large and unregulated factories began to emerge. In the beginning there were no laws to protect workers, who consisted largely of women and children, who were favoured by the profit-driven industrialists.

Initially it was thought that the government should not interfere with the labour market, as the market mechanisms were the most efficient method of determining what was produced and at what costs. This was known as a *laissez-faire* market.

The workplace conditions were so appalling that eventually governments began to regulate the workplace to ensure minimum standards of safety and rates of pay. **Trade unions** were legalised in England in 1832.

From the 1840s onwards, trade unions pressured governments and employers to improve hours of work, rates of pay and safety. The rise of trade unions and effective pressure groups, and the metamorphosis of these into political parties, corresponded with the continued improvement of working conditions provided by a growing body of workplace law.

With respect to the workplace there are two main types of workplace contracts. These are **contracts of service** and **contracts for service**. A contract of service is a legal agreement between an employee and an employer that outlines the rights and duties of both parties in the employment arrangement. For example, under a contract of service an employer is required to provide an employee with safe working conditions and compensation in the event that the employee is injured. The employer must also provide the employee with annual leave, sick leave and superannuation.

A contract for services is when an independent contractor agrees to provide a particular service for an agreed payment to either a consumer or another business. Once the service has been provided there are no other legal obligations.

All workplace contracts include terms that outline the purpose of the contract. These terms may be **express** or **implied**. **Express terms** are terms that are included in the contract, either verbally or in writing, and agreed to by both parties. These can make explicit hours of work, rates of pay, entitlements to leave such as maternity, illness and family leave, etc. Workplace agreements also have **implied terms**, which are included in the contract even though they are not explicitly referred to. These terms usually have been created through precedent or legislation in the past. Provision of a safe workplace is implied in all workplace contracts.

The workplace is also regulated by **awards** and **agreements**. An **award** is a legally binding agreement that sets out the minimum condition for workers across a whole industry working for specific employers. **Awards** are usually vetted by industrial courts. In Australia there are state and federal awards which workers can be employed under. At present, under the Labor federal government, a process of rationalisation of existing federal awards into what has been termed 'modern awards' has been taking place. As governments come and go, awards may be amended to suit the political ideology of the party in power. Whatever the case, awards set workplace conditions across the whole of an industry that is not characterised by individual workplace contracts.

There are various workplace **agreements** that exist and these either complement awards or have taken the place of them. **Enterprise agreements** were introduced to allow greater flexibility across varied workplaces. **Enterprise bargaining** is the process of developing enterprise agreements. Where they are entered into, the workers must be no worse off than they would be under their relevant award. This is called the **no-disadvantage test**, which sets up a **safety net** for workers entering into an enterprise agreement. These are also known as **certified agreements** and are approved by the **Australian Industrial Relations Commission (AIRC)** if the above conditions are met. These allow workers and employers flexibility to bargain beyond the parameters of the award system if it is in the interests of both parties.

Workers not covered by an award would usually have signed an **individual work contract**. Under the *Fair Work Act 2009* (Cth), these are now referred to as common law contracts, which also contain minimum standards that are to be included. Many workers have their workplace conditions set out in an individual workplace agreement.

At a federal level the main **statutory provision** for the regulation of the workplace is the *Fair Work Act 2009* (Cth). It provides for the National Employment Standards (NES), which are 10 minimum standards for employees' pay and conditions that all workplace arrangements must meet. The Act also introduced the development of **'modern awards'** that aim to establish a minimum set of standards for people working in industries across Australia. These awards will also have in-built flexibility arrangements so that individual workplaces can negotiate an agreement to suit their particular circumstances, keeping in mind the 'no-disadvantage' test. The modern awards will be reviewed by **Fair Work Australia** (now the **Fair Work Commission**) every four years, and minimum wage provisions will be reviewed annually.

The Fair Work Act also makes provision for enterprise agreements. They can be negotiated with or without union involvement, and, as mentioned earlier, workers cannot be worse off under the agreement compared to the award which must be agreed to by the majority of workers. **Greenfields agreements** are allowed under the Act, providing for future employees of a new enterprise to be established by one or more employers. The agreement is made when it has been endorsed by each employer and by the trade union or unions that cover the prospective employees.

From 2010 all employees of sole traders and partnerships, as well as employees of constitutional corporations, are covered by the industrial relations system governed by federal law under *The Industrial Relations (Commonwealth Powers) Act 2009* (Cth). This is because the NSW Government referred these matters (such as employees of sole traders and partnerships) to the federal government and therefore they are dealt with by Fair Work Australia (now the FWC).

Regulation of the workforce
Both the state and federal governments have the power to make laws with respect to industrial relations. This has caused confusion over the years for both employers and employees. It has been possible for some business enterprises to have employees on both state and federal arrangements at the same time. When the state and federal law conflicts, Section 109 of the Constitution (inconsistency provisions) is invoked, which ensures that federal law prevails to the extent of the inconsistency.

Industrial relations refers to the relationships between employers, employees, the government and trade unions. Each of these groups is considered a stakeholder in the process of negotiating what is in the best interests of each in terms of awards, enterprise agreements and individual workplace arrangements. In NSW the Industrial Relations Commission negotiates these disputes or oversees the bargaining process that occurs periodically in various industries.

At the federal level, the *Fair Work Act 2009* (Cth) has established **Fair Work Australia** (now the FWC) to approve collective agreements and assess against the 'no disadvantage' test.

Both tribunals were created to set salary and working conditions in the form of awards, resolve industrial disputes, and hear and determine any industrial matters. An industrial dispute can concern various matters, including unfair dismissal, discrimination or occupational health and safety.

At times employees and employers will disagree on matters pertaining to pay and/or working conditions and both may take action to assert their points of view. During a negotiating period to draw up a new enterprise agreement both parties may engage in what is known as **'protected industrial action'**. Fair Work Australia (now the FWC) acts to ensure that the bargaining process complies with industrial laws. In order to commence a claim in support of a new enterprise agreement after an existing agreement has passed its expiry date, employees must first obtain an order from Fair Work Australia allowing them to proceed, with a protected action ballot endorsing industrial action.

Negotiations between employers and employees are commonly known as workplace bargaining. As mentioned earlier, enterprise agreements are negotiated across an industry or a workplace involving a number of employees who have similar concerns and issues in respect to their workplace. Generally in these situations, employees have greater bargaining power and hence get more favourable conditions. Employees hired on individual employment contracts may get similarly advantageous conditions but these cannot be worse than what is provided for in the award.

Industrial disputes may arise in the workplace over issues such as working conditions, pay and entitlements, and discrimination. **Dispute resolution mechanisms** centre on mediation and other consensual forms of resolution. If disputes cannot be resolved then the matter will move to arbitration.

Under both the *Fair Work Act 2009* (Cth) and the *Industrial Relations Act 1996* (NSW), all awards and agreements must contain dispute resolution procedures (the NSW legislation exempts businesses employing fewer than 20 people from this requirement). The most efficient way to resolve these types of disputes is through negotiation via **mediation** and **conciliation**. Matters that cannot be negotiated for various reasons move to **arbitration**. This can be costly and time-consuming where a decision is imposed on both parties by the Fair Work division of the Federal Court or the Federal Magistrates Court. Fair Work Australia (now the FWC) will advise the parties if it believes the matter to have no reasonable prospect of success in court.

The **Fair Work Ombudsman** also has jurisdiction to deal with complaints about pay and entitlements, employers breaching the law and discrimination. The main approach will be to resolve the matter in a consensual manner. If investigation reveals that a party has broken the law, the inspector can give the party notice to remedy the breach, and if the party fails to do so, the matter may go to court.

There are specialist courts and tribunals set up to deal with workplace disputes. In NSW the **Industrial Relations Commission**, which refers matters to the **NSW Industrial Relations Tribunal**, investigates alleged breaches of state industrial legislation, awards and enterprise agreements. It will first order a compulsory conference between the parties, then conciliation. It will only employ arbitration to deal with an industrial dispute if conciliation is unsuccessful. Its orders are binding.

At the federal level, **Fair Work Australia** (now the FWC) is the industrial relations **tribunal**. It can arbitrate matters and also make rulings on unfair dismissal and other matters emanating from industrial disputes. The *Fair Work Act 2009* (Cth) created a **Fair Work Division** of the **Federal Magistrates Court,** which can hear small claims matters under the value of $200 000. It also created a **Fair Work Division** of the **Federal Court**.

There are a number of **governmental organisations** at the state and federal levels to support various courts and tribunals and also undertake other specific roles with respect to industrial relations. The **NSW Industrial Relations Commission (IRC)**, apart from the adjudicating role mentioned earlier, also engages in the formulation of awards and approving enterprise agreements for workers operating under the state system. The commission can also regulate and register employer associations.

Fair Work Australia (now the FWC), in addition to being an industrial tribunal, also oversees the federal industrial relations system. It can modify awards, provide advice about the industrial framework to businesses and workers, make decisions concerning minimum wages and review and approve enterprise agreements.

The **Fair Work Ombudsman**, as outlined in Section 68 of the *Fair Work Act 2009* (Cth), is to advance 'harmonious, productive and cooperative workplace relations and to ensure the provisions of the Act are complied with'. It does this by providing education and advice in addition to investigating and enforcing breaches of the Act, awards and agreements.

Trade unions have historically been the main bodies that have agitated for and improved employee pay and working conditions, as far back as the Industrial Revolution. Today, union membership has fallen to approximately 20% of workers in Australia. Unions provide education and advice to their members as well as advocate in matters involving members who may have a genuine grievance with their employers. Unions also collectively bargain on behalf of their members during the process of updating awards and negotiating enterprise agreements.

The **Australian Council of Trade Unions (ACTU)** is the national peak body for all Australian unions. It was formed in 1927. The ACTU represents Australian labour organisations internationally, articulating positions and advocating on behalf of human rights and other issues.

Employer associations are composed of employers from similar industries. Like unions, they represent their members when awards are being updated or when enterprise agreements are being negotiated. They provide education and research to their members and inform them of the rights under the industrial framework. Employer associations include the Australian Chamber of Commerce and Industry, the Chamber of Commerce (NSW), the Business Council of Australia, and Master Builders Associations of Australia and the various states and territories.

Non-government organisations (NGOs) also provide research, carry out education programs and make submissions to governments voicing concerns they may have with respect to an aspect of workplace relations. There are various NGOs and they may receive funding from government, or they could be established under statute and may have developed from a community grassroots organisation. Irrespective of origin, NGOs are independent from government and respond to issues as they see fit.

Many issues to do with workplace relations may also be addressed by the **media**. The media can be a very effective non-legal mechanism to ensure justice is achieved in the workplace. For example, the *Sydney Morning Herald* ran a series of articles about workplace safety for workers aged between 16 and 24. It researched the damning statistics for this sector of the workforce and looked into the reasons for it. The media has also highlighted other issues such as discrimination and sexual harassment in the workplace as well as the many facets of occupational and workplace safety. The media may also be biased depending on the proprietor's priorities, which may see it slightly favour either workers or employers when various disputes or negotiations are under way.

Remuneration refers to size of a worker's salary and additional package or wage that they receive annually or weekly. Employees earning a salary may package a number of additional items into their remuneration, such as superannuation, share portfolios, use of a company car, etc. The remuneration package must satisfy the NES as to minimum award rates of pay and entitlements. It may also include an 'incentive package', which is based on the employee's performance.

In addition to this is the **Superannuation Guarantee Scheme**, which is provided for under the *Superannuation Guarantee (Administration) Act 1992* (Cth). Under this scheme employers must pay 9% of an employee's annual earnings into a fund of the employee's choosing.

Contemporary issues concerning the workplace

Discrimination in the workplace has always been an issue and the law has responded to make this behaviour illegal. Discrimination is treating a person unfavourably because of a characteristic or feature that may be a part of their make-up. This could be on the basis of age, gender, sexual orientation, marital status, race, pregnancy, etc. There are two types of discrimination. These are **direct discrimination** and **indirect discrimination**.

The main legislation in NSW is the *Anti-Discrimination Act 1977* (NSW) which is a broad-based Act that covers many types of discrimination. The *Industrial Relations Act 1996* (NSW) also has provisions making discrimination illegal. More specific laws exist at a federal level, including the *Sex Discrimination Act 1984* (Cth), the *Race Discrimination Act 1975* (Cth) and the *Age Discrimination Act 2004* (Cth). These Acts all have **tribunal mechanisms** for complaints to be mediated or adjudicated depending on the nature of the complaint. The Fair Work Act also has provisions in regard to discrimination.

Discrimination in the workplace still occurs, and women are more likely than men to make a complaint under state or federal law. Sexual harassment is still a major concern but many victims do not make complaints under the various legislation. The NSW Council of Social Services (NCOSS) and the Federation of Ethnic Communities' Councils of Australia (FECCA) are examples of some of the non-legal bodies that highlight aspects of discrimination with respect to the areas of concern.

In the last 20 years, **workplace safety** has become one of the core compliance issues for businesses and any other organisations that have paid employees. A safe workplace includes safe equipment, safe work systems and appropriate training procedures. Many Australians every year are injured in the course of their work and a significant proportion of these injuries are preventable.

Employers may be subject to court action under the common law of negligence as a result of injuries or other harm suffered. The tort of negligence requires that employers provide a proper **standard of care** to ensure they fulfil their **duty of care** owed to employees.

Apart from common law standards, employees also have statutory obligations with respect to safety in the workplace. In NSW there are numerous pieces of legislation that regulate occupational health and safety in the workplace. The main ones are the *Occupational Health and Safety Act 2000* (NSW), the *Workers Compensation Act 1987* (NSW) and the *Workplace Injury Management and Workers Compensation Act 1998* (NSW). Employees also participate in workplace safety, and one way in which this occurs is the statutory obligation for employees to be members of an 'Occupational Health and Safety Committee' at their workplace.

Unions have been the major non-legal mechanism, with a long history of working to improve workplace safety in Australia. Education and training will continue to be the most effective method of preventing injuries in the first place. Strong coercive regimes are still needed to ensure that non-compliant employers face the full weight of the law.

The fourth stage of the employment relations cycle is **separation (termination) of employment**. Employment can be terminated by resignation and this occurs when an employee for various reasons decides to leave their current employment. There is no official **retirement** age given we have an aging population and may face a future skills shortage, but age does determine when a person is entitled to take all of their superannuation.

At times employees will be **dismissed** and this can be **without notice** because they are incompetent; have engaged in some form of serious misconduct; or they have been warned about an issue by the employer a number of times but have failed to rectify the problem. Some employees can be dismissed **with notice** as long as the employer meets their legal obligations. If a dismissal is harsh, unjust or unreasonable, the employee can file a claim of unfair dismissal with Fair Work Australia (now the FWC) or the NSW IRC. If an employee is unfairly dismissed they may be reinstated or may receive a monetary payout.

At times some employees may face **retrenchment** and this happens when there is no longer a job for that person.

Leave is a fundamental right of employees and can be found within International Labour Organization conventions and UN treaties. Minimum leave entitlements are included in all modern awards and enterprise agreements, and are protected under both state and federal legislation. The various types of leave that workers may be entitled to are annual leave, sick leave, long service leave, community-based leave, parental leave or carer's leave.

A major issue facing working families today is juggling work and family life. There have been many calls for workplace law to be more flexible for employees, but it must be remembered that the rights of employers have to be considered in this. The Paid Parental Leave scheme began in Australia on 1 January 2011. Australians work some of the longest hours in the developed world. The continued debate about a flexible workplace that meets the needs of employees and employers is important, as the quality of family life is a key factor in the type of society that is developed.

Sample examination questions

Question 1
Assess the extent to which the law reflects changing values and ethics in the community in achieving justice for individuals in the workplace.

[25 marks]

Question 2
Describe how agencies of reform meet the need for law reform in the workplace, how well they meet the needs of employees and employers, and under what conditions these needs arise.

[25 marks]

Question 3
'In order to achieve justice, it is necessary to have compliance with the law.'
In the context of workplace law, discuss this in relation to compliance and non-compliance.

[25 marks]

Question 4
Assess the ability of the legal system in resolving conflict and encouraging cooperation in negotiations between employers and employees and other aspects of consumer law.
[25 marks]

Question 5
Explain how changes in Australian society have been reflected in law in the workplace.
[BOS 2009]   [25 marks]

Question 6
Examine why justice in the workplace has been hard to achieve.
[BOS 2010]   [25 marks]

Question 7
Explain the role of legal measures in balancing the rights and responsibilities of employees and employers.
[BOS 2011]   [25 marks]

Question 8
How effective has law reform been in dealing with contemporary issues in the workplace?
[BOS 20011]   [25 marks]

Question 9
Assess the role of the government in resolving conflict in the workplace.
[BOS 2012]   [25 marks]

Chapter 9

Option 5 – World Order

The nature of world order

The world has striven for peace and security for centuries. Preventing conflict has often proven difficult, as people continue to compete for resources. In addition, our social, political, moral and religious differences create a constant tension between nation states.

In essence, therefore, the central aim of world order is to promote international peace and harmony, and to reduce conflict. The main obstacles to achieving this are due to sovereignty and the differing moral and ethical standards evident in different nation states throughout the world.

For the purposes of this topic, a world order issue is anything that threatens peace and security on a regional or global level. It also includes any incidences of crimes against humanity, as these are mass atrocities that in most cases cannot be confined to one nation state. For example, crimes against humanity in the Darfur region of Sudan saw many flee to neighbouring Chad, escalating the conflict to a regional level and making it a world order issue.

The world today is interdependent to the extent that communities around the world interact with each other on a scale never before witnessed. As such, the impact of conflict regionally or globally has enormous implications for all nation states that act out of economic and political self-interest first and foremost.

This definition becomes important for the operation of international law because being a state brings with it fundamental rights and responsibilities. First, once a nation is recognised as a state, it becomes an international 'person', empowered to enter into a relationship with other states and to act in world affairs.

Many issues confronting the world today are therefore dealt with in a multilateral manner.

Sovereignty is the second consequence of statehood. A state has a right to be autonomous and in so doing has the exclusive right to control its own people and territory through domestic legislation and government policies. Sovereignty allows a state to act independently, reflecting its own unique culture. As such, the sovereignty of nation states can promote world order (as will be seen in later examples) or it can be an impediment to world order.

Conflict today is characterised by being either **inter-state** or **intra-state**. There are many forms of inter-state conflict. Some of these are:
- **Conventional war:** the use of large, well-organised military forces. During such a war, soldiers wear clearly identified uniforms and there is a clear command structure. The majority of wars in history have been conventional, although the trend seems to be that these may become a thing of the past due to technological advances.

- The development of nuclear weapons at the end of World War II saw the emergence of weapons of mass destruction and the possibility of a **nuclear war**. The trend today is for nations to reduce their nuclear stockpiles and hence create an environment where there is an intent to minimise the likelihood of a nuclear conflict. This is contrasted by some nations agitating for the right to develop nuclear technology, including Iran and North Korea.
- Another form of conflict that has emerged, especially over the last 10 to 15 years, is the possibility of **cyber warfare**. Due to the interconnectedness of the world through the internet, the potential to disrupt important infrastructure and defence systems is very real.

The main form of conflict in the world today is intra-state conflict. Forms of intra-state conflict include the following:
- **Guerrilla warfare:** an unconventional warfare where a small group of combatants use mobile tactics (ambushes, raids, etc.) to combat a larger and less mobile formal army. The Taliban are using these types of tactics against coalition forces in Afghanistan as they are facing a superior force with technologically better weapons.
- **Civil war:** a conflict between two or more sides within one country. There are many examples throughout history of conflict within nation states.
- There continue to be many conflicts **where governments wage war against their own people**. At times this results in crimes against humanity as a result of mass atrocities. These types of genocide have been newly termed 'democide'.

A further cause of conflict is **access to resources**. As the world comes under increased pressure for resources, it is likely that conflict will eventuate over the ownership of or the right to access resources. Oil reserves continue to diminish and access to fresh water is becoming increasingly scarce for some nations.

Responses to world order

The United Nations
The United Nations was founded after World War II. Its purpose is to strive for peace and security and act in a manner that reduces conflict. This is evident in its Charter, the main articles being:
- Article 2, which details how members of the UN should act if the stated purposes are to be achieved, for example:
  - Article 2(3) All members shall settle their international disputes by peaceful means in such a manner that international peace and security, and justice, are not endangered.
  - Article 2(4) All members shall refrain in their international relations from the threat or use of force against the territorial integrity or political independence of any state, or in any other manner inconsistent with the Purposes of the United Nations.
  - Article 2(5) All members shall give the United Nations every assistance in any action it takes in accordance with the present Charter, and shall refrain from giving assistance to any state against which the United Nations is taking preventive or enforcement action.

The laying down of these guidelines is significant because it is an attempt to set standards that any state can choose to follow and introduces the idea that states should join together to prevent war and maintain peace. The problem for the United Nations is that it does not have coercive powers to get nation states to agree to its agenda for peace and security in the world. As mentioned previously, every nation has the right to sovereignty, and it usually acts in its own economic and political interests first.

The **Security Council**, one arm of the UN, consists of 15 member states with only five of those being permanent members: the USA, Britain, France, the Russian Federation and China. The other 10 states are elected for two-year terms as representatives of the world, taking into account their contribution to international peace and attempting to ensure an equitable geographical distribution of non-permanent states (UN Charter Article 23). Any of the five permanent member states has the power of veto over an otherwise majority decision, and this custom reflects the dominance of members in the world order.

The UN Security Council's powers come from the UN Charter and they include (Article 39) that 'the Security Council shall determine the existence of any threat to the peace, breach of the peace, or act of aggression and shall make recommendations ... to maintain or restore international peace and security'. In resolving a threat to the peace, the Security Council may (Article 41) 'advocate complete or partial interruption of economic relations and of rail, sea, air, postal, telegraphic, radio and other means of communication, and the severance of diplomatic relations'. If these measures are inadequate, the Security Council may (Article 50) 'use demonstrations, blockades and other operations by air, sea or land forces'.

The UN (and the Security Council) faces mounting criticism that it is out of date and that its Charter is very Eurocentric in its views. In essence, its Charter cannot adequately deal with the threat of terrorism to world order, as terrorism is not confined to the sovereignty of a particular nation state. The veto power of the Security Council has seen many crises unresolved, resulting in humanitarian disasters such as those that occurred in Rwanda and Darfur. Some argue that the UN should reflect the current world order by including a Muslim nation among the permanent members of the Security Council.

International instruments
International instruments are documents, which are binding once they have been ratified, and are usually called treaties, covenants, conventions, protocols, agreements or pacts. Treaties are referred to as hard law. A treaty is an international agreement between states where parties agree to the terms of the treaty and are therefore bound by it. A treaty can be bilateral (between two countries) or multilateral (between more than two countries). Treaties are also guided by the principal of **jus cogens**, which means that when the context of a treaty becomes out of sync with the global public morality that the treaty no longer remains a viable and binding international agreement. For example, treaties signed by nation states to regulate the trade in slavery would not be recognised. Similarly, nation states that sign security treaties that breach the rules of the Geneva Convention would also not be recognised or binding.

A document that is not legally binding is called a declaration. It clarifies the international opinion on a specific issue, and this is called soft law.

International instruments relevant to world order issues are those instruments that are related to peace and security issues on a regional or global level. Some examples include:

- Recognition of the increased stockpiling of nuclear weapons and hence the signing of the Nuclear Non-Proliferation Treaty (NPT) 1966 did reduce the stocks of nuclear weapons held by nuclear nations.
- The more recent Comprehensive Nuclear Test Ban Treaty (CNTBT) was another important step in the right direction but it has been limited due to the fact that only nine of the 43 signatories have ratified it. This indicates a lack of political will to comply. A good example is North Korea's weapons testing in October 2006. Despite non-legal attempts at negotiation, it was decided that a UN resolution for sanctions against testing would be utilised. These were ineffective due to the sovereignty of North Korea.
- **ANZUS** is a more immediate example of an international treaty in our own region to promote stability and good relations.
- **'Lombok Treaty'** – Indonesia and Australia signed a security treaty in 2006 aimed at smoothing ties through greater security cooperation, and underlining support for Jakarta's sovereignty over restive provinces. The signing of the treaty enhances anti-terrorism cooperation and joint naval border patrols, as well as formalising military exchanges and training.
- Other world order instruments that could be referred to include the South Pacific Nuclear Free Zone Treaty (1986), the Sea-Bed Treaty (1971) and the Geneva Protocol.

Courts and tribunals

The International Court of Justice (ICJ) is the principal judicial organ of the United Nations, according to Article 7(1) of the UN Charter, and is sometimes referred to as the World Court. It has limited jurisdiction and only states can be parties to cases before the ICJ, not individuals. The ICJ's jurisdiction applies when there is a special agreement about a specific dispute, when parties to a treaty nominate the ICJ as the resolution mechanism or when nations make a unilateral declaration.

The ICJ can be used to solve international disputes by interpreting treaties between states, but only if the states consent to the ICJ's arbitration in advance. It can also be used to give advisory opinions on issues such as the legality of actions of other organs of the United Nations, but only if those organs request that opinion. Limitations on its powers reduce the ICJ's ability to take the initiative and to judge a state's behaviour, or that of a United Nations organ, independent of a request by that party itself. This is quite unlike the operation of any other type of court.

A decision of the ICJ has no binding force upon anyone other than the states that are parties to the case. There is therefore no doctrine of precedent operating to determine the decisions in future cases.

The International Criminal Court (ICC) convened for the first time in The Hague on 1 July 2002. It is empowered to bring prosecutions against world leaders, army officers and others thought responsible for war crimes or crimes against humanity. Its powers are not retrospective so it can only convict for human rights abuses committed after 1 July 2002. Complaints can be made to the court by an individual or a state. For a case to be eligible to be heard by the court, the incident has to have occurred in one of the ratifying countries or have been committed by one of their nationals. Therefore, it would not have power to hear a case against a US, Chinese or Israeli perpetrator. Offenders are punished by imprisonment in any of the ratifying states.

Another feature of the ICC is that it has complementary jurisdiction. This means that some accused can be tried within their own country under the auspices of the ICC. This can create problems. The 51 people named for crimes against humanity in Darfur, Sudan are all high-ranking government officials. If the ICC believes these men should stand trial, Sudan could implement the complementary jurisdiction provision of the Rome Statute. This may reduce the likelihood of the victims of these crimes against humanity seeing the perpetrators brought to justice. (See your criminal law notes on the ICC.)

The success of the ICC in effectively and more efficiently bringing perpetrators of crimes against humanity to justice remains to be seen. It is certainly an improvement on the ad hoc war crimes tribunal of Rwanda and Yugoslavia. At present, three British soldiers have been indicted for crimes against humanity (war crimes) in Iraq. The fact the USA has not ratified the Rome Statute certainly has weakened it as an instrument. The ICC potentially has an important role to play in world order in representing the view of the world that even leaders of nation states cannot hide behind the sovereignty of their countries. Once indicted, they may be apprehended when leaving the safety of their own borders. The chief prosecutor of the International Criminal Court issued warrants for the arrest of the Libyan leader, Muammar Gaddafi, and two members of his regime because they 'appear to bear the greatest responsibility for crimes against humanity' committed in Libya since 15 February 2011. In July 2010, the ICC issued a warrant for President al-Bashir's arrest for three counts of genocide.

Ad hoc tribunals were set up by the UN Security Council in the 1990s to deal with the crimes against humanity that had occurred in the Balkans [the International Criminal Tribunal for the former Yugoslavia (ICTY)] and in Rwanda [the International Criminal Tribunal for Rwanda (ICTR)].

Intergovernmental organisations
Intergovernmental organisations (IGOs) play an important role in the promotion of world order. They promote global standards as well as regional issues. Many IGOs work closely with their equivalent United Nations bodies; however, their primary role is to advocate for the interests of their own region.

NATO (the North Atlantic Treaty Organization) is a regional organisation operating as a defence pact since 1949. Starting out with 12 member states, it now has 19 member states from Europe and North America: Belgium, Canada, the Czech Republic, Denmark, France, Germany, Greece, Hungary, Iceland, Italy, Luxembourg, the Netherlands, Norway, Poland, Portugal, Spain, Turkey, Britain and the USA.

The NATO Charter details its powers and responsibilities; for example, Article 5 states, 'the parties agree that an armed attack against one or more of them in Europe or North America shall be considered an attack against them all; and consequently they agree that, if such an armed attack occurs each of them … will assist … by taking … action … to restore and maintain security of the North Atlantic area'.

NATO cooperates with the United Nations to promote the concept of collective security by providing methods of collectively keeping the peace. In the past decade, NATO has played a key role under the authority of the United Nations in former Yugoslavia, providing armed patrols and air strikes against warplanes violating the air space above Bosnia.

The European Union (EU) stands out as the most successful and influential regional intergovernmental organisation because it has created unprecedented wealth and security for its members and has revitalised European influence in the world. Furthermore, it has made the prospect of war between any of its 27 members unthinkable. A large number of states seek admission to the EU and it is emulated by other regional organisations, including the African Union.

The International Crisis Group (ICG) was founded in 1995 by a number of retired international leaders in response to the failure of the international community to anticipate and respond effectively to the genocides that occurred in Somalia, Rwanda and Bosnia in the early 1990s. With a budget of around $16 billion a year, the ICG monitors 60 conflicts and potential conflict situations. The ICG's aim is to be an accurate source of information for governments, IGOs and NGOs that are working to respond directly to conflict situations.

Other IGOs include the **African Union**, which is working in conjunction with the UN to resolve the crisis in Darfur, Sudan.

Non-governmental organisations
Non-government organisations (NGOs) are organisations that are not established by governments and therefore act independently of government and have no political role. They have played an important security role in particular situations. NGOs such as Community Aid Abroad, International Red Cross (known as the Red Crescent Movement in Islamic countries) and Amnesty International have attained a high profile in the pursuit of humanitarian relief and fostering local economic and social development. In doing so, these NGOs promote peace and security.

Australia's federal government
Australia became an internationally recognised nation state with its own legal identity after Federation in 1901. Like any nation state, Australia has the ability to promote peace and security or be an impediment to it within our own region.

In essence, it is the structure and systems of the Commonwealth and state governments that enable Australia's stance on many issues to be communicated effectively to the international community via the external affairs power in Section 51 of the Constitution. This gives it the power to ratify international agreements that form the main basis for the search for regional peace and security. An example of this was the Lombok Treaty signed between Indonesia and Australia, which was an important step to greater security and stability in the region.

Australia plays an important role in the peace and security of the Asia Pacific region. It has brokered many diplomatic solutions to international crises, e.g. East Timor, and has been a willing participant in many United Nations peacekeeping missions.

The media
It should be remembered that all media outlets are influenced by the culture and values that permeate the community they exist within. Hence, no media outlets are completely free of bias. Having said that, the media has played a crucial role in highlighting world order issues that were at the heart of incredible human suffering and the commission of crimes against humanity. Examples include Rwanda, Darfur in Sudan, East Timor – especially the Dili massacre. In fact, it was media pressure on the Security Council

during the Darfur crisis that eventually assisted in getting some form of sanctions against the Sudanese Government for alleged crimes against humanity.

Political negotiation, persuasion and the use of force

Force is a non-legal remedy because the UN Charter (Article 41) specifically states that 'the Security Council may decide what measures not involving the use of armed force are to be employed to give effect to its decision …'. The use of force invariably leads to retaliation and an escalation of hostilities. The United Nations has attempted to prevent force being used and advocates peaceful measures.

The United Nations Charter states that 'All members shall refrain in their international relations from the threat or use of force against the territorial integrity or political independence of any state, or in any other manner inconsistent with the purposes of the United Nations': Article 2(4) United Nations Charter. The Charter, however, does go on to state that nation states are able to use force in self-defence or on the grounds of humanitarian intervention.

Political negotiation is the simplest and most frequently used means of working with other states and resolving disputes. Communication between states now occurs at many levels of government, and each country has a vast array of experts who can negotiate the details of international agreements. These changes in the means available for political negotiation have increased the scope for greater cooperation. When disputes cannot be solved through political negotiation, the next option is the use of persuasion.

Persuasion is an alternative non-legal method. Its effectiveness depends upon whether persuasion is backed up by threats. A former British Prime Minister flew to meet with the Sudanese President to try to persuade the government to stop the attacks on civilian populations in the Darfur region. He was unsuccessful.

Nation states can be persuaded by UN reports, membership to certain IGOs or other incentives to resolve certain differences.

Contemporary issues concerning world order

Responsibility to protect

The 'responsibility to protect' is a new international security and human rights norm, designed to address the international community's repeated failure to prevent and stop mass atrocity crimes such as genocide and war crimes.

The principle, known in abbreviated form simply as R2P, came about in response to the controversy that raged over whether the international community had the 'right of humanitarian intervention' in the conflicts of Rwanda, Bosnia and Kosovo. Supporters of humanitarian intervention argued that the UNSC could use its Chapter VII powers to intervene, while opponents argued that the principle of state sovereignty, upheld by Article 2.7 of the UN Charter, did not permit humanitarian intervention. R2P was aimed at bridging the gap between these two views of state sovereignty.

This means that states have the responsibility to warn populations, to generate effective prevention strategies, and, when necessary, to mobilise military action. For NGOs and individuals, R2P means the responsibility to draw policy-makers' attention to what needs to be done, by whom and when. Evidence of the acceptance of R2P was evident in NATO and UN airstrikes on Libya and the Ivory Coast, respectively, in 2011.

Regional and global situations that threaten peace and security

A range of situations could be raised here to illustrate and apply some of the course content. Crises in countries where crimes against humanity have occurred may be raised. Some of these may be historical, such as Kosovo and Rwanda. More current ones could be Darfur or the Congo crisis. A further issue that could be examined may be the nuclear threat as outlined in *Cambridge Legal Studies HSC* (2nd edition) in Chapter 14, the world order topic. Whatever issue is examined, the effectiveness of the legal and non-legal measures to combat it must be looked at.

The success of global cooperation in achieving world order

The best way to examine this topic is through various case studies. Obviously world order is an ideal that has been around for many centuries. Lasting peace has always been unobtainable due to varying interests of nation states around the world. The notion of state sovereignty has generally seen most states put their own or regional interests before the common good. Lack of resources, social, ethnic and religious differences have also highlighted competing interests, especially on a regional level.

This is highlighted by the fact that more conflicts are intra-state conflicts than inter-state conflicts, and the ability of the treaty system and the United Nations to resolve these differences can be very limited at times.

Two case studies that could be researched and highlighted could be the instability of the Korean peninsula, or East Timor and UN intervention towards nation state status.

Rules regarding the conduct of hostilities

The formalised development of rules regarding the conduct of hostilities started after World War II. Some aspects of these rules had been in operation in various ways over time but not been incorporated into the modern treaty system in a consistent, coherent manner. The rules regarding the conduct of hostilities are also known as International Humanitarian Law (IHL). IHL refers to the body of treaties and humanitarian principles that regulate the conduct of armed conflict and seek to limit its effects. The main treaties that make up the body of IHL include the following:

- The Hague Conventions, which prohibit the use of chemical weapons, aerial bombing, etc.
- The four Geneva Conventions of 1949, which deal with the treatment of prisoners of war, the sick and civilians
- The Geneva Protocol of 1977, which further strengthened the protections offered to civilians, and in 2005 strengthened protections for international workers with the Red Cross/Red Crescent.

The introduction of the International Criminal Court (ICC) created under the Rome Statute is a further mechanism placed to deal with war crimes and crimes against the international community.

Sample examination questions

Question 1

Assess the extent to which the law reflects changing values and ethics in the community in achieving world order.

[25 marks]

Question 2
Describe how agencies of reform meet the need for law reform in world order, and under what conditions these needs arise.
[25 marks]

Question 3
'In order to achieve justice, it is necessary to have compliance with the law.'
In the context of world order, discuss this in relation to compliance and non-compliance.
[25 marks]

Question 4
Assess the ability of law in resolving conflict and encouraging cooperation in the implementation of international agreements and other aspects of world order.
[25 marks]

Question 5
The law reflects the culture and values of different societies and groups within society. Evaluate this statement in relation to legal issues and remedies affecting world order, and include a discussion of the nature and sources of conflict.
[25 marks]

Question 6
'The law is fundamental to achieving world order.' Assess this statement.   [25 marks]

Question 7
Discuss whether the nation state limits the effectiveness of law in achieving world order.
[BOS 2009]   [25 marks]

Question 8
Assess the difference the law can make in achieving justice regionally or globally where peace and security are threatened.
[BOS 2009]   [25 marks]

Question 9
Why is world order hard to achieve?
[BOS 2010]   [25 marks]

Question 10
Explain the role of nation states in achieving world order.
[BOS 2011]   [25 marks]

Question 11
How effective is global cooperation in responding to challenges to world order?
[BOS 2011]   [25 marks]

Question 12
Discuss how the nature of conflict provides challenges for achieving world order?
[BOS 2012]   [25 marks]

Chapter 10

Suggested responses

Section I: Crime and Human Rights

Sample multiple-choice questions

Chapter 1 – Crime

1	C	A significant feature of a crime is that it is punished by the state.
2	D	*Actus reus* is Latin for 'guilty act'.
3	C	A, B, and D all contain inaccurate information and act as distractors.
4	A	B is correct but not the most correct. C and D are distractors.
5	A	B and C are examples of social prevention. D is simply incorrect.
6	D	Stem of question refers to not being released.
7	B	C is also correct but a time limit applies. A and D are incorrect.
8	C	Arrest or release has been a fundamental civil right afforded to all police interrogation suspects.
9	D	A, B and C mostly identify matters starting in the District Court.
10	D	Key is mention of the state and beyond reasonable doubt.
11	B	A, C and D contain partial defences.
12	A	B is correct but not the most correct.
13	C	A is correct but not the most correct.
14	A	D can occur but not always.
15	B	A, C and D contain some incorrect information.
16	A	An accused can seek bail as they are presumed innocent until their matter is determined by the courts
17	B	A committal is a first look at the evidence. It tests the strength of the state's evidence.
18	B	A, C and D do not contain all post-sentencing options.
19	D	Parole is post-sentencing.
20	B	In NSW, a child is considered *doli incapax* under the age of 10.
21	C	Laws require at least one of these to be present.
22	C	Only hears summary matters.
23	A	B, C and D are all factually incorrect.
24	D	B is a distractor.
25	C	A is correct but not the most correct.
26	A	The standard is universal where rule of law applies.
27	A	Complementary jurisdiction.
28	B	B is most accurate.
29	B	A and C are distractors.
30	B	The presumption of innocence is universal where the rule of law applies.
31	D	Surveillance cameras aim to monitor environmental factors.
32	B	Fulfils the judge's role primarily as an umpire when the law is in doubt.
33	C	Simple knowledge of the objectives of punishment.

34	A	Shane's involvement after the fact – did not plan or carry out the crime.
35	B	Robbery is a property crime.
36	B	Dale both planned the crime and carried it out.
37	C	One will be classed as an indictable offence, the other a summary offence.
38	C	A committal proceeding to decide if a 'prima facie' case exists. Is there enough evidence to go to trial?
39	A	Police have wide-ranging discretion for minor offences.
40	D	Age is one of a number of aggravating factors that can be considered.
41	B	They have no place during the trial.
42	D	Is committed across national borders.
43	A	This is a strict liability matter – the *mens rea* does not have to be established.
44	A	Arrest will deprive Lou of her liberty – it also allows the police to detain, interrogate and fingerprint her if she is charged. Interrogation can occur without arrest if the suspect is willing to do so.
45	B	The ICC since 2002 under the Rome Statute.
46	A	All people regardless of age are permitted the right to silence.
47	B	The crimes identified are minor crimes to be heard in the Local Court.
48	C	Ariel was under duress – she was forced to commit the offence.
49	D	All minors must have an interview friend present when being interviewed by the police.
50	C	Police must contact the parents or guardians to ensure the evidence gathered will be permissible in court.
51	D	Possession of spray cans may be a strict liability offence in some situations depending on the legislative provisions.

Chapter 2 – Human Rights

1	A	Sovereignty overrides C.
2	B	Australia has no 'charter of rights' – statute law greatest coverage.
3	D	D is the most correct – it provides legal rights with Australia.
4	C	B is partially correct.
5	C	All others are non-legal measures.
6	C	All others are individual rights.
7	D	Arbitrary use of power by governments infringes fundamental civil and political rights
8	A	Reflect one of the strengths of a Statutory Bill of Rights as opposed to rights that may be entrenched.
9	A	The rest are all collective human rights.
10	B	A is partially correct.
11	A	The right to assemble and protest is an important civil and political right.
12	A	Section 116 of the Constitution provides one of the few express rights such as freedom of religion.
13	C	Human rights are problematic to enforce due to sovereignty.
14	C	Ratification allows the passing of domestic law to embody all or part of an international treaty signed by the Australian Government.
15	B	The person would be denied the right to earn an income which is an economic right.
16	C	Separation of the 3 powers fundamental to a democracy. No distractors in this question.
17	C	Other responses are all NGOs. C is an official body set up by the UN.

Section II: Core – Crime and Human Rights

Chapter 3 – Part A: Human Rights

Past examination short answer questions

Question 1
There are a number of human rights issues that can be referred to within Australia. The answer below is too lengthy but has been provided to give some background information. Below are some examples where there is non-compliance, failures and violations of human rights around the world and within Australia.

Discrimination on the basis of a criminal record: this type of discrimination is widespread throughout countries such as the United States and Australia, but is lawful in many states and territories. It is argued that this form of discrimination affects a person's health, housing and employment status.

Art 2(1) and 26 of the ICCPR and Art 2(2) of the ICESCR put an obligation on all Australian governments to guarantee equal and effective protection from discrimination, including on the grounds of criminal record. This form of protection can reduce marginalisation, disadvantage and poverty, all of which are causal factors and risk indicators of criminal activity. Reducing this type of discrimination promotes rehabilitation, integration and participation.

Some examples of this can be zero-tolerance policing, and some of the checks conducted on employment applications as outlined in various domestic legislations. In addition, increasing restrictions on bail in NSW for some repeat offenders is seen to be a further erosion of a fundamental human right.

Other domestic human rights issues that can be used include domestic violence against women; the plight of Aboriginal and Torres Strait Islander peoples; the right to social security and to adequate housing; and strip searches, DNA sampling and forcible cell extractions in prisons.

Question 2
Individual human rights are derived from natural law and are those rights that all human beings have. Human rights are said to be inherent, inalienable and universal by the mere fact of being human. Examples of individual human rights are civil and political rights and economic, social and cultural rights. Examples include the right to vote, freedom of speech and the right to an education.

Question 3
Collective human rights are those that are received by people as members of a group, as distinct from their rights as individuals. The right to peace and environmental rights are considered to be collective because they affect large groups of people rather than individuals.

Question 4

Child executions violate international law. The international consensus against putting child offenders to death for their crimes reflects the widespread recognition of the capacity of young people for growth and change.

International law prohibits the use of the death penalty for crimes committed by people younger than 18, yet some countries continue to execute child offenders or sentence them to death. Nations that continue to execute minors are in breach of the following international laws:

- The **International Covenant on Civil and Political Rights (ICCPR)**, one of the primary human rights treaties, states in Article 6: 'Sentence of death shall not be imposed for crimes committed by persons below 18 years of age … ' The ICCPR had been ratified by 152 states at mid-August 2004.
- The **Convention on the Rights of the Child** states in Article 37: 'Neither capital punishment nor life imprisonment without the possibility of release shall be imposed for offences committed by persons below eighteen years of age'. The Convention on the Rights of the Child has been ratified by 192 states – all countries except Somalia and the USA. Both Somalia and the USA have signed the Convention, indicating their intention to ratify it at a later date.

It has also been argued that because so many countries have demonstrated uniform and constant practice in refusing to execute minors it is said to be a part of international customary law. This is a direct result of these nations complying with their international obligations under the above treaties.

Reference to the issue of sovereignty being an obstacle to human rights or a vehicle for them must be addressed here. Countries that continue to follow this policy can continue to do so until they can be convinced it is not in their interest to do so. Domestically in many countries around the world the law prohibits this from occurring. In Australia capital punishment is outlawed for all citizens.

Question 5

Nation states are not to execute a child for committing a crime. A person under the age of 18 at the time the crime is committed is considered a child for the purposes of international law. Some examples of how this human right is protected by international law include:

- The **International Covenant on Civil and Political Rights (ICCPR)**, one of the primary human rights treaties, states in Article 6: 'Sentence of death shall not be imposed for crimes committed by persons below eighteen years of age.' The ICCPR had been ratified by 152 states at mid-August 2004.
- The **Convention on the Rights of the Child** states in Article 37: 'Neither capital punishment nor life imprisonment without the possibility of release shall be imposed for offences committed by persons below eighteen years of age.' The Convention on the Rights of the Child has been ratified by 192 states – all countries except Somalia and the USA. Both Somalia and the USA have signed the Convention, indicating their intention to ratify it at a later date.

Question 6
Domestic legal measures within Australia protect human rights in the following ways: constitutional rights can be entrenched and therefore they cannot be removed, but they can become dated. These rights are protected by the High Court of Australia. The Constitution has limited recognition as it guarantees very few explicit rights.
Statute law is wide sweeping and can offer protections to all people in society. It can be repealed by subsequent governments, and enforced by the courts and/or tribunals when a person has had their rights breached, i.e. discrimination legislation.

Common law is an ad hoc protection of human rights. Judges have no control over what matters will come before them. At the same time, common law through precedent recognises individual human rights in the decisions handed down. *Dietrich v The Queen* recognised a limited right to legal representation in a criminal trial. Ultimately, without a bill of rights the human rights of minorities are hard to guarantee.

International human rights treaties are very much dependent on the economic and political will of all nations. Nation states on the whole do not wish to be outside of international law and the international community, but will, when necessary, act in their own national interests. Sovereignty, as mentioned previously, is integral to a discussion on the effectiveness of international law in protecting human rights.

Question 7
The collective right to self-determination refers to the rights of people to be allowed certain forms of sovereignty, which may include the right to control certain parts of land and to utilise certain laws. Article 1 of the International Covenant on Civil and Political Rights states that 'all peoples have the right of self-determination. By virtue of that right they freely determine their political status and freely pursue their economic, social and cultural development'.

Question 8
Arguments for a Charter of Rights (Bill of Rights) for Australia include:
- There is inadequate protection currently.
- Common law rights would gain greater influence as judges would be called on to decide on disputes over rights in the Bill.
- A Bill of Rights would improve the quality of government policy-making and administrative decision-making. It would be more likely to be consistent and predictable in its recognition of human rights.
- It would bring Australia into line with the rest of the world and help it meet its international human rights obligations.
- It would enhance Australian democracy by protecting rights of minorities, by empowering marginalised Australians.
- It would take the politics out of human rights protection and educate the public as to the role and nature of human rights.

Arguments against a Charter of Rights (Bill of Rights) for Australia include:
- Human rights are already well protected and our democracy has adequate checks and balances on state power.
- The judiciary would become politicised. Enabling judges to enforce the Bill of Rights or to strike down legislation which is inconsistent with an entrenched Bill of Rights undermines the doctrine of parliamentary sovereignty and is undemocratic.

- To define a right is to restrict it, and society would be unable to cope with the changing understanding of some rights over time.
- Rights can also become 'fossilised'. They might well be the values held by society today but they could become outdated in the future.

Question 9
Child executions continue to be a contemporary human rights issue in the world today. International law prohibits the use of the death penalty for crimes committed by people younger than 18, yet some countries continue to execute child offenders or sentence them to death.

Article 6 of the International Covenant on Civil and Political Rights (ICCPR) states that the 'sentence of death shall not be imposed for crimes committed by persons below 18 years of age'. This treaty has been ratified by 152 states as of August 2004. In addition to this treaty is the Convention of the Rights of the Child (CROC). Article 37 of CROC states that 'neither capital punishment nor life imprisonment without the possibility of release shall be imposed for offences committed by persons below 18 years of age'. CROC has been ratified by 192 states.

The enforceability of these two international treaties, CROC and ICCPR, is restricted due to state sovereignty. In order to achieve universal abolition of child executions, all states must ratify and implicate the provisions of both treaties into domestic law. In some states where child executions are taking place, accessibility to the law may not be available. For example, in third world countries, child offenders may not have access to the law itself or to the resources necessary for proper legal representation. Therefore, resource efficiency, along with the application of the rule of law, also impedes a child offender's chance of achieving equal justice. The law, in theory, protects a child's right to life and not to be executed as punishment for a crime, but in practice this is not always the case.

NGOs such as Amnesty International believe that the death penalty violates the right to life and is an inhumane and degrading punishment. Amnesty International activists from around the world joined with other organisations in an international campaign aimed at ending the use of the death penalty against child offenders worldwide by December 2005. Amnesty International has been successful in promoting this issue globally. Although it is hard to directly attribute the change to them, there has been a slow development where nearly all countries in the world now refuse to carry out child executions.

The media also shapes public perceptions and opinions about significant political and social issues. Legal and non-legal responses are publicised through the media. For example, the American media drew international attention to the case of Napoleon Beazley, who was sentenced to death for a crime he committed when he was 17 years old. Beazley was executed in 2002; in 2004, the US Supreme Court banned the practice of executing offenders who were under the age of 18 when they committed their crimes.

Question 10
Two non-government organisations that promote human rights are Amnesty International and Human Rights Watch.

Question 11
The right to self-determination is a collective human right afforded to groups of people being able to determine their own political status. Article 1 of the International Covenant on Civil and Political Rights states that 'all peoples have the right of self-determination. By virtue of that right they freely determine their political status and freely pursue their economic, social and cultural development'.

Question 12
Universal suffrage, the right to vote, is a civil and political human right gradually being recognised around the world with increased democratisation of the world. By 2011, 89 countries, representing 46% of the world's total population, are classified as freely democratic. Forty-seven countries, or 34% of the world's population, are still classified as 'not free'. The right to vote was recognised as a universal human right in Article 21 of the Universal Declaration of Human Rights.

It is also recognised in Article 25 of the International Covenant on Civil and Political Rights.

In Australia today, legislation at a federal and state level recognises universal suffrage as a civil and political human right.

Question 13
There are numerous contemporary issues that can be discussed with this question. See the answer to Q11 above for a response to the human rights issue of child executions. Irrespective of the issue undertaken your response should address the following:
- Define the issue.
- Outline what the law provides – domestic/international (whichever is relevant).
- Describe the non-legal responses to this issue – NGOs, media.
- Evaluate the effectiveness of both legal and non-legal responses in addressing this issue. (Explicit reference to sovereignty is required.)

Question 14
The sovereignty of states is one of the most essential components of the international system. State sovereignty refers to the ultimate law-making power of a state – its independence and freedom from external interference in its own affairs. Sovereignty is the source of a state's legal and political power to make laws over its own population and to enforce those laws. As such, state sovereignty can be used to promote and enforce human rights or it can be used as an impediment to people accessing their human rights, as is the case in numerous nation states around the world.

Chapter 4 – Part B: Crime

Sample extended response questions

Question 1
Sample introduction

To remain relevant and effective, the criminal justice system must be a reflection of the morality and ethics of the community it purports to regulate. Crimes are those behaviours outlawed by the community because it deems them to be harmful to society. Decisions about this behaviour constitute a society's 'public morality', which reflects those shared values and ethics. Therefore, the criminal law must reflect the public moral and ethical standards of the community.

Not all behaviour is subject to the criminal justice system, as the law must allow a degree of personal ethics that is not subject to the criminal law. It is sometimes uncertain as to whether some behaviours should be criminalised. As a society's sense of public morality shifts, so must the criminal law.

The Wolfenden Committee in England in 1957 – a report that contributed greatly to the decriminalisation of homosexual conduct between consenting adults in private – stated 'there must remain a realm of private morality and immorality which is, in brief and crude terms, not the law's business'. However, it is quite apparent that many moral values are still evident in our legal system, especially in the area of criminal law.

In essence, then, in a democratic society, the law is not inclined to interfere with an individual's personal ethics and beliefs, so long as they do not lead to conduct that is harmful to others. Most crimes are the result of moral and ethical judgements by society (public morality) about behaviour that may be deemed harmful, and that therefore warrant sanctions by the state.

Notes about the response
In order to assess the extent to which law reflects moral and ethical standards, it may be useful to cite examples used in your coursework in the first two sections of the criminal law syllabus. In other words, consider what laws now exist that reflect public morality, what ways these laws have changed to respond to shifts in public morality, and what areas are now subject to legal change for these reasons. The law evolves to maintain the balance between community rights and the rights of individuals.

Some other examples of shifting public morality may include:
- Specific domestic legislation – the Crimes Act and the *Law Enforcement (Powers and Responsibilities) Act 2002* (LEPAR) are just two pieces of legislation that reflect public morality. The law creates social order through educating each subsequent generation about right and wrong. Anti-terrorism legislation that allows a suspect to be held without charge increases police powers. Is this driven by government ideology or a genuine shift in public morality because of a real fear of terrorist activity within Australia?
- International treaties are all to a degree a reflection of the community's public morality. For example, the ICC via the Rome Statute reflects the international public morality that crimes against the international community, such as mass atrocities,

must be punished. The growing recognition of the need for international cooperation to combat transnational crimes has come as a result of the growing awareness of the damage these crimes do to the community and the belief (morality) that authorities need to be more effective in this area.

- One area where there has been legal change as a result of shifting public morality is sentencing laws. The move to restrict the discretion of judges is seen as an interference in the rule of law, as parliament is blurring the separation of powers by increasingly dictating what judges do when sentencing. Cite examples of the legislation in this area.
- Sexual assault laws – changes to the onus on proof of consent and the increased use of transcript evidence are examples where the public, through the parliament, has judged that the outcomes in sexual assault trials do not reflect public morality, i.e. that victims of alleged sexual assault should not be traumatised by the legal process of trying to prove the assault against them.
- Restrictions on bail for certain offences seem to fly against the long-held belief that a person is innocent until proven guilty, and that they have a presumption to bail if they are not a danger to society or a flight risk. The *Bail Amendment Act 2007* has added to restrictions to bail as outlined by the other bail amendment Acts. It limits the number of bail applications that can be made by a person accused of an offence, and allows refusal of a second bail application unless the person was unrepresented when the previous application was made.
- What aspect of the criminal justice system currently is in a state of flux? Some examples could be victimless crimes or other areas of the criminal justice system that are calling for some type of change – high recidivism rates, coupled with the burgeoning prison population, would suggest the traditional objectives of punishment (values about what punishment should achieve) are not being met in this area.
- The use of covert search warrants, modelled on Commonwealth anti-terrorism legislation. These laws enable the police force to search people's homes without their knowledge. The warrants will be issued through the Supreme Court and are limited to investigations of suspected serious offences punishable by at least seven years' jail. These include the manufacture of drugs, computer crimes, the sale of firearms, homicide and kidnapping. This would seem to be an enormous increase in police powers.

Question 2

International crime has always been evident throughout the world, but the extent to which it is increasing is changing the way the international community is responding to it, and poses considerable challenges legally, financially and socially. Increased cooperation between nation states is fundamental if aspects of international crimes are to be addressed and justice delivered to the international community.

International crime can be said to be any act or omission that has international consequences on nation states, their citizens and international law.

There are a number of incidences of transnational crimes evident in the scenario. The growth of these and other international crimes is a cause for concern for the international community. The domestic and international legal systems are lagging behind in their approach to managing the types of international crimes evident today.

In this response it would be important to outline or describe the different types of international crimes that exist and then to evaluate them with the use of examples and/or case studies.

Crimes against the international community are in breach of natural law by the very nature of the types of acts committed on groups of people in various communities throughout the world. The violence perpetrated by crimes against the international community are as James Catano said 'the gravest conceivable crimes', and therefore they require international attention. Domestic law and domestic institutions cannot effectively respond to such acts and they are a global concern, which is why they are classed as international crimes. Examples of these types of crimes are explained below.

Genocide involves acts which have the intention of destroying 'all or part of a national ethnic, racial or religious group'. According to Article 6 of the Rome Statute, genocide can take the following forms. It can be perpetrated in a number of ways, from outright murder to inflicting conditions to bring about the loss of life, methods to prevent births, and the systematic rape of women to dilute the ethnicity of a group. It can also involve the destruction of cultural identity through policies of assimilation, or the imposition of a language or religion upon a group. Genocide can also be implemented through the transferring of children from one group to another, preferred one.

Crimes against humanity consist of knowledge of a sanctioned widespread or systematic attack against any civilian population. There may be legal distinctions between genocide and crimes against humanity but both have similarly devastating effects if perpetrated.

War crimes are constituted by a breach of the rules of conflict as outlined by the Geneva Conventions and any other customary rules of conflict that exist. War crimes can include things such as the unnecessary destruction of towns, villages and/or other infrastructure without any military importance, murder of civilians and rape. It is universally understood that during the hostilities of armed conflict there is a need to protect innocent civilians and their communities from any violence not justified by military or civilian necessity.

Transnational crimes are crimes that cross international borders. Due to the nature of these crimes, traversing international borders is an essential requirement for the commission of the crime. Transnational crimes can also be crimes committed in one country that may have significant negative implications for other countries. Some transnational crimes have been around for centuries, whereas others are relatively new due to the rapid development of technological highways that have made the world interconnected.

Some of the main types of transnational crimes are:
- Human trafficking and people smuggling
- International fraud and white-collar crime, which has been greatly facilitated by the rapid development of computer technology
- Terrorism, including cyber terrorism, such as the disruption of infrastructure; for example, electrical systems or computer networks
- The creation and trafficking of child pornography.

Methods of dealing with international crime include the following:

- **Extradition** is the process of legal surrender of a fugitive to the jurisdiction of another state, country or government for trial. It is used in situations where an offender is not residing in the state or country where they have been accused, or convicted, of a criminal offence. Reference is required here to the *Extradition Act 1988* **(Cth)**, which sets out the guidelines for the federal government to follow. These guidelines include that it must be determined that the accused has a case to answer on *prima facie* evidence, and that the accused will receive a fair trial in the state or country to which they are being returned. It must also be determined that the offence is a crime in both the state and country of which the accused is a citizen, and the one in which they currently reside.

- The federal government passed the *International Criminal Court Act 2002* **(Cth)** and the *International Criminal Court (Consequential Amendments) Act 2002* **(Cth)** to ensure Australia's domestic criminal justice system complies with the Rome Statute. This in effect **ratifies the International Criminal Court (ICC) – the Rome Statute 2002.** The Rome Statute is having its presence felt internationally by indicting key figures in crimes against the international community and humanity such as, for example, Muammar Gaddafi in Libya in 2011.

- **Transnational crimes** – there are a number of agencies set up to deal with these types of crimes. Some of these are the Australian Crime Commission, the Australian Federal Police, Australian Customs Service and the Australian High Tech Crime Centre (AHTCC). References to these and others can be found in *Cambridge HSC Legal Studies, 2nd Edition.*

Evaluation

The ease with which some transnational crimes are committed, as well as the sophisticated measures taken to avoid detection, highlight some of the problematic areas of enforcing the law in this area. Authorities around the world have to combat identity fraud, internet crime, paedophilia rings and the trafficking and smuggling of people and contraband, to name just some of the crimes being tackled on a transnational level. Technology is a double-edged sword, in that the reliance and convenience that the world enjoys as a benefit of a technology-driven world is a 'Trojan horse' within our communities.

It is suggested that nation states will have to cooperate and share information and resources on an unprecedented scale if they hope to combat the many types of transnational crimes. To date, the authorities have responded in kind, and perpetrators are being discovered and prosecuted, but this is a reactive approach which at times can be sporadic in terms of success.

The three main issues as to whether transnational crime continues to thrive will be dependent upon:
- The extent of international cooperation between states and the provision of adequate resources
- The effectiveness of coordination among international agencies, reliant on exchanges of information
- The level of compliance among weaker or poorer states. Where rule of law may be weak, states run the risk of becoming targets, especially by organised crime groups.

It has also been suggested that extradition procedures may be archaic in their inability to deal with offenders committing transnational crimes.

The move to prosecute offenders who have committed the worst types of **crimes against the international community** on a large scale has been a recent development over the last 20 years. Events in Rwanda in the early 1990s saw the move to set up ad hoc tribunals to deal with matters where domestic criminal justice systems were not equipped to do so. Other tribunals followed and eventually the global community set up a permanent court – the International Criminal Court (ICC).

The effectiveness of the international community to deal with crimes of genocide and crimes against humanity is mixed. Obviously, a permanent court such as the ICC is symbolically powerful. Its existence sends the message that despotic leaders can no longer hide behind the immunity of their own sovereignty and commit despicable acts against their own citizens.

The extent to which courts such as the ICC can stop such atrocities occurring is limited. The ICC is essentially reactive, in that it responds to such crimes as they occur. In addition, the extent to which the ICC can make those highly placed in governments think twice before acting remains to be seen. Essentially, the reasons why such mass atrocities occur would be a more proactive starting point for the world community to try and counter. According to Steven Freeland in his article *The Effectiveness of International Criminal Justice*, internal conflicts continue to increase. He says, 'more and more, armed conflicts – indeed the majority of wars now being fought – are internal conflicts. In this context, it appears to the observer that more, rather than fewer, horrendous acts of violence are being perpetrated, even in the face of this evolving system of international criminal justice'.

Question 3

Sample introduction (in an exam situation you would spend less time on this).
The general aim of law in Australia is the preservation of society's beliefs and ideologies. Law develops and establishes rules about relationships between individuals, and between individuals and society. One of the main aims of the criminal justice system is to punish and prevent crime, protecting society from the wrongful actions of individuals. One of the many purposes of punishment is its importance as a symbolic public declaration of society's opinion towards the offence and the offender. Many forms of punishment have differing outcomes and objectives, each aimed at achieving a specific purpose depending on the seriousness of the offence and the offender.

There are different types of penalties that a person may face when they have broken the law. These penalties can be separated into three sections:
- Custodial: detention
- Semi-custodial: some supervision
- Non-custodial: without detention/supervision.

The punishment given will depend on the severity of the crime committed, whether the accused is less than 18 years of age and the judge's discretion. Various forms of punishment include a fine, bond, probation order, community service order, home detention, periodic detention, imprisonment, work release, admonishment, diversionary program, forfeiture of assets, restitution, reparation and compensation. These forms of punishment aim to act as a form of retribution on behalf of the community, to reform the offender as far as possible, and to act as a punishment in its own right by depriving the offender of some of his or her freedoms or money. *(Some of these are as follows.)*

Fines can be an appropriate and inexpensive (on the part of the state) form of punishment for minor offences. When a judge imposes a fine they should not make it so expensive that the offender will be unable to pay it. The amount of money set as a fine will depend on how severe the offence is. While fines have the advantage of being flexible, they may not deter people from reoffending. Fines can also disadvantage offenders from low socio-economic groups, as they will have trouble finding money to pay the fine. Another disadvantage of fines is that they do not rehabilitate the offender.

On-the-spot-fines replaced a number of offences on 1 November 2007, despite a public outcry. They also replaced court appearances – and a resulting criminal record – for a range of offences. Some of the offences decriminalised were shoplifting of goods worth under $300, larceny under $300, goods in custody, offensive behaviour, offensive language, unlawful entry to a boat or vehicle, obstructing traffic, and obtaining a benefit by deception. This move was meant to be a resource-efficient move by the then Iemma Government, but statistics reveal it failed to attract a successful compliance rate, as approximately 30% of fines imposed since their introduction have not been paid. The police, on the other hand, support on-the-spot-fines as they free police personnel from being tied up in court. There is no evidence to suggest that these fines are a better deterrent than the court appearances that were previously in place.

Community service orders require the offender to perform unpaid community work in his or her leisure time. This is an inexpensive form of punishment that assists the general community. For example, the offender may correct damage they have caused; hence, the punishment becomes a form of retribution. The downside is that the offender has the opportunity to reoffend.

Compensation is a penalty that the offender may have to deal with if the victim chooses to sue the offender. Compensation is usually dealt with by the Victims Compensation Tribunal. The maximum amount that can be paid to a victim of a crime is $50 000 and the minimum is $2400. Again, this method of punishment does not deter the criminal from reoffending, and since many offenders do not have the ability to pay, the state picks up the cost.

Probation orders require the offender to report to a probation officer regularly in order to be monitored. Because of the regular reports, it is easy to supervise conditions imposed on the offender. These orders are inexpensive and can rehabilitate an offender. Yet the offender can still reoffend, and probation orders are time-consuming for police.

Imprisonment is a serious punishment that is used for people who have committed serious crimes. It has its advantages, one being that offenders are unable to reoffend against the public for the term of their sentence. One of the disadvantages of imprisonment is that it does not rehabilitate offenders, and may have a negative effect on their behaviour.

In New South Wales, 41% of inmates who finish their prison sentences will be back in prison again within two years. What's more, the Probation and Parole Service will sentence a further 10% to community service or other supervision within two years of finishing their sentence. With such a high rate of recidivism, the effectiveness of many forms of punishment must seriously be questioned. Obviously, prison is minimally effective as a deterrent, and the corrective service's attempts to rehabilitate, educate and equip offenders with sufficient skills so as to provide legal means of obtaining revenue once out of prison is failing.

Average prison sentences are becoming longer, and a higher proportion of offenders than ever before are being sentenced to prison terms. Hence, alternatives to the common 'gaol term' approach to sentencing need to be seriously considered. These could involve application in sentencing of one or more different types of punishment, proportionally to the seriousness of the offence. Courts need to assess the harm done and the degree of culpability of the offender and handcraft a sentence tailored specifically to the individual offender. The resulting extended time needed by the courts, and the additional costs, would be outweighed by the later economic and social benefits felt by the wider community as a result of a lowered prison population. Greater emphasis needs to be placed on rehabilitation and the needs of the individual as well as the corresponding needs of the community. *(Refer to the Sentencing Act and other legislation that has eroded judicial discretion in sentencing – Cambridge HSC Legal Studies 2nd Edition.)*

Periodic detention allows an offender to serve his or her sentence on a periodic basis, which is usually on weekends. Periodic detention is advantageous for reducing recidivism as it allows offenders to keep their jobs and/or remain in education (Hamper et al., 2001, p. 118). It is also less costly than imprisonment. However, like many of the other punishments it may not deter and gives the offender the ability to reoffend.

In December 2007 the NSW Sentencing Council released its Review of Periodic Detention. The majority of the Council found that the Review's concerns were strong enough to recommend the replacement of periodic detention with an alternative sentencing option. The proposed alternative was the Community Correction Order (CCO), which is a form of intense community supervision. Attached to the CCO would be certain conditions that would need to be met, including but not limited to:
• Curfew or residential requirement
• Compulsory participation in rehabilitation or educational programs
• The performance of community work.

At this stage, the NSW Government has not implemented the Sentencing Council's recommendations, and periodic detention is still a sentencing option.

Home detention is a relatively new form of punishment, which requires offenders to wear a bracelet or anklet that must be attached to a phone line when the supervising officer rings or sends a signal. If the bracelet or anklet is not attached, the supervising officer visits the offender's home to ensure the offender has not breached the conditions of his or her home detention. Offenders are encouraged to seek employment and are regularly tested for drugs and alcohol.

Home detention is appropriate for people convicted of a non-violent crime as they do not mix with career criminals, and therefore the differential association theory is prevented from coming into effect (Brassil, 2001, p. 83). Home detention also allows offenders to remain at home with their family, providing more opportunity for rehabilitation. Furthermore, the offenders take care of themselves, greatly reducing the cost to society as well as the prison population. There are disadvantages to home detention, however.

Home detention is only available in city courts, and discriminates against individuals from low socio-economic groups who do not have a phone line.

The compliance rate for home is generally high with some figures up to 80% being cited. Given its resource efficiency and other benefits to the community and the offender, and its relatively high compliance rate, home detention appears to be a sentencing option worth exploring for offenders of non-violent crimes.

This question therefore assesses the types of penalties handed down in NSW, and evaluates their successes, or otherwise, in achieving the objectives (purposes) of sentencing.

Question 4

Law reform refers to any change to the law. The criminal justice system must reflect the public morality of the community it purports to regulate. Generally, the law will lag behind development in the Australian and international community. Law reform *per se* is not necessarily law reform for the better. The following examples of law reform need to be assessed by including the intention behind the changes and its impact. It should also be noted that law and order arguments from both sides of the political debate have meant most reform has been more punitive, and has achieved a political objective, but has not necessarily improved outcomes.

Some examples include:

- Restorative justice has been introduced over the last 15 years. Examples include youth justice conferencing and circle sentencing. There have been proposals to apply restorative justice to sexual assault cases but critics argue this is not suitable, as the victim may not want to be in the same room with the offender. Restorative justice, when applied in the appropriate situations, has produced positive outcomes in terms of reducing reoffending behaviour.
- The failure of the prison system to achieve the traditional objectives of punishment, evident in the make-up of the prison population. A significant percentage of prisoners (about a third) have mental health problems, others are there for non-violent crimes, and the prison population continues to climb. Rates of recidivism also point to a failing of the system to achieve the objectives of punishment. When discussing imprisonment, refer to some of the issues raised by extended questions from Crime: Chapter 4, Question 3. Sentencing laws need to be examined here, as well as the erosion by Parliament of the discretion of the judiciary when sentencing. Continuing detention orders and preventative detention orders are relatively new, and are designed to protect the community, but at the expense of the rights of the accused/offender.
- The introduction of the International Criminal Court (ICC) as a measure to deal with crimes against the international community, via the Rome Statute. The ICC is a new mechanism that tries to ensure that crimes of mass atrocities do not go unpunished. The growing recognition of the need for international cooperation to combat transnational crimes has also come about as a result of the growing awareness of the damage these crimes do to the community, and the belief that authorities need to be more effective in this area. Ratification of this treaty by the federal government, and greater cooperation by authorities around the world to combat the increasing number of transnational crimes committed, are examples of law reform in the area of international crime.

- Calls for a specialist court to deal with sexual assaults because of low reporting and conviction rates. Transcript evidence is now allowed for retrials. Changes to the law of consent putting the onus of proof on the defendant are also relatively new. 2009 figures reveal the conviction rate for these types of crimes hasn't improved.
- The abolition of the death penalty has not changed rates of homicide. This gives an insight into deterrence of criminal punishment – for example, a harsher sentence does not equate to reduction in reoffending.
- Australia is frequently signing new extradition treaties with other countries. The extradition of Gordon Wood from the UK to face trial in Australia is an example of the benefits of such treaties.
- Improved evidence-gathering techniques have led to new powers to collect DNA, as well as the need for laws to clarify the rights of citizens with respect to using and storing that evidence on file. The rights of citizens to have this destroyed also have been clarified. DNA evidence has been an extremely successful tool in the solving of serious crimes, but a general criticism is that the police rely too much on it. The judiciary has also been criticised for convictions on DNA evidence without other corroborating evidence.
- The number of scenarios where the presumption of bail is being denied to offenders has increased. This has had a significant impact on adult and juvenile incarceration figures.
- It is difficult to gather evidence and achieve convictions in cases of white-collar crime. Should there be increased police powers in this area?
- Agents of change for law reform can also be mentioned. NSW and Australian Law Reform Commissions investigate areas of law and make recommendations, which can be used or ignored. All or parts can be utilised. The 2002 Samuels Review with respect to plea bargaining is an example of this.
- Governments play a pivotal role in law reform as they obviously have the power to introduce sweeping and specific laws.
- Courts do not consciously try to change the law. Judges can only respond to cases presented to them. Agents of law respond to precedent cases such as *Dietrich v The Queen*.

This is a broad question, so there are many areas to examine with respect to law reform. Correct use of legislation, cases and media reports are needed and a judgement needs to be made about the place of law reform in the criminal justice system.

Question 5
Plea bargaining is sometimes mentioned as a solution to trying to resolve the lengthy delays that are evident in the criminal trial process. This generally can occur in three ways.
- If the accused is facing several charges in relation to the same crime, the prosecution may drop some charges if the defendant pleads guilty to some of the remaining charges. This is called *charge bargaining*. This may also occur when the accused agrees to assist the police in other matters under investigation.
- The charge may be reduced to a lesser one if the accused pleads guilty. For example, murder might be reduced to manslaughter.
- In some courts a *sentence indication hearing* may be held, in which a judge will indicate the kind of sentence the accused might expect if they plead guilty.

Advocates of plea bargaining argue that the prosecution achieves a conviction, while the court saves time and money because there is no lengthy trial. Advocates who disagree with this process argue that reducing the charges means there is no consideration of the victim.

In 2000, a district court judge set minor sentences for a group of boys charged with the aggravated sexual assault of two girls in Sydney after plea bargaining negotiated a lesser offence. After a public outcry, the Samuels Review recommended that laws be changed so that witnesses and victims are kept informed and consulted, and the views of the police and the victims are sought before any 'statement of agreed facts' is adopted and any plea bargaining occurred.

There may also be cases where prosecutors threaten more serious charges so as to intimidate the accused into pleading guilty to a lesser charge. The accused gets a lesser penalty than he or she risked with the more serious charge. In Australia this was generally not an open and officially recognised practice.

The concept of fairness in criminal matters is not only about fairness to the person accused of a crime. The legal system generally, and the courts in particular, have to reconcile different areas of interest that come into conflict.

One area of interest is the need to maintain respect for the dignity, privacy and human rights of individuals. The law is required to protect each of its citizens from illegal, irregular or excessive invasions of their liberties by police, prosecuting authorities, or judicial procedures.

It could be argued that plea bargaining does not respect the dignity of the victim, as it lessens the seriousness of the crime committed. The victim of the crime may feel the offender has not received an adequate punishment for their offence.

In addition to this, some victims want their story to be made public, and for the offender to be held accountable in front of the community and receive the full punishment they deserve. Still, it could be argued that plea bargaining does achieve a conviction, so in this sense the rights of the victim have been protected to a degree.

The main aim of the criminal justice system is to 'safeguard individual rights via a focus on the wellbeing of the community' as mentioned above. The *Victims Rights Act 1996* (NSW) includes a range of statutory provisions relating to victims, including a 'Charter of Victims Rights'. Plea bargaining may seem to override the spirit of the above legislation. Amendments to the *Criminal Procedure Act 1986* introduced by the *Victims Rights Act 1996* allow for Victim Impact Statements in the Supreme and Federal Courts in serious criminal cases. It could be also argued that plea bargaining may lessen any Victim Impact Statement given before a court.

An equally significant area of interest to this is the state's interest in suppressing crime for the benefit of all, and for the preservation of a peaceful and ordered community (i.e. rights of the community). This is part of the requirements of a fair trial, where the accused have certain rights but are submitted to certain procedures to get at the truth in a criminal matter. Plea bargaining upholds the rights of the community by ensuring that certain offenders are punished. It also provides a measure of resource efficiency, as stated earlier, in that lengthy trials can be avoided.

However, with respect to the efficiency of the court system, plea bargaining certainly saves time and money, but does it defeat the purpose of it? The court system, with its rules of procedure and adversary manner, allows crimes to be prosecuted in front of the community. It allows justice to not only be done but to be seen to be done. Plea bargaining could defeat this important function of the court system.

Even without plea bargaining, the accused has the right to throw themselves at the mercy of the court and make a guilty plea. This may give the offender a chance to make amends in some cases. In addition, in some courts a sentence indication hearing may be held, in which a judge will indicate the kind of sentence the accused might expect if they plead guilty. This is a good compromise to plea bargaining as it still can save time and money, but doesn't water down the crime and the impact upon the victim.

Question 6
This question is directly related to the principal focus of the Crime topic in the 2010 syllabus. There is a constant tension between the state and individuals' rights and freedoms in ensuring that criminal law is enforced. In doing so, the state (through legislation) has empowered the police, the Director of Public Prosecutions (DPP), and the judiciaries to investigate crimes and to prosecute and punish offenders. Throughout this process the state must ensure that rights of individuals and their freedoms are respected, otherwise a 'police state' will be created where ultimately the rights of the community will be undermined, and its ability to deliver justice to all will be seriously questioned. The community has a right to be protected and the criminal justice system is the main vehicle for this to occur.

The extent to which the state balances the rights of the community and individuals can be analysed through aspects of the criminal justice system. Some of these areas are:
- The investigation stage. The state empowers police to carry out the task of investigating crime and apprehending offenders by granting them police powers. These powers must have checks and balances. The *Law Enforcement (Powers and Responsibilities) Act 2002* (NSW) (LEPAR) is the main piece of legislation that regulates police powers in NSW, and analysis of these checks and balances is required. These checks and balances are examples of the state attempting to balance the rights of the community with those of individuals. At present most police services use a 'nominative system' of investigation where a prime suspect is identified and a case is built around this. This approach can have fundamental flaws, as discovered in the United Kingdom, which has moved to an 'eliminative system' of investigation where suspects are eliminated as the evidence is analysed.
- These powers are at times abused and the rights of individuals are put at risk, especially in the area of search and seizure. In *DPP v Leonard (2001)* 53 NSWLR 227, it was held that a person may validly consent to a search even if not aware of the right to refuse (although it was held that such lack of awareness may be relevant to the issue of consent in some cases). Give practical examples to further your

arguments, such as the increase in police powers to investigate crime and apprehend offenders due to perceived public safety issues or the threat of terrorist activity. The effect of this has seen an erosion of the rights of accused individuals.

- Since 2001 the NSW Government has introduced 17 pieces of legislation to enhance the state's powers in the cause of fighting terrorism. These laws arguably favour the rights of the community but erode individual rights. Some examples are the *Terrorism (Police Powers) Act 2002* (NSW), which allows police acting on credible information to stop, search and demand the names and addresses of anyone who fits the broad description of a potential terrorist. It entitles police to enter and search cars and properties. It also gives police the power to search and bug premises of suspected terrorists for six months without notifying the suspect. The *Freedom of Information (Terrorism and Criminal Intelligence) Act 2004* (NSW) restricts people from obtaining security sensitive information under freedom of information laws.

- Considerations as to whether to grant bail weigh up the rights of an accused to bail and the right of the community to be protected from an accused who may offend further or take flight. The Bail Act gives judges this discretion, although there have been increasing restrictions on the right to bail, such as the *Bail Amendment (Terrorism) Act 2004* (NSW), which restricts the right of an accused terrorist to be granted bail, and the *Bail Amendment Act 2003* (NSW), which has made it harder for repeat offenders to get bail. With magistrates' discretion reduced, bail refusal rates have risen 15%.

- Plea bargaining: See the response notes to Question 5.

- The criminal trial, with rules of evidence and procedure, attempts to balance these competing rights. Some fundamental rights that an accused has are the presumption of innocence and the right to silence. These rights are the cornerstone in ensuring that a person receives a fair trial.

- The factors affecting the sentencing process are a further example of the judiciary attempting to balance the rights of the community and the victim with the rights of the accused. Circumstances of the offence, the offender, and mitigating and aggravating factors are all weighed up in this process. Judges must also carry out this process. The *Crimes Sentencing Procedure Act 1999* (NSW) is one of the main laws that set out the guidelines for sentencing. The *Crimes (Sentencing Procedures) Amendment (Standard Minimum Sentencing) Act 2002* was passed to ensure tougher sentences for very serious offences such as murder, gang rape and aggravated robbery. Both of these laws limit the discretion of judges, and critics have argued they favour the rights of the community over that of the accused.

- The victim can be a 'bit' player in the criminal justice process, especially during a trial. The rights of victims are contained in the *Victims Rights Act 1996* (NSW), which contains a range of statutory provisions relating to victims, including a 'Charter of Victims Rights'. It also makes provisions of compensation to be made to victims by offenders and/or the state. Amendments to the *Criminal Procedure Act 1986* introduced by the *Victims Rights Act 1996* (NSW) allow for Victim Impact Statements in the Supreme and Federal Courts in serious criminal cases. The implications of plea bargaining for victims are highlighted in the response notes to Question 5.

The criminal justice system must continue to attempt to balance the rights of the community with the rights of the accused and victims in order for the community to continue to have confidence in its processes and procedures.

Question 7

'The administration of criminal justice in Australia is essentially a discretionary decision-making process: an offence may or may not be reported; the police may or may not respond to a report and they may do so in different ways; the offence may or may not be prosecuted; there may or may not be a conviction; and some decision has to be made as to the type of punishment imposed. The whole law enforcement process depends on decisions made by victims, police and other law enforcement officers, prosecuting authorities and accused persons.' ('Multiculturalism: criminal law', *Discussion Paper*, no. 48, May 1991)

This question is taken from one of the themes of the Crime topic. As indicated in the quote above, discretion is used at all stages of the criminal justice process. The decisions made at each step of the process need to be explained in terms of the competing rights of the community against the rights of individuals, such as the accused and the victim.

Question 6 provides suggestions for some of the content that can be discussed here. It is not possible to provide justice for all, and the role of discretionary decision-making allows for individual situations and circumstances to be taken into account in an attempt to create a fairer system.

It should be noted that successive state governments have continually eroded or undermined the discretionary role of the DPP and the judiciary, as outlined in Question 6. The tenure of the DPP will revert from a 'life or retiring age' to a five-year term after the retirement of the current Director.

Question 8

The criminal justice system adopts a combination of the 'welfare' model (take into account factors around offending behaviour), and the 'justice' model (get tough on crime). With respect to Brad and Jamal, the system needs to balance the seriousness of the offences they have committed with the likelihood of them being able to be rehabilitated.

There are a number of ways outlined as follows that the criminal justice system differentiates between young offenders and adult offenders.

- The *Children's (Criminal Proceedings) Act 1987* (NSW) clearly outlines the age of criminal responsibility. It states: 'It shall be conclusively presumed that no child who is under the age of 10 years can be guilty of an offence'. This is the same in all criminal jurisdictions. Between the ages of 10 and 14 a child may be found guilty of a criminal offence, but the prosecution must rebut the notion of *doli incapax* and show that the child, at the time of the alleged offence, could distinguish between right and wrong. From the ages of 14 to 17, children and young people are held fully responsible for their actions. As both Brad and Jamal are aged 13, the prosecution must have succeeded in determining that both boys could distinguish between right and wrong.
- Critics of the notion of *doli incapax* argue that the age of criminality should be lowered because children are now better educated and that the criminal law is not as harsh as it once was. In addition, it is stated that the rule can be unfair, especially to victims of crimes, and that it makes the prosecution's role in a criminal trial more difficult as there is not always enough evidence to rebut the presumption of *doli incapax*. Defenders of the notion believe that different children develop their understanding of right and wrong at different stages of life, and that it may slow down the prosecution

but ultimately does not stop them if there is proof of a guilty mind for children aged between 10 and 14.

- When arrested, both Brad and Jamal had certain rights as a result of their age, as outlined under the *Law Enforcement (Powers and Responsibilities) Act 2002*. Their guardians or carers should have been notified as soon as they were arrested and they should have had an interview friend with them prior to any interrogation. The interrogation should not have proceeded without this and the interrogation should have been limited to no more than two hours. There is no right for Brad and Jamal to have legal representation during these interviews, but *R v Cortez* (CE, ME, Ika & LT, unreported, NSWSC, Dowd J, 3 October 2002) held that for a young person to be given the opportunity to seek legal advice, they must be informed about the Legal Aid Hotline and have the opportunity to ring it.

- Application needed to be made to the Children's Court for someone above the rank of sergeant to get permission to take a photograph, finger or palm print, and ensure that both boys not be held in custody while such an application is made. If the matter is not proved, then under the *Children (Criminal Proceedings) Act 1987* these records can be destroyed.

- When Brad and Jamal were sentenced, the court would have taken into account their age, background and prior offences, if any. Essentially, the court should have regard to the following:
  - Children have rights equal to adults and have a right to be heard and to participate in the proceedings.
  - Children are responsible for their actions but require guidance and assistance.
  - Where possible, the education of a child should proceed without interruption.
  - Where possible, a child should be able to reside in his or her home.
  - The penalty imposed on a child shall be no greater than that of an adult for the same offence.

Both Brad and Jamal received a custodial sentence, presumably due to the seriousness of the offence. At times the court will disregard the age of the offenders and may treat them the same as adults if they are satisfied that juvenile offenders engaged in what is called 'grave adult behaviour'. This, in the eyes of the law, is when a juvenile has acted like an adult and therefore other sentencing objectives come into play.

Had the offences that Brad and Jamal committed been minor offences that they admitted to, they may have been dealt with by the *Young Offenders Act 1997* (NSW) which focuses on diversionary methods such as youth justice conferences. A recent evaluation of youth justice conferences has indicated they are not reducing recidivism rates of participants, unlike the Victorian model which includes more serious offences in its conference regime. (See the BOSCAR site under media releases.)

Understanding the effectiveness of the criminal justice system to young offenders should start at an understanding that from a young age children cannot control a lot of the circumstances they find themselves in. Children who have been neglected or maltreated, or who have simply received poor and dysfunctional parenting, generally find it challenging to make good decisions. This at times puts them at odds with the criminal justice system.

As previously stated, the Young Offenders Act attempts to take a holistic view of a young person's offending, and has a high success rate. As discussed earlier, though, it should not be seen as a soft option, and could possibly be used for a variety of less serious offences. Brad and Jamal did not have this option.

It is acknowledged that more can be done to take into account the totality of a child's or young person's situation and sentence accordingly, especially in the case of more serious matters. To what extent did the judge consider the dysfunctional upbringing of both Brad and Jamal? This is always a problematic exercise.

In addition to this, the number of juveniles in detention has grown exponentially. A major reason for this (as outlined in the report *Recent trends in legal proceedings for breach of bail, juvenile remand and crime, 2009*) has been changes made to section 22A of the *Bail Act 1978*. This amendment reduced the amount of times a juvenile could apply for bail. For juvenile offenders, usually the reason for denial of bail is welfare-related, not offence-related; they are mostly remanded for a failure to comply with curfew conditions and not being in the company of an adult. The report also went on to say that the increased rate of juvenile remand saw no evidence of a fall in property crime as a result.

This adds another negative: experience of the criminal justice system for young offenders may exacerbate their situation. In her article 'Teenage detention centres too crowded' published in the *Sydney Morning Herald* on 27 October 2009, Louise Hall points out that 80% of young offenders held on remand are not subsequently given custodial sentences. Having said this, there are some young offenders who must be detained without bail in order to protect either them or the community. It could be argued that if Brad and Jamal were denied bail it would be in the interests of the safety of the community.

There have been calls for specific legislation to introduce a specific bail law for young offenders. At the time of writing, the NSW Government is planning to review section 22A of the Bail Act to place no limit on the number of applications that can be made for bail if there is new evidence about a child or young person's circumstances. The community has the right to be safe, and young people who are a danger to the community need to be dealt with appropriately. However, greater rates of incarceration are not the answer, as indicated by the finding of the 2009 study. At present the NSW Government is considering amending again section 22A of the Bail Act due to the adverse effects of suspected young offenders increasingly being placed on remand.

Increasing the prison population among young offenders is resource inefficient and usually produces worse long-term outcomes. The projected rate at which adult and juvenile detention centres will need to be constructed to cope with increases in this population is verging on maladministration, and is a poor use of community resources.

The criminal justice system must also be assessed on the manner in which it deals with young people, especially in their use of public space. Some legislation that restricts a young person's use of public space, although they may not be young offenders at the time, may make this likelihood greater. The *Crimes Legislation Amendment (Police and Public Safety) Act 1998* was introduced in response to the increased offences related to knives between 1996 and 1997. The Act made it an offence to carry a knife in a public place and gave the police the power to search people for knives and other weapons. It also gave the police the power to search people in public places if their behaviour appeared to cause fear, obstruct, harass or intimidate. While knife offences continue to rise, it is argued that young people are unfairly targeted and searched by the police.

The Youth Justice Coalition and other groups have argued that police stop and search powers should be consolidated into one piece of legislation; at present there are a minimum of six Acts giving police the power to stop and search people, which can cause confusion for the police and citizens alike. *Seen and heard: priority for children in the legal process*, the report of a national inquiry into the status of children in the legal system in Australia, stated that the legislation has problems. It outlines that police can scrutinise the behaviour of children and young people even if it is not criminal, and it allows the police to act on stereotypes about young people.

As is often the case, the criminal justice system is usually dealing with the symptoms as opposed to addressing preventative measures that could assist children who may be at risk. In fairness, approximately 85% of offenders do not reoffend after appearances in the Children's Court. For offenders like Brad and Jamal, by the time of their court appearance, it may already be too late to turn their situation around. Incarceration will not improve their outlook on society, and, if anything, may make them more anti-social.

The law and order debate has won out to date, and the right of the community is winning out over individuals, especially with respect to search and seizure laws and bail laws regarding young offenders.

Question 9
The most difficult function of a judge is to pass sentence while keeping in mind the purposes of punishment, and factors affecting the sentencing decision, to arrive at an appropriate penalty. Judges are regularly criticised in the media for failing to hand down sentences that do not reflect public morality – community standards. Punitive sentences, while appearing to appease community expectation, generally have the opposite effect for the community in the long term.

A sentencing hearing is conducted after the trial has been completed. It is at this stage that the judge must consider what penalty will satisfy the community and be fair to both the victim and the accused. The purpose and effectiveness of possible punishments are discussed in the response notes to Question 3. These things are weighed up with the other factors considered during the sentencing process.

The court must attempt to balance the rights of the individual with the rights of society. The judge must ensure that society is protected and that future offenders will be deterred by the punishment handed down. The judge must also consider the rights of the accused, who is entitled to a fair trial and reasonable punishment. Sentencing is usually the most difficult task of the judicial officer as he/she must consider what society will gain from the sentence. The judicial officer has two choices:
- A harsh sentence that acts as a deterrent
- A lighter sentence that allows for rehabilitation.

Circumstances of the offence
The circumstances of the crime, referred to as 'objective features', are put forward by the prosecution to reinforce the severity of the crime. These include:
- The use of a weapon
- Threat or use of violence
- Level of preplanning of the crime
- Whether the crime is becoming more prevalent and therefore requires a deterrent.

Circumstances of the offender
The judge will not only take into account the circumstances of the offence but also those of the offender before determining the most appropriate sentence. The judge will consider the offender's age, any prior convictions, mental or physical disabilities, whether other people rely on the case, whether the offender was of assistance to police, and any other mitigating circumstances, known as 'subjective features'.

Aggravating and mitigating circumstances
A crime is said to be *aggravated* when it is a particularly severe example of that offence. Aggravating circumstances are those where:
- The victim is young, elderly or disabled, making the impact of the crime more damaging
- The offender was in a position of trust
- Gratuitous violence was involved.

The *Crimes (Sentencing Procedure) Amendment Act 2007* added additional aggravating factors such as an offence committed in the presence of a minor, use or threatened use of a chemical or biological agent and actions that are a risk to national security, to list a few. Aggravating circumstances are most likely to increase the sentence of the offender.

Mitigating factors may partly excuse the defendant's actions and may achieve a reduced sentence. Mitigating factors that are commonly used include:
- The offender is young or inexperienced.
- The offender was forced to commit the crime by others.
- The offender has experienced poverty or previous abuse.
- The offender has experienced drug and alcohol addiction.

The *Crimes (Sentencing Procedure) Amendment Act 2007* has clarified that remorse will only be a mitigating factor if offenders have acknowledged the injury/loss caused by their actions and provided evidence that they have taken responsibility for their actions. Mitigating circumstances are not complete defences for crimes; showing mitigating circumstances is a bid to reduce the severity of the sentence.

See *McCartney v R* [2009] NSWCCA 244 for a consideration of mitigating and aggravating factors.

Judicial discretion and the limits of discretion
Judicial discretion is the right of the judicial officer to make a decision on what he/she considers is right based on the evidence. Without this discretion it would be impossible for a judge to consider the specific circumstances of individual cases when making a ruling. This right has limits placed on it. Judges must follow sentencing guidelines or precedents set by higher courts. The *Crimes Act (1900)* and other statutes set out maximum sentences for certain crimes, and judges are not permitted to exceed the maximum sentence. Judges can impose a sentence less than the maximum due to the factors discussed above.

Parliament can and does limit judicial discretion through Acts of Parliament that impose certain restrictions on the sentences handed down. Some examples are:
- The *Crimes Sentencing Procedure Act 1999* (NSW) contains the provisions for sentencing first established under the original Act, *The Sentencing Act 1989*, also known as the 'Truth in Sentencing Act'. This was the first in a series of legislation to restrict the discretion of the judiciary in sentencing by providing that:

- A prisoner may not be released on parole until they have served three-quarters of the total sentence. This increased prison time spent.
- Any sentence of six months or less is fixed with no parole.
- If a judge sentences someone to life imprisonment, they will never be released except in exceptional circumstances.
- Remissions mean time taken off the original sentence for good behaviour. Prisoners can also receive extra time in prison for misbehaviour.

- The *Sentencing Procedure Act* has been seen as political. Since the original Act was passed in 1989, the prison population has continued to rise steadily. Politically, it was argued that this brought sentencing in line with community expectations.
- *The Criminal Procedures Amendment Act 1986* was amended in 1998 to enable the NSW Attorney-General to ask the court and the judge to give a 'guideline sentence' for a certain criminal offence. This means that the sentence a judge gives in a particular case is the sentence that would be given to all similar offences. This, it is argued, maintains consistency and public confidence in the sentencing system. The arguments against these amendments are that it erodes judicial discretion and that sentencing guidelines do not take into account the circumstances surrounding the offence and offender.
- The *Crimes (Sentencing Procedures) Amendment (Standard Minimum Sentencing) Act 2002* was passed to ensure tougher sentences for very serious offences such as murder, gang rape, aggravated robbery, etc. The Act provides for mandatory minimum sentences for these offences, e.g. 15 years' imprisonment for gang rape. This Act has removed judges' discretion to make sentencing decisions for these offences. The reason for this change was to reflect community concerns about judges giving lenient sentences. This Act also provides for retrospective mandatory sentences for some vicious murderers. This part of the Act has been subject to challenges in the High Court, because it was felt that it is not legal to change a sentence once given.
- The *Crimes (Sentencing Procedure) Amendment Act 2007* has added standard non-parole periods for the following offences:
- Murder of a victim under 18 years: 25 years
- Reckless causing of grievous bodily harm: four years
- Reckless causing of grievous bodily harm in company: five years
- Reckless wounding: three years
- Reckless wounding in company: four years.
- Preventative and continuing detention orders are controversial because offenders who have served their time, or offenders who may cause harm 'in the future', may be detained. In some ways these measures that have been designed to protect the community also erode the rights of the accused or offender. This further erodes judicial discretion by undermining the original decision handed down, or pre-empting a decision before it has even come before a court.

While considering the above process it should also be remembered the suggestions of studies do not always fit with the resources available or the political cycle. Prevention is always better and more cost-effective (especially if it is well-targeted) than dealing with the symptoms of crime. Allocation of resources is always scarce, and the fact that governments face re-election every three to four years means that not enough is done to prevent crime from occurring in the first place.

Another dimension to this is that prevention is more long-term, as the benefits may not be seen straight away, which does not suit the agenda of most governments. It is easier for governments to implement policies that get tough on crime, have an immediate impact and are usually more popular with the electorate.

Nicholas Cowdery (the NSW DPP) states 'only social and educational programs can really deter in advance … by and large people who are well-educated, in good health, comfortably housed, in employment … do not commit crime'. Further to this it has been shown that harsher penalties have little or no impact on deterring crime or on rehabilitation.

Having said this, there are some offenders that must be sequestered from the community for everyone's safety. Although aspects of their judicial discretion have been eroded by statutory controls, judges are able to weigh up all factors when deciding on an appropriate penalty, thus implementing a sense of justice tempered with mercy and common sense. This occasionally puts them at odds with the community's attempts to understand the reasoning behind some sentences. It is true the judiciary does not always get it right, and at times it fails to reflect community standards when sentencing.

Diversion methods, such as youth justice conferencing and circle sentencing for Indigenous offenders, seem to have made a positive impact on reducing offending. The Drug Court in NSW has also been successful in taking a holistic approach to offending behaviour, and has been successful for those who have been able to meet the demands put on them by the court.

While the criminal justice system continues to be reactive to crime by using punishments as a means of confronting crime within our community, it will always fall short, especially if we use the objectives of punishment as the measure of success. Hence, they will never truly reflect what the community expects. Again, as the NSW DPP Nicholas Cowdery states, '…maybe the question to ponder is: should we reconsider the objectives of punishment?' Then we may have new measures of effectiveness to develop. Or perhaps we should consider how we go about the objective of preventing crime in the first place and apply more resources to that.

Question 10
The majority of individuals within a society obey the law most of the time. Individuals also enjoy the freedoms and protection that a largely well-organised and well-regulated society gives. It is partly for this reason that the majority comply with the law. The law can also enforce compliance and sanction violations on behalf of society where individuals do not comply.

Some of the reasons for why people do not comply with the law include:
- Psychological or pathological factors may be relevant to the commission of an offence, with many forms of mental illness affecting a person's behaviour.
- Social factors influencing a person's attitude towards crime may include their family situation or personal relationships. The social groups that people associate with will often influence a person's attitudes and views of acceptable behaviour. This may be particularly relevant, for example, in the area of drug offences or public order offences. In other areas of crime, it may be the environment in which a person has been raised that influences their behaviour as an adult.

- Economic factors present some of the most substantial reasons for the committing of crimes in NSW. People from disadvantaged backgrounds are more likely to commit crimes and appear before courts than any other group. For example, statistics released by the Australian Institute of Criminology show that one-third of males and half of female offenders receive a welfare or government payment as their main source of income. Poor education and lack of skills will often be closely related to economic factors, with such criminals often perpetually unemployed and unskilled. Even where people are employed in menial or poorly paid jobs, they are more likely to commit offences than those with better jobs and better education.

- Genetic theories surrounding criminal behaviour have long been a topic of interest for scientists and criminologists. For example, in the early 19th century the pseudoscience of phrenology was born. Using this approach, criminals' heads were measured to determine whether there were any physical characteristics that could allow scientists to pick potential criminals. Fortunately, recent studies have been more advanced. They have investigated and compared the DNA of prisoners to see if there are any common genetic markers that can predict criminal behaviour. None of these genetic studies has been conclusive in showing that individuals with certain genes are more likely to commit crimes. This suggests that external factors (social, economic or psychological) play the greatest role in criminal activity.

- Although not the most influential factors in criminal offences, political factors have played a role in influencing criminal behaviour for centuries. Most obviously, offences against the sovereign or offences against the state are likely to have some political factors behind them, but public order offences such as riots may also have politically motivated factors, especially in situations where public protests become politically intense.

- Self-interest will usually play some role as a motivating factor in committing a crime, such as committing drug offences for profit or for use, property offences for profit, offences against the person for self-interested revenge, and white-collar crimes such as embezzlement or insider trading.

Issues that could also be critiqued could include how the criminal justice system tries to ensure greater compliance through the following:

- Crime prevention (situational and social) aims to improve compliance with the law through either improving or altering the physical environment or using preventative measures on societal influences. On the whole, as indicated in the response notes to Question 7, resources are rarely sufficient to adequately implement preventative measures.

- More effective investigation of crime through an increase in police powers such as search and seizure, covert warrants and anti-terrorism legislation (to name a few) has been introduced to ensure greater compliance (these measures have been referred to in the response notes to previous questions). It has been argued that some of these measures may result in breaches of civil liberties.

- The purpose of punishment is to reduce reoffending through the balance of the objectives (refer to the prison system, recidivism rates and tougher sentencing regimes). Tougher sentencing aims to encourage greater compliance, but it could be argued that it is having the opposite effect. The Crimes (Serious Sex Offenders) Act 2006 (NSW) was introduced to deal with offenders who are unlikely to comply with the law and therefore a 'continuing detention' order is required. (Make reference to the response notes to Questions 3 and 4.)

- It could be argued that the failure of sexual assault laws has encouraged non-compliance.
- Measures to combat international crime: the ICC brings cases for crimes against the international community. Greater measures and cooperation to combat transnational crimes attempt to ensure greater compliance with the law. Review the effectiveness of international law in response to international crime. (Make reference to the response notes for Question 2.)

These are some suggestions as to the coursework that could be covered in this question. The question is derived from one of the themes of the Crime topic.

Question 11

Most of the content to address this question can be found in the 'Criminal trial process' section of the Legal Studies Stage 6 Syllabus on page 18. The question is specifically addressing the 'learn to' dot-point under this section – 'discuss the use of the adversary system as a means of achieving justice'.

Some of the following may be referred to in the context of this question.

- The role the court hierarchy plays in ensuring specialist courts deal with particular matters through their original jurisdiction. The system of appeals is also crucial to ensure an ongoing focus on the right outcome.
- The features of the adversary system and its ability to arrive at the truth. The process of plea and charge bargaining, the problems around legal representation and the application of the rules of evidence (in particular the use of DNA evidence). The use of some controversial defences, such as provocation, which reduces liability to manslaughter, and the ongoing arguments for and against the use of juries. The move to majority verdicts could also be addressed. Appropriate cases should be used to highlight some of these issues.
- Sentencing can be a hot topic for debate; for example, the extent to which sentences reflect community standards and hence provide justice to offenders, victims and the community. (This is a large area in itself and aspects of the sentencing process by the courts could be discussed.)
- Non-legal responses should also be discussed, as some non-government organisations and the media continually scrutinise the ability of the courts to provide justice.

Reference should be made to the answers provided in questions 4, 5, 6 and 9.

Section III: Options

Past examination questions

Option 1 – Consumer Law

Question 1
This question about changing community values and ethics goes to the heart of one of the key themes and challenges of this topic, and addresses consumer law as a reflection of changing values and ethical standards. This is a broad question that traverses much of the course content covered. Critical analysis is required of the legal and non-legal responses to the shift in community values and ethics about consumer issues.

The following are some of the areas that could be addressed in this question:

- The **historical development of the need for consumer law** resulted in a growing awareness of the need for consumer protection. The nature of the commercial world has continued to evolve since the time of the industrial revolution, when there was little protection for consumers when making purchases. *Caveat emptor* ('let the buyer beware') was the way in which the marketplace was regulated. It was the consumer's responsibility to ensure the purchases they made were fit for the purpose intended.
- In a *laissez-faire* economy there was no government intervention in the buying and selling process that occurred in the marketplace. The market itself was seen to regulate matters between buyers and sellers. Eventually, governments began to pass laws to protect consumers as the marketplace developed and became more complex, which resulted in a range of ethical issues around consumerism.
- Historically the common law was used to resolve consumer issues related to contracts. Due to the growth of the modern economy and increasing complexity of consumer contracts, the Parliament responded by implying certain standards into consumer contracts. Some of the main legislation is the *Sale of Goods Act 1923* **(NSW)**, the *Competition and Consumer Act 2010* **(Cth)** and the *Fair Trading Act 1987* **(NSW)**. These acts imply conditions into contracts, and make illegal misleading and deceptive behaviour, unconscionable behaviour and selling defective or dangerous products. The *Contracts Review Act 1980* **(NSW)** allows the court to grant relief for unjust contracts. There was a consensus (values) in the community that these behaviours should be made illegal.
- Laws protecting consumers from **deceptive advertising and marketing practices** are also examples of a shift in values that showed consumers needed legislative protection from false and misleading promotions. This is provided for in the *Competition and Consumer Act 2010* **(Cth)** and the *Fair Trading Act 1987 (NSW)*. These Acts also make provision to protect against:
  - Unscrupulous suppliers using their greater bargaining power to obtain an advantage over vulnerable consumers
  - Consumers being enticed to buy products through the offer of gifts, prizes or other free items without the intention of providing the advertised gift
  - Bait and switch tactics where consumers are lured into premises with the lure of a very good discount or deal that does not exist, only to be switched to a more expensive product once in the store
  - Engaging in referral selling, sending unsolicited or unordered goods to consumers and the use of coercion, force or harassment in obtaining a sale.

- There was also a development in the regulation around **occupational licensing** to ensure that certain standards be met prior to an organisation operating in an industry.
- Section II of the course work can also be reviewed from the perspective of the place of the state and federal governments in establishing organisations to raise **awareness** and provide **consumer redress**. There is a belief in the community (values) that it is in the community's interest to monitor the behaviour of businesses and educate the public about consumer issues in order to reduce the societal costs of consumer problems.
- **Contemporary issues** continue to raise moral and ethical issues that face consumers in contemporary society. Lawmakers must continue to evolve the law with the onset of technological developments that impact consumer credit, product certification and marketing innovations. *(For more detail on these see Question 2.)*

Question 2

The answer outlined below has been adapted to reflect the key theme and issue, 'the role of law reform in recognising the rights of consumers'. The law generally lags behind shifts in societal values and changes in technology. It should be remembered when discussing law reform that not all reform is for the better. In the area of consumer law there has generally been an incremental increase in the rights of consumers and ongoing clarification of the responsibilities business entities are obligated to operate under.

This question can be approached by looking at an historical development, from the concept of a *laissez-faire* economy to the development of the rights of consumers through the courts and (increasingly) from the parliaments. Some consumer law has been listed above and referred to in Question 1. Any precedent decision or Act passed in Parliament can be considered law reform, and therefore the range of issues that can be covered in this question are broad. A good approach to the topic of consumer law reform is to examine the contemporary issues in the area.

Credit: Our modern society depends on personal and corporate credit to function. There are many forms of credit, but ultimately it is where a person/group obtains goods and services in the present but pays for them at a later date.

The Commonwealth has received powers from the state with respect to consumer credit under the ***Trade Practices Amendment (Australian Consumer Law) Act 2009* (Cth)**. This has standardised laws regulating consumer credit for providers and users, and is a reflection of the desires for common standards to protect consumers in an increasingly complex marketplace. The **Uniform Consumer Credit Code (UCCC)** also ensures that all laws relating to all forms of consumer lending, and to all credit providers, are uniform in all jurisdictions in Australia. This is further evidence of an understanding of the damage an unregulated and unscrupulous credit market can do to individuals and the community.

There are a number of **non-legal measures** in place to assist in addressing concerns around the provision of consumer credit. Some of these include the NSW Office of Fair Trading, community Justice Centres and the Financial Ombudsman. These push agendas that reflect the need for law reform to ensure better, more effective regulation in the area of consumer credit.

The levels of personal debt in Australia are a cause for major concern. The standardisation of consumer credit contracts, assessing an individual's ability to repay a loan, and the other obligations of credit providers are positive developments.

Product certification: This is a process to ensure that all goods meet certain standards with respect to quality and performance. Products sold in Australia have to meet industry standards, communicate effectively how the product is to be used, and continue to improve safety standards over time. Product certification has continued to develop over time, with the understanding (values) that a lack of standards may pose a risk to the community. This also can be viewed in the context of the globalised economy; many of our products are now made outside of our legal jurisdictions.

The Australian Competition and Consumer Commission (ACCC) regulates information standards and product safety under the *Competition and Consumer Act 2010* **(Cth)**. The Office of Fair Trading is also responsible for monitoring the safety of products that are used in NSW, and is empowered to do so under the *Fair Trading Act 1987* **(NSW)**. Historically it was expected that the market would regulate such things, but law reform was necessary in this area to ensure some government oversight.

The ACCC and the Office of Fair Trading both have powers to remove unsafe goods from sale. This might include recalling dangerous products or a public warning of a particular defect.

There are a number of **product certification marks** that have been developed in the various markets that they operate in. **Standards Australia** grew out of a need to ensure all products made in Australia meet minimum benchmarks with respect to safety and information.

There has been incremental law reform in this area; even so, unsafe products still find their way onto the market and constant vigilance is always required by Australian authorities. Consumers who shop around based not only on price but quality, as indicated by product certification, reaffirm the mantra that self-help in a globalised market place is the best protection.

Marketing innovations: Marketing is the process by which a business entity makes the consumer aware of its product or services. With the advent of technological advancement, marketing has become sophisticated and at times invasive. Some unscrupulous methods of marketing include spam on the internet, offers of unrealistic deals from all over the world, and phone calls from call centres from other countries, to name a few. Illegal practices such as internet fraud and **phishing** are also of concern. Now more than ever, the law needs to monitor ways in which the internet is used to market products and services to consumers in an intrusive or illegal manner.

The problem for lawmakers in Australia is that no one government has jurisdiction over cyberspace. Some examples of law reform in this area include the *Spam Act 2003* **(Cth)**, which made it a civil offence to use address-harvesting software to construct distribution lists of recipients. Despite this, its use is on the rise by e-marketing companies.
Phishing, a form of internet fraud, is the use of computer programs to steal valuable information such as credit card numbers, user IDs and passwords. Federal and state

criminal jurisdictions around Australia have amended their criminal laws to include this type of criminal behaviour.

Technology: Technology has broadened the consumer marketplace to a global phenomenon, allowing unscrupulous traders to escape national jurisdictions. Once consumers and businesses engage in online transactions outside of Australia, they forgo the consumer protection afforded to them by state and federal laws. As such, the types of redress they receive will depend on the existence of international treaties. The details of the online provider may assist in the freezing of assets or the pursuing of court orders in other national jurisdictions.

The current provisions of legislation within Australia are inadequate to protect Australian consumers from the majority of problems they encounter in the global marketplace due to the advancement of technology and the growth of the internet. Amendments to the *Telecommunications Act 1997* **(Cth)** give the ACCC authority to regulate dealings with international telecommunications operators, where there are a range of problematic areas requiring vigilance.

Ultimately, law reform can never keep pace with technological developments, but constant vigilance is necessary. As stated earlier, no government has exclusive jurisdiction over the internet. E-commerce has and will deliver many benefits to consumers, but it has increased the vulnerability of uniformed and susceptible users.

Case studies that highlight law reform should be integrated into this question, especially in the area of contemporary issues.

Question 3
This question is derived from the key themes and challenges of the course, 'issues of compliance and non-compliance'. This is a broad question that fundamentally looks at the ability of the law to effectively regulate the marketplace with respect to consumers. It is also possible to discuss non-legal measures that complement legal attempts at achieving justice for consumers.

Some areas that could be discussed are:
The law of contract: This regulates the agreements between parties that satisfy the elements of a contract. It encourages compliance by ensuring that specific contracts be in writing, that the terms to the contract are identified and that breaches of contract are dealt with by adjudicating bodies. It has also implied standards into contracts to ensure providers of goods or services cannot contract themselves out of certain compliance issues.

Some of the main legislation is the *Sale of Goods Act 1923* **(NSW)**, the *Competition and Consumer Act 2010* **(Cth)** and the *Fair Trading Act 1987* **(NSW)**. These Acts imply conditions into contracts, and make illegal misleading and deceptive behaviour, unconscionable behaviour and selling defective or dangerous products. The *Contracts Review Act 1980* **(NSW)** allows the court to grant relief for unjust contracts.

Some contracts are harsh or unfair, and the law attempts to remedy these to ensure greater compliance and justice for consumers. Redress through the courts is expensive, untimely and stressful. Some examples of redress through the courts for harsh or unfair contracts include:

- A contract must be fairly negotiated without any undue influence – *Johnson v Buttress (1936)* 56 CLR 113.
- A contract must be entered in the absence of duress or coercion – *Hawker Pacific Pty Ltd v Helicopter Charter Pty Ltd (1991)* 22 NSWLR 298.
- A product purchased must be of merchantable quality – *Australian Knitting Mills Ltd v Grant (1933)* 50 CLR 387.
- A product must match its advertised description – *Beale v Taylor (1967)* 1 WLR 1193.
- Manufacturers/suppliers cannot engage in deceptive or misleading marketing behaviour – *Qanstruct Pty Ltd v Bongiorno Ltd (1993)* 113 ALR 667.

Regulation of marketing and advertising: The law attempts to ensure that providers of goods and services are truthful in the claims they make about their products. Laws protecting consumers from deceptive advertising and marketing practices are provided for in the *Fair Trading Act 1987* **(NSW).**

The Competition and Consumer Act makes provision regarding the making of false representations. The Competition and Consumer Act and the Fair Trading Act also make provision for:

- Unscrupulous suppliers preying on vulnerable consumers by using their greater bargaining power to obtain an advantage
- Enticing consumers to buy their products by offering gifts, prizes or other free items with the intention of not providing the advertised gift
- Bait and switch tactics, where consumers are lured into the premises with the lure of a very good discount or deal (that does not exist) only to be switched to a more expensive product once in the store
- Engaging in referral selling, sending unsolicited or unordered goods to consumers and the use of coercion, force or harassment in obtaining a sale.

There are many vulnerable consumers with poor financial literacy skills who are subject to such claims outlined above. The extent to which the law can prevent such tactics from unscrupulous businesses is reliant on the reporting of such conduct and obtaining sufficient proof that it has occurred.

Occupational licensing encourages compliance with the law and industry standards in the delivery of goods and services to the marketplace. It is argued that some regulators of 'occupational licensing' are too close to those they are regulating, and at times fail to consider consumer interests in balance with the interests of the industry.

Self-help and awareness are the most effective and efficient ways of dealing with consumer issues. Self-knowledge can ensure consumers are more discriminating and therefore avoid situations that require some form of redress. It also keeps providers of services and goods honest and ensures greater compliance with the law when consumers are aware of their rights. Resolving the issue at the place where it began saves personal and community resources being invested.

Some consumer problems are not able to be resolved without some form of intervention, and there are state and federal organisations to assist with this:

- There are a number of **state and federal government organisations** that provide education, advice, investigative procedures and mediation and adjudicating mechanisms. The **Office of Fair Trading** in NSW is one such organisation. It also is the place where small businesses register the owner of their organisations.

Federal government organisations include the **Australian Competition and Consumer Commission (ACCC)**. The ACCC is an independent statutory body that administers the *Competition and Consumer Act 2010* (Cth) and other Commonwealth Acts. Its role is to promote competition and fair trade in the marketplace. The **Australian Securities and Investments Commission (ASIC)** is an independent statutory body which regulates Australia's corporate, markets and financial services sectors and ensures that Australia's financial markets are fair and transparent.

All of these bodies attempt to ensure greater compliance with the law. They have at times been criticised because the Corporations Law they work under does not have enough 'clout' to punish corporate offenders heavily enough. Gathering sufficient evidence that will hold up in court can also be problematic for these bodies.

- Some industries have developed their own style of **ombudsman.** This office acts on behalf of the whole industry and consumer complaints can be dealt with at this level. Examples include the **banking ombudsman** and the **Energy and Water Ombudsman NSW**. These types of industry initiatives attempt to ensure greater compliance with industry standards, but some critics question the extent to which they are independent. They have no statutory authority to punish offenders.
- There are particular **courts and tribunals** that adjudicate on consumer conflict. The *Consumer, Trader and Tenancy Tribunal Act 2001* **(NSW)** established the Consumer, Trader and Tenancy Tribunal. The Act outlines the operation of the tribunal. The role of this tribunal is to resolve disputes between entities involved in consumer relationships. Some of these are tenants, landlords, traders and consumers. Like most tribunals they are a relatively cheap and fast way to resolve disputes, making the law more accessible to consumers for matters not involving large sums of money and providing a much needed avenue of justice.
- There are a number of non-legal measures that can be highlighted, along with their ability to encourage greater compliance through pressure, persuasion and media attention.
- Contemporary issues such as the development of uniform credit laws and increased product certification can be raised, especially in ensuring greater compliance with the law and achieving justice for consumers. *(See Question 2.)*

Case studies need to be used to provide concrete examples that assist in the critical analysis of some of the areas highlighted in this question.

Question 4

Conflict with respect to consumer issues arises in many areas. The ability of the law to encourage cooperation and resolve conflict is a challenging proposition. The law sets out the rights and obligations of both consumers and providers of goods and services. The law has made significant progress historically to ensure that consumers are better informed, information supplied to them is accurate and truthful, and products are safe. Self-help and awareness are obviously the most resource-efficient ways to minimise conflict and encourage cooperation. Informed consumers have a knowledge of their rights and are able to negotiate a solution to their own consumer problems. This question specifically asks for a discussion of the regulation of marketing and advertising; a brief overview of this is provided in the response notes to Question 3. The extent to which the state and federal governments can eliminate false and misleading advertising is a measure of its ability to encourage businesses to be truthful in their marketing and advertising. This is not always possible, so community awareness is essential, and codes of practice that operate parallel to legislation are important in encouraging cooperation in this area.

Other areas of the course work that can be referred to through the perspective of resolving conflict and encouraging cooperation include the laws regarding contracts, negligence and occupational licensing. *(Refer to the response notes to Questions 1 and 3 above for Consumer Law in this section for an overview of some of this content.)*

Also address the problems raised by the contemporary issues referred to on page 23 of the syllabus. *(See the response notes to Question 2 of Consumer Law discussed earlier in this section.)*

Question 5
Legal methods include any legislation, precedent decisions or bodies set up to regulate the area of consumer law. Consumer redress is referred to in previous answers.

Non-legal measures can also assist consumers in seeking redress for consumer problems they experience. Some examples include:

- **Awareness and self-help** are the most effective and efficient ways of dealing with consumer issues. Self-knowledge can ensure consumers avoid situations that require redress. Resolving the issue when it begins saves personal and community resources. Some consumer problems cannot be resolved without some form of intervention, and there are state and federal organisations to assist with this.
- **Industry groups** have set up mechanisms to resolve consumer issues at an industry level. Some industry organisations are customer-focused and may provide training for staff and develop their own systems for handling complaints. This can be an effective way of building positive customer relationships and ensuring greater resource efficiency by reducing consumer-related problems. It can also assist with consumers who have complaints and want them resolved at the point of sale.
- Some industries have developed their own **industry ombudsman**. This office acts on behalf of the whole industry and consumer complaints can be dealt with at this level. The ombudsman is supposedly independent from the major organisations in that industry. The banking ombudsman is a good example. As a result of a growing perception that the major banks within Australia charged excessive fees and were unresponsive to genuine consumer complaints, the industry sought to set up a complaints mechanism that was independent of the businesses in the industry.
- **Non-government organisations** exist to represent the interests of consumers by raising concerns with governments, educating the public about specific issues or supporting consumers in advocacy matters. Some examples of consumer non-government organisations include **Choice, Consumer Credit Legal Centre (NSW)** and **Incorporated and Consumers' Federation of Australia**. A number of these pressure government to act on areas that may pose problems for consumers.
- **The media** is another important non-legal measure for raising awareness of consumer problems within society. All media is biased to some extent, but can still provide an invaluable service in putting pressure on governments and informing consumers of recent developments that may put consumers at risk financially or physically. It can at times call for redress of problems, and exposure may spark a more immediate response.

A combination of legal and non-legal mechanisms is required to address many issues facing consumers in a global economy. Government and the courts change and develop the law, and at times non-legal responses to a consumer problem may not influence the resolution of the problem. Generally, though, their influence is incremental, especially where research is conducted and education programs are implemented.

Question 6

This question can be dealt with historically by examining the development of the need for consumer laws. The nature of the commercial world has continued to evolve since the time of the industrial revolution, when consumers had little expertise in making consumer purchases. *Caveat emptor* ('let the buyer beware') was the only regulation; consumers were responsible for ensure the purchases they made were fit for the purpose intended.

In a *laissez-faire* economy there is no government intervention in the buying and selling process. The market itself was seen to regulate matters between buyers and sellers. Eventually governments began to pass laws to put in place protections for consumers, as the marketplace developed and became more complex.

Developments in the market economy continue to challenge and shape the nature of the concept of the consumer. The complexity of the commercial world has seen the evolution of modern contract law and laws around the marketing and advertising of consumer goods. It has also seen the drive to ensure some form of occupational licensing. As consumer complaints grew, so did a need to introduce various tribunals and other forms of alternative dispute resolution to divert problems away from the expensive and time-consuming court system.

With the onset of the global marketplace, many consumers shop online in other parts of the world. This has raised some concerns in relation to consumer credit, product certification, marketing innovations and the technological revolution. These contemporary issues should be explored in light of the extent to which they have changed the concept of the consumer.

Question 7

As a topic of study, consumer law generally focuses on the rights of consumers, because historically they had little or no protection at all.

From the perspective of consumers, many legal protections exist in the area of contract law where there are implied standards that manufacturers/suppliers must meet. Unfair and unjust contracts can also be made void if the manufacturer/supplier acts in an unconscionable manner. However, provisions in some contracts (such as credit contracts) provide protections for manufacturers/suppliers, as they spell out the consumers' obligation under the terms of the contract.

Similar protections exist in laws regulating advertising and marketing with respect to false and misleading statements about goods or services. While the consumer has particular rights, the law also serves the needs of honest and ethical manufacturers and suppliers by ensuring that unscrupulous ones are detected and made answerable to the law.

There are other areas that could be addressed in this broad question. It does not matter what content areas you specifically discuss, so long as you address the balance the law tries to achieve with respect to the rights and obligations of both consumers and manufacturers/suppliers.

Other areas that may be addressed include occupational licensing, avenues of redress, and the rights and obligations of both consumers and manufacturers/suppliers, outlined in one or more of the contemporary issues identified on page 23 of the syllabus.

Question 8
Government regulation certainly has improved the rights of consumers and the awareness that consumers have about their rights. It has been acknowledged for a long time now that governments do have a responsibility to protect the more vulnerable consumers within our communities. Legislation and the regulatory bodies set up to respond to consumer redress are the main components for this regulatory framework.

This is a broad question that can be answered by referring to many of the content areas in the Consumer topic. Each area would need to be addressed in terms of its ability to protect consumers and provide justice in resolving consumer disputes. It should be noted, however, that 'caveat emptor' will always apply to consumer protection and the ability of the law to keep pace with the globalised marketplace is becoming increasingly challenging.

Non-legal measures can be included in the discussion as they prompt governments to regulate in certain areas or highlight deficiencies in areas of government regulation that are failing to meet the needs of consumer redress.

Some areas of government regulation that may be included in this question can be found through reference to Questions 1 and 3 in Chapter 5. The solutions to these can be found in Chapter 10.

Reference to non-legal measures can be found in Question 7 Chapter 5.

Question 9
This question is similar to Question 8 but can be discussed again in a very broad manner addressing the ability of the regulatory framework to protect and provide justice to consumers. Justice for consumers has, and always will be, a challenge as there is only so much the legal system can achieve.

Having said this, legislative frameworks dissuade certain behaviour and provide dispute resolution mechanisms while outlawing deceptive, misleading and unsafe practices.

The ability of legal and non-legal measures to deliver better outcomes for consumers needs to be critiqued in this question. Examples of content that may be covered include the regulation of:
* Contracts (refer to Question 3: Chapter 5)
* Marketing and advertising (refer to Question 1: Chapter 5)
* Occupation licensing (refer to Question 3: Chapter 5).

It could also examine the role of:
- Government organisations (refer to Question 3: Chapter 5)
- Non-legal measures (refer to Question 7: Chapter 5).

One could focus on the contemporary issues section of the topic. These continue to develop, some faster than the law can keep up with. More uniform consumer credit laws have been developed across the country to ensure consistency of consumer rights. As technology continues to pervade Australian homes, which are often now points of sale, the law is failing to reflect these changes and protect the rights of consumers.

Some of the above issues need to be addressed with the inclusion of cases, legislation, media reports and critical analysis of the extent to which the law reflects changes in the market economy in its attempts to protect the rights of consumers. (Refer to Question 2: Chapter 5.)

Option 2 – Global Environmental Protection

Question 1
This question relates directly to the theme and challenge, 'the impact of changing values and ethical standards on environmental protection'. There has been significant change in the way most of the world views environmental protection issues. Historically, most environmental management was limited to the relevant jurisdiction within a nation state. Humankind did not generally perceive the Earth's resources as finite, and the need to think sustainably only took on importance in the last 30 years. This shift in changing community values (in the international community) can be mirrored in the development of global environmental law and the consensus of the need for global environmental protection.

It should be noted and clarified in a discussion of this question that while there is a general consensus around the world on issues concerning global environmental protection, there is significant disagreement as to how it is to be achieved. There is a disparity in values between nation states, and this is reflected in the difficulty of getting agreement among various international instruments and at conferences such as Copenhagen in 2009.

International thinking on the issue of **sustainability** is an example of changed community values and ethics. Work such as the Brundtland Report, commissioned in 1987, defined sustainable development as 'development that meets the needs of the present without compromising the ability of future generations to meet their own needs'. The international community began to understand that by working sustainably the community can aim to meet the needs of society today, including the alleviation of poverty, while managing natural resources, energy and waste in ways that can continue into the future without destroying the environment or endangering human health.

Further concepts such as **biodiversity**, **intergenerational equity**, **intragenerational equity** and the **precautionary principle** (with respect to scientific findings on climate change) are all relatively new ideas and could be included in discussions regarding global environmental protection and how they are influential in evolving values and ethics.

The issue of nation state sovereignty should also be addressed, looking at the ways in which it can promote or impede global environmental protection. Examples of the growth of **international instruments** and **conferences** and their outcomes should be cited as they reflect the changed community values over previous decades.

The increased focus by the **United Nations** on global environmental protection is a further example of changed community values and ethics, driven in part by the numerous scientific papers that have been written on the topic, especially on the subject of climate change. This is the case with **intergovernmental organisations** such as the **European Union (EU)** and the establishment and increased activities of **non-government organisations** such as **Greenpeace**.

The emergence of a number of **climate change sceptics**, some of whom have received extensive media coverage, indicates that there is still a way to go before there is true consensus about the way forward with respect to global environmental protection.

Question 2
There is no question that there has been substantial law reform with respect to the need to protect the global environment. This question relates directly to the theme and challenge 'the role of law reform in protecting the environment'.

Continued **technological advancement**, dating back to the Industrial Revolution, has seen the developed world harvest the Earth's resources at increasingly unsustainable levels, to the point where it is causing changes in the climate. This has caused a shift in international **social values**, resulting in the emergence of numerous international conferences and instruments. This reform has primarily occurred in the United Nations and intergovernmental organisations, with continued pressure from NGOs.

Examples of changed social values can be seen in the evolution of attitudes towards sustainable development and certain key principles:
* **Biodiversity** is the variation of life forms within an ecosystem. (An ecosystem is a set of relationships among the plants, animals, microorganisms and habitats in an area.) Biodiversity is important because diverse ecosystems are better able to withstand and recover from disasters, and are more sustainable in the long term because of the wide variety of interdependence that exists within them.
* **'Intergenerational equity'** is the idea that ecosystems, and the environment in general, should not be passed on in any worse condition from one generation to the next. Decision-makers need to consider intergenerational equity when determining how each society is going to meet its needs from year to year.
* **Intragenerational equity**, in contrast to intergenerational equity, refers to fair and just treatment of groups of people within a generation. It is accomplished through policies that endeavour to raise the standard of living of disadvantaged peoples and nations, and ensure that the management and use of their environment does not exploit them. The extent to which the developed world consumes the resources of the planet is clearly unjust. If China and India were able to give all their citizens the same standard of living as people in the West, the world would go into meltdown. Some fundamental shifts will be required if intragenerational equity is to be addressed, while at the same time working towards intergenerational equity.
* Convincing the developed world to work towards ecologically sustainable living has proven to be difficult, and some sceptics argue that the scientific research is not

conclusive enough. The **precautionary principle can be used to** argue that if the science tends to argue that a particular course of action will cause long-term harm, then corrective action needs to be taken now. Waiting for the science to firm up will be too late.

Examples of law reform can also be cited, such as a number of international instruments developed in a bid for greater global environmental protection. Some of these are:
- **Convention on International Trade in Endangered Species of Wild Fauna and Flora (CITES)** 1975. Considered hard law. It aims to ensure that international trade in wild animals and plants, and products made from them, does not threaten their survival.
- **Convention on Wetlands of International Importance (the Ramsar Convention)** 1971. Considered hard law. It provides a framework for national action and international cooperation for the conservation and wise use of wetlands and their resources.
- **Vienna Convention for the Protection of the Ozone Layer** 1988. It presents non-legally binding targets for reducing substances that deplete the ozone layer (notably chlorofluorocarbons). Its aim is to protect human health and the environment from adverse effects resulting from human activities that alter the ozone layer.
- **Montreal Protocol on Substances That Deplete the Ozone Layer** 1989. Considered hard law. It sets out a mandatory timetable for the phasing out of ozone-depleting substances.
- **UN Convention on Biological Diversity** 1993. Considered hard law. It is concerned with the conservation of biological diversity, the sustainable use of its components, and the fair and equitable sharing of the benefits from the use of genetic resources.
- **Agenda 21** 1992 and the **Rio Declaration on Environment and Development** 1992. Considered soft law. It provides principles for guiding sustainable development; it defines humans' responsibilities to safeguard the common environment, as well as the rights of the people to be involved in the development of their economies.
- **UN Framework Convention on Climate Change** 1994. Its goal is to stabilise atmospheric concentrations of greenhouse gases at a level that would prevent harm to the climate system. It has no legally binding targets or enforcement mechanisms.
- **Kyoto Protocol** 1997. Considered hard law. It set binding targets for 37 industrialised countries, and the European Community, for reducing their greenhouse gas emissions by an average of 5%.
- **Copenhagen Accord** 2009. Considered soft law. It was intended to establish an ambitious global climate agreement, starting in 2012 when the Kyoto Protocol expires, but sets no binding targets. It recognises that global temperature rises must be kept below 2 degrees Celsius but includes no specifics for achieving this.

Question 3
Compliance with the law has been difficult to achieve, especially with respect to global environmental protection. The issue of global compliance with the law has only become an issue since the development of a global ethic around the issue of environmental protection.

Compliance and non-compliance at this level can be viewed in a number of ways. Some nation states refuse to sign up to international instruments, such as Australia and the

United States when the Kyoto protocol was being signed. They may sign certain instruments but include a number of reservations that water down their commitment. Lastly, some nation states may simply fail to meet their obligations once they have committed to certain targets or programs.

The need for greater compliance with the law developed in the latter half of the 20th century when nation states recognised the need for a coordinated approach. As businesses began to operate on an international scale, environmental problems also became globalised. These new issues – e.g. acid rain, the hole in the ozone layer, the depletion of fish stocks, climate change – could not be adequately dealt with at a national level. In addition, the affluence of industrialised nations has been built on the use and exploitation of the resources and workforces of developing countries. Poverty, population growth and the accelerated pace of industrial development in Third World countries have all contributed to the environmental challenges faced.

The 1970s and 1980s saw a number of international conferences and multilateral treaties on the environment in response to global threats, in a bid to increase compliance globally. These occurred as many developed countries realised that a purely national approach to environmental protection was inadequate to address what was becoming a transnational phenomenon.

Globalisation of the economy saw further increases in consumption and development, which led in turn to detrimental environmental effects on a global scale. Pollution, global warming and ecological catastrophes are not confined by national boundaries. However, globalisation has not extended to worldwide political integration. Hence, there is a need for international environmental law to attempt to achieve compliance among nation states.

Attempts to increase compliance and discourage non-compliance can be discussed by reference to the role of the **United Nations, international instruments** *(see Question 2)*, **courts** and **NGOs**. The successes of these must be viewed through the eyes of sovereign nation states that ultimately act out their own economic and political interests, even if this means being out of step with international consensus.

Question 4
Resolving conflict at a global level is and will continue to be problematic. Multinational treaties that address global environmental protection issues rarely achieve the original desired outcomes, due to the need for cooperation of nation states that act in their own national interest most of the time.

Conflict over global environmental issues can come from many sources and can be evident in many countries, from developed nations to developing and third world nations. For example, developing countries whose economies depend on the export of primary natural resources (such as metal ores) or agricultural products (for food, housing and other uses) have been less likely to regulate the methods and extent of production. One million hectares of forest are cleared per year in Indonesia – the highest rate of deforestation on the planet – for illegal logging and to convert the land for palm oil plantations. Palm oil is found in 40% of the products on supermarket shelves in Australia and other industrialised countries.

A further example can be seen with the dumping of electronic waste. With the increasing demand for computers, televisions and mobile phones, the United Nations Environment Programme estimates that 50 million tonnes of electronic waste containing lead, cadmium, mercury and other hazardous substances are discarded each year, and that much of this waste is being dumped in Asia and Africa.

Within countries like Australia there is still no political agreement on the way a price should be put on carbon. A carbon tax was introduced in 2012 with a starting price of $23 a tonne. It was planned that three years later the price of carbon would be determined by the international carbon market. However, the Coalition Government, elected in 2013, vowed to repeal the 'carbon tax' and move to a program of direct action.

Global environmental law has the potential to reduce conflict and encourage greater cooperation between nation states. The United Nations has attempted to reach global consensus on a range of environmental priorities. This has been haphazard and sporadic, as consensus across such a broad range of cultures and socioeconomic situations lowers the debate to the lowest common denominator. The Copenhagen conference is an example of this lack of political will.

Having said that, while these international environmental instruments may not enjoy excellent compliance, they can educate the world and provide a way forward that may not have been there previously.

The following entities may be discussed in the context of the extent that they have encouraged greater cooperation and reduced conflict in environmental protection:

- The **United Nations** has increasingly focused on global environmental protection over the last 30 years. Several programs and specialised agencies have been established by the UN to deal with environmental issues and encourage cooperation in these areas. Some of these include the **Food and Agriculture Organization of the UN** and the **United Nations Development Programme (UNDP)**. The UN established the **United Nations Environment Programme (UNEP)** in 1972, following the UN Conference on the Human Environment ('the Stockholm Conference'). The UN also created the **Intergovernmental Panel on Climate Change (IPCC)** which is involved in reviewing and assessing the most recent scientific information from around the world relating to climate change, in a bid to convince stakeholders of the need to address carbon reduction.
- **International instruments:** See the response notes to Question 2 in this section on global environmental protection.
- **Intergovernmental Organisations:** A significant example is the **European Union (EU)**, which has developed an Environment Section whose function is implementing environmental policies for the 25 nation states now comprising the EU. This also includes an **EU Sustainable Development Strategy** that took effect in 2006.
- **NGOs** use a combination of action and advocacy to advance their agendas. Some operate nationally (within a single nation state) and others are international. Significant examples of environmental NGOs are Greenpeace, the World Wide Fund for Nature and Friends of the Earth.
- To what extent have constitutional constraints and Australia's federal structure affected its role in the Pacific region?

Reference to the contemporary issue ('the conflict of the increasing demand for resources and global environmental protection') can also be made. The need to resolve the conflict between resource use and global environmental protection is at the core of sustainable development. The legal system must take into account an enormous range of competing interests (including developers, financial institutions, NGOs, governments, corporations, and future generations in both rich and poor countries) and somehow balance their competing rights. These competing interests are a major source of conflict and pose enormous challenges for the law to encourage greater cooperation.

Question 5

This question asks for a discussion of international tribunals. Prior to the establishment of the United Nations (and thus the **International Court of Justice**), there was practically no court or tribunal in place to settle environmental conflicts between nation states, since few issues had arisen.

Only nation states can be parties to a case before the ICJ. It has the power to decide a case only when the parties to a dispute have consented to its jurisdiction, either by special agreement, where it is specifically provided for in a treaty, or where the parties to the Statute of the ICJ recognise its jurisdiction as compulsory in relation to any other state. Where the parties have consented, it is rare for a decision of the court not to be implemented. However, a state can raise 'preliminary objections' to the court's jurisdiction, or refuse to appear before the court because it totally rejects the court's jurisdiction. This limits the effectiveness of this judicial body.

A range of environmental cases have been heard since the establishment of the ICJ in 1945. An example is the nuclear test cases (1974–75) involving Australia and New Zealand against France, which was concerned with testing nuclear devices in French Polynesia. The cases did not proceed to the merits stage, as the ICJ decided that once France stated that it was ceasing the atmospheric tests of its own accord, the cases no longer had any object. Later, France commenced underground nuclear testing.

One problem with the ICJ's role in settling global environmental disputes is that its jurisdiction depends on whether two or more states have consented to be bound by it. This seriously constrains its jurisdiction, given that corporations are responsible for a vast number of the environmental problems today.

Some cases heard by the IJC include:

- The nuclear test cases (1974–75) involving Australia and New Zealand against France, which was testing nuclear devices in French Polynesia (see above).
- Nauru's case against Australia for failing to remedy the environmental damage caused by 90 years of phosphate mining. In 1992 a negotiated settlement was reached, whereby Australia agreed to pay $107 million in compensation for the extensive damage caused to Nauru prior to its independence.
- The Danube Dam Case of 1997 concerned a dispute over water resources between the neighbouring countries of Hungary and Slovakia, and allegations of transboundary environmental harm. After Hungary withdrew from the joint venture to build a dam to drive a hydroelectric plant, Slovakia diverted the river to operate the dam on its own. The ICJ found both Hungary's withdrawal and Slovakia's diversion of the river unlawful. It held that the 1977 treaty between the countries was flexible enough to take account of new international environmental norms, that the Slovakian

action was unjustifiable in light of shared water resources and equitable use, and invoked the principle of ESD (ecologically sustainable development).

Question 6
International efforts
This question is a broad question and could include reference to efforts of Australian laws to protect and regulate the environment domestically and internationally. Domestic responses are now seen as an important aspect of legislative protections that contribute to global environmental protection.
Refer to the response notes for Questions 2 and 5 in this section for numerous examples of international efforts to protect the environment.

Domestic efforts
Domestic legislation has been evident in NSW since the 1960s and 1970s. New South Wales passed a number of laws that were clearly aimed at the protection of the environment, including the *Clean Air Act 1961, Clean Waters Act 1970, Pollution Control Act 1970* (all since repealed by the *Protection of the Environment Operations Act 1999* (NSW), which consolidated these Acts and added some significant new provisions); the *Heritage Act 1977*, the *Pesticides Act 1978* (repealed and superseded by the *Pesticides Act 1999* (NSW)), and the *National Parks and Wildlife Act 1974*.

Prior to 1979, environmental law and town planning law developed separately. The creation of the NSW Land and Environment Court in 1979 indicated a major shift in policy and direction. It was instituted as a superior court of record, with exclusive jurisdiction in environmental and planning law. In that same year, the *Environmental Planning and Assessment Act 1979* (NSW) was passed, mandating that town planning decisions must take account of environmental considerations.

At a federal level, the main environmental law is the *Environment Protection and Biodiversity Conservation Act 1999* (Cth) ('EPBC Act'). It provides the legal framework for the protection and management of nationally and internationally important animals, plants, ecosystems and places, which are defined in the Act as matters of national environmental significance. Under this Act, any activities involving those matters may require assessment and approval from the Minister for the Environment.

Continued cooperation between the states and the federal government has been important because of constitutional constraints. This has posed difficulties for Australia in meeting its international obligation under some international instruments concerning global environmental protection.

An important initiative to define state and federal roles more clearly, reduce jurisdictional disputes, foster a cooperative approach and ultimately provide better environmental protection was the **1992 Intergovernmental Agreement on the Environment (IGAE)**, which reflected some elements of the Rio Declaration as well as setting out the agreed areas of responsibility between the Commonwealth and all state and territory governments.

The **National Environment Protection Council (NEPC)** was set up under the *National Environment Protection Council Act 1994* (Cth) ('NEPC Act') to oversee the implementation of the IGAE. As stated in Section 3 of the NEPC Act, the objects of the legislation are to ensure that people enjoy the benefit of equivalent protection from air, water, soil or noise pollution, wherever they live in Australia, and to protect businesses and markets from inconvenient effects of jurisdictional variations.

Another means of streamlining federal and state responsibilities is the use of bilateral agreements between the Commonwealth and each of the states and territories. In 2007 the federal and NSW governments signed a bilateral agreement that allows the Commonwealth to accept an environmental assessment done by the state if it fulfils certain conditions. In other words, some assessment procedures under the *Environmental Planning and Assessment Act 1979* (NSW) can replace the need for assessment under the EPBC Act, although they still require approval from the Commonwealth Environment Minister.

Often the various levels of government attempt to operate collaboratively, as with the **Murray-Darling Basin Ministerial Council**, which comprises the relevant ministers from NSW, Victoria, South Australia, Queensland and the Commonwealth. The council was established by the *Murray-Darling Basin Agreement in the Water Act 2007* (Cth), and it has a decision-making role in federal-state plans for sustainable use of the resources of the Murray-Darling Basin, which is used by all of these states.

Question 7
Refer to the response notes for Question 2 in this section on global environmental protection for reference to international instruments.

Reference could be made to the international conferences regrading global environmental protection. The success of these (as outlined in previous questions) is very much dependent on political will, especially of the big economies in the world. There has definitely been a shift in community values in this area, and there seems at times to be greater consensus, especially in the light of emerging scientific data on climate change. It may be that the world will need to edge closer to environmental disaster before it sees the imperative of action on climate change.

Some of the development in global environmental law has been moved forward, and in some cases created, through the increasing regularity of international conferences. Prior to 1972, international instruments promoting environmental protection were predominantly reactionary. They addressed discrete areas of environmental protection as the need arose. Early international law in this area was ad hoc and generally regional in its approach, such as the Protocol Amending the Agreement on the Protection of the Salmon in the Baltic Sea, adopted in 1972.

During the 1960s it was recognised that this sort of piecemeal approach was insufficient to address the global threats facing the environment. Under the guidance of the United Nations, the first international conference to focus on the global environment was organised for Stockholm in 1972. Since then a so-called 'mega-conference' has been held every decade to look at global environmental issues. In 2012 Brazil will host the 'Rio Plus 20' Earth Summit with a focus on low-carbon economies.

A number of other conferences have been held, focusing on specific issues. These often relate to a particular treaty or convention. Meetings of the parties to a framework convention are generally held at intervals to continue negotiations for specific, legally binding commitments from the state parties. For example, the Conference of the Parties to the UN Framework Convention on Climate Change of 1992 meets every year; the 1997 Conference of the Parties in Kyoto, Japan gave rise to the Kyoto Protocol.

The **Stockholm Conference (1972)** was influential, according to the United Nations Environment Programme (UNEP). The main aim of this conference, officially titled the UN Conference on the Human Environment, was to consider 'the need for a common outlook and for common principles to inspire and guide the peoples of the world in the preservation and enhancement of the human environment'. It was the first international gathering to consider the natural environment and material human needs (economic development) together.

This conference produced the **Stockholm Declaration**, which can be credited with providing the impetus for sustainability becoming the focus of global environmental protection. Declarations have no binding legal effect, but they do have an undeniable moral force and provide practical guidance to nation states about how they should behave.

While it can be argued that the Stockholm Conference produced nothing concrete in international law, it did result in the formation of UNEP. Stockholm's real success lay in the foundations it provided for all subsequent international environmental law. It produced non-binding guidelines that were open to wide interpretation, but also introduced the concept of ecologically sustainable development (ESD). UNEP became the major forum for promoting global environmental protection.

The **Nairobi Conference (1982)** was to mark the 10th anniversary of Stockholm and reaffirm the participants' and the world's commitment to the Stockholm Declaration and Action Plan. The conference did not generate as much worldwide interest as Stockholm (possibly due to international political tensions at the time between the USA and the Soviet Union, and Kenya's internal difficulties) and for that reason is not considered an official Earth Summit. The Nairobi Declaration urges 'all governments and people of the world … to ensure that our small planet is passed over to future generations in a condition which guarantees a life of human dignity for all'.

It was hoped that the **Rio Conference (1992)** would produce a range of binding environmental agreements, but the different perspectives of the 180 represented nation states and non-government organisations (NGOs) made it difficult to reach consensus. Still, while Stockholm provided the general guidelines for ecologically sustainable development, it was Rio that produced the framework for domestic and international law aimed at global environmental protection.

The **Rio Declaration** contains 27 principles for utilising the environment in a sustainable manner. **Agenda 21** is a comprehensive, voluntary plan of action for all levels of government to work towards sustainable development. It covers the efficient use of resources, fostering an equitable world, protecting global resources, making the world habitable and increasing the input of disadvantaged groups (such as children, women and indigenous communities). It also recommended the strengthening of communication and partnerships between governments and non-government organisations (NGOs). The main achievement of Agenda 21 is that it placed pressure on nation states to implement ESD.

The **Johannesburg Conference (2002)** aimed to put the concepts of sustainable development into practice. In particular, its focus was to establish time plans and enforcement mechanisms. As usual, state sovereignty provided the biggest obstacle, as expressed on the UN website for the event: 'Sadly we have not made much progress in realising the grand vision contained in Agenda 21 … it is no secret that the global community has not demonstrated the will to implement it.'

Despite the intentions of the conference, the final result was disappointing as not all of the commitments were sufficiently firm. For example, no specific targets were set for one of the key aims: diversification of energy sources.

Reference should also be made to the Kyoto and Copenhagen conferences, to address the issue of reducing carbon emissions.

At the time of writing it is acknowledged that the 10th International Conference on Climate Change (ICCC-10) will take place in 2015. In light of this America and China have signalled the need to take further action on climate but the extent to which they may agree to binding resolutions will remain to be seen.

Question 8
One recurring theme when dealing with international law is the ability of sovereign nation states to promote or impede the effectiveness of the implementation of international instruments. This is especially the case with respect to global environmental protection. Many nation states are at different stages of development with respect to economic prosperity and growth, and culturally they view environmental issues through various paradigms.

Refer to previous questions to highlight such international instruments and conferences, and the extent to which they have fulfilled their potential for global environmental protection. The ability of the United Nations and intergovernmental organisations to facilitate consensus among nation states may also need to be analysed. The failure of the Copenhagen Conference in 2009 is one of many examples that could be highlighted where the diversity of interests of nation states around the world proved problematic in moving global environmental protection forward.

Question 9
This question addresses the phenomenon of the gradual recognition that many environmental issues confront the world today; while being of national significance, they are also of global concern. This question asks 'Why' and implicit in this is a higher order approach to analysing the ability of the global community to achieve consensus on how best to approach global environmental problems and its failure to effectively do so today.

The **development of global environmental protection** has been a feature of the last 20 years. Many environmental issues reach beyond a domestic jurisdiction solution. Domestic legislation of industrialised nations in the 1970s, including Australia, focused on pollution prevention and control. Much of Australian state and federal legislation relating to the environment falls into two general categories, those of environmental impact and pollution control.

As a result, with the recognition of the limitations of domestic jurisdictions, the 1970s and 1980s also saw a number of **international conferences** and **multilateral treaties** on the environment in response to global threats. (Refer to Question 2: Chapter 6).

Driving the push **for why a coordinated global approach to environmental problems is required** is the idea of **Ecologically Sustainable Development (ESD)**. The **Brundtland Report** commissioned in 1987 defined sustainable development as 'development that meets the needs of the present without compromising the ability of future generations to meet their own needs'. It aims to meet the needs of society today, including the alleviation of poverty, while managing natural resources, energy and waste in ways that can continue into the future without destroying the environment or endangering human health.

The keys to ecologically sustainable development are four important elements. These are as follows:
- **Biodiversity** is the variation of life forms within an ecosystem, a biome, or the planet.
- **Intergenerational equity**, or 'equity between generations', is the idea that ecosystems and the environment in general should not be passed on in any worse condition from one generation to the next.
- **Intragenerational equity**, in contrast to intergenerational equity, refers to fair and just treatment of groups of people within a generation.
- The **precautionary principle** states that if an action is suspected of causing long-term harm, even if there isn't a scientific consensus about that action, then the action should not be done.

Having established the need for a global approach to environmental protection, the problematic approach to achieving this should also be examined. **National sovereignty** is the implicit recognition under international law that a nation has authority over its citizens and territory, and can govern as it sees fit. The tension between a consistent global approach to environmental protection and national sovereignty is apparent. At times what is best for the environment is not considered the best option for a country.

This should be critiqued in the context of the limitations in trying to achieve a global approach to global environmental protection. Underlying this is a lack of political and economic will, which ultimately is driven by differing values and ethics in responding to global environmental problems. National sovereignty therefore underpins the ability of the world community to take effective and decisive action, and should be a central theme when critiquing this question.

Further responses to this need can also be examined and analysed through the roles and limitations of intergovernmental organisations, court and tribunals, with regard to the ways in which they are attempting to respond to the need for global environmental protection.

Question 10
This question is taken from the contemporary issues section of the topic. It requires a discussion on the extent to which the law has responded to the conflict of the demand for resources and the need to protect the environment around the world.

A discussion of the essential issues that arise from this tension needs to be addressed. The following is a brief overview of the problem.

A fundamental issue facing the world today is **the conflict between the increasing demand for resources and global environmental protection**. A non-renewable resource is a naturally occurring resource that cannot be produced, re-grown, regenerated, or reused on a scale comparable with its rate of consumption. Non-renewable resources are generally considered finite because their consumption rate far exceeds the rate at which nature can replenish them; examples include coal, uranium, petroleum and natural gas. Renewable resources are those that can regenerate themselves via natural or human management processes, meaning they can be replenished for future generations – for example, timber, fish, solar energy and wind power. If a resource such as fish or timber is over-harvested it will not have the opportunity to reproduce at a rate that is sufficient to ensure that it can last indefinitely.

There is obviously a strong link between resource usage and sustainability. Resources are the fundamental component of the economic system in both industry and agriculture. The legal system has in recent times intervened in the resource markets to provide a more equitable outcome. The paradox is that the use of resources generates revenue, which provides wealth and raises living standards, but if the resources are non-renewable, they will not be available to future generations. The problems for future generations will be compounded by the 'side effects' of resource use, such as global warming, species extinction and pollution.

The 'ecological footprint' and 'The Story of Stuff' highlight the global use of resources and clearly illustrate the inequities in resource consumption between nations. Redressing this imbalance to provide justice for nation states and societies creates numerous dilemmas. Nation states have their own expectations of what they hope to achieve and are averse to external standards imposed by the international community. The need to resolve the conflict between resource use and global environmental protection is at the core of sustainable development.

The legal system must take into account an enormous range of competing interests (including developers, financial institutions, NGOs, governments, corporations, and future generations in both rich and poor countries) and somehow balance their competing rights.

The extent to which the law has achieved this is questionable. Examples could be provided of the manner in which legal responses have attempted to collaboratively address the many environmental issues confronting the world today.

The following are some suggestions of responses made by the law to address the issue of sustainability:
- Examination of the number of **international conferences** and **multilateral treaties** on the environment in response to this issue of sustainability. (Refer to Question 2: Chapter 6).
- The **United Nations** has increasingly focused on global environmental protection over the last 30 years. Several programs and specialised agencies have been established by the UN to deal with environmental issues and encourage cooperation in these areas. Some of these include the **Food and Agriculture Organization of the UN** and the **United Nations Development Programme (UNDP)**. The UN

established the **United Nations Environment Programme (UNEP)** in 1972, following the UN Conference on the Human Environment ('the Stockholm Conference'). The UN also created the **Intergovernmental Panel on Climate Change (IPCC)** which is involved in reviewing and assessing the most recent scientific information from around the world relating to climate change, in a bid to convince stakeholders of the need to address carbon reduction.

- **Intergovernmental organisations:** A significant example is the **European Union (EU)**, which has developed an Environment Section whose function is implementing environmental policies for the 25 nation-states now comprising the EU. This also includes an **EU Sustainable Development Strategy** that took effect in 2006.
- **NGOs** use a combination of action and advocacy to advance their agendas. Some operate nationally (within a single nation-state) and others are international. Significant examples of environmental NGOs are Greenpeace, the World Wide Fund for Nature and Friends of the Earth.
- To what extent have constitutional constraints and Australia's federal structure affected its role in the Pacific region?

Question 11

Achievement of global environmental protection action will require nation states to cast aside political and economic considerations and forgo aspects of their sovereignty in order to achieve consensus on how best to tackle the pressing environmental issues facing the world today. This is because many of the world's environmental problems are beyond domestic jurisdictions and require a coordinated international approach due to the transnational nature of these concerns. In order to achieve sustainability and inter-/intra-generational equity, and to put into action the precautionary principle, an international framework is essential.

Reference should be made to the effectiveness of the responses from the groups identified in Section 2 of the syllabus, 'Responses to global environmental protection', on page 24, as well as Section 3 of the syllabus, 'Contemporary issues concerning global environmental protection', specifically 'barriers to achieving an international response to global environmental protection' (page 25).

Reference should be made to the answers to questions 2, 4, 6 and 9 above. These address the role the UN, international conferences/treaties, and courts and tribunals play in achieving global environmental protection. The role of IGOs and non-legal responses should also be highlighted and critiqued.

Option 3 – Family Law

Question 1

Family law, possibly more than any other area of law, is filled with issues that reflect changing family values. As family values evolve, so does the law. Changes have been made to existing legislation, new legislation has emerged, changes to court procedures have occurred and demands upon legal practitioners have increased. This is essential if the law is to be truly reflective of the public morality (community values) of the time in order to ensure the rights of people are protected and they receive just outcomes, usually when their relationships are in crisis.

The extent to which the law is reflective of community values and ethics in its attempt to deliver just outcomes to family members can be illustrated in some of the following family areas:

- The incorporation of some of the **principles of CROC**, i.e. 'the best interests of the child' and many other provisions into parts of state and federal legislation. It also reflects that the Australian community has a shared sense of public morality on this issue with international standards.
- The **definition of marriage** as outlined in the Marriage Act does not recognise same-sex marriages. It could be argued that this does not reflect the values of all as it excludes same-sex couples. Due to 2009 reforms for de facto couples, it seems the Marriage Act in its current form specifically excludes symbolic recognition of equality for same-sex couples.
- The recognition of **de facto relationships** (and later same-sex relationships) through the *Property Relationships Act 1984* (NSW) and *the Family Law Amendment (De Facto Financial Matters and Other Measures) Act 2009* (Cth) is evidence of a mainstream shift in thinking on these issues. The community generally believes that all couples should have their rights protected in relationships.
- The development of legal and non-legal measures to combat **domestic violence** in Australian communities. Historically the law offered very little immediate protection of victims of domestic violence, but since the early 1980s there has been an attitude in the community that domestic violence is a crime and should be dealt with by the law. This eventually led to the introduction of a standalone piece of legislation in the *Crimes (Domestic and Personal Violence) Act 2007* (NSW). Rape-in-marriage laws, domestic violence legislation and public education programs reflect the changed values of the community, but have also have helped educate the community about why domestic violence is wrong.
- The move to favouring the rights of the child over the rights of adults in certain situations through developments in **child protection legislation**, via the *Children (Care and Protection) Act 1998* (NSW), has reiterated the public's belief about the dangers to society if child abuse is not investigated and dealt with effectively.
- Changes to **dissolution laws** through the Family Law Act in 1976 reflected a major shift in the morality and ethics of the community to make divorce easier and no-fault. This reflected increased recognition that people, especially women, wanted more control over the relationships in their lives when they were in crisis.
- **Recognition of non-financial contributions to property** showed a shift to favouring the protection of women's economic rights in property settlements. The Children's Cases Program is a continuing development of the rights of children in having primacy over the rights of parents in guardianship matters in the case of matters that are resolved in an adversarial manner in the Family Law Court.
- The focus given to **shared parental responsibility** for separating couples going through dissolution has been a controversial shift in the presumption given at the time of deciding guardianship issues, as outlined under the *Family Law Amendment (Shared Parental Responsibility) Act 2006* (Cth). It has been argued that it does not represent the values of all the community in relation to this issue, i.e. some women's groups within society are opposed to this being the starting point in these matters.
- **Birth technologies** continue to raise moral and ethical issues. Technological developments in this area are occurring at a rate that the law struggles to keep up with. At the moment it is possible to create sperm cells from a female through stem cell research and procedures; the ethical and moral implications of this are not known. Much more discussion and education are needed before recognising these

procedures legally. The Status of Children Act that provides for the rights of children born of these procedures may very quickly become out of date. Legislators need to decide if they are going to allow certain developments and whether they reflect what we value as a society. All women (regardless if they are single, married or in a relationship with another person) are permitted **access** to IVF treatment under the *Assisted Reproductive Technology Act 2007* (NSW). The *Miscellaneous Acts Amendment (Same Sex Relationships) Act 2008* (NSW) recognises co-mothers as legal parents of children born through donor insemination and provides birth certificates allowing both mums to be recognised.

- The *Surrogacy Act 2010* recognised 'altruistic surrogacy' and allowed for commissioning parents to apply for a parentage order. It also outlawed commercial surrogacy and makes an offence for people within NSW to enter into a commercial arrangement with a surrogacy agency overseas.

There are many other areas of your course work you can refer to, but ensure that you make the link to how it is a reflection of community values and analyse whether or not it provides just outcomes for family members.

Question 2

The main issues facing family members today are many and varied. The main ones can be categorised into some of the following areas:

- **Domestic violence:** Historically, victims of domestic violence did not have access to the law under the Crimes Act via the law of assault, because of the standard of proof required and the lack of immediate protection. ADVOs have improved this in many ways and this should be explored. Ultimately, the law can only provide so much protection, and if an offender wants to breach the law they will. *(See also Question 1.)*

- **Child protection:** The evolution of law in this area has provided better access to the law for children 'at risk'. Community education has significantly improved reporting, but, as seen in NSW, lack of resources and poor procedures and processes by Community Services NSW have seen a number of children fall through the cracks. The Dean Shillingsworth and Baby Ebony cases are two such matters. The new tier of reporting may hopefully streamline more serious cases that deserve greater attention. *(See also Question 1.)*

- **Dissolution of marriage or the ending of a de facto relationship:** Most of these issues are now covered under family law legislation in the Family Law Court. The main issues still to be resolved centre around guardianship, maintenance and property.

  With respect to guardianship, the rights of the child to have contact with both parents are the focal point of the *Family Law Amendment (Shared Parental Responsibility) Act 2006* (Cth). It has defined what it considers shared parental responsibility to be. Parents must develop a parenting plan and outline the types of parenting orders they want. The court will examine these to determine what it believes is in the best interest of the child. Family relationship centres have also improved access, even though attendance is mandatory. Where parents cannot agree, the court will decide these matters in an adversary manner. The Children's Cases Program has improved children's access to the law in those matters. The judge puts the child at the centre of the deliberations.

  The *Child Support (Assessment) Act 1989* (Cth) improved access to the primary carer's right to maintenance, as it improved the rate of collection via the taxation office. A recent move to refuse overseas visas to a parent who is behind on paying maintenance also saw a significant increase in the payment of these monies. Having said this, some parents do not pay maintenance and it can be difficult for the Child Support Agency to track this down.

The recognition of non-financial contributions to property and superannuation as a family asset has improved access to predominantly stay-at-home or part-time working parents. That said, the Family Law Court struggles to hear matters in an appropriate time frame; a certain number of women appear in the court unrepresented, and it is routinely criticised for delivering inconsistent outcomes from case to case. An issue that may further impact access is the increased number of de facto couples entering the Federal Court to have their matters heard.

- **The recognition of same-sex couples:** The *Property Relationships Act 1984* (NSW) recognised same-sex couples in the same way that de facto couples were recognised. Prior to this they had no access to the law, as their relationships were not recognised. The *Property Relationships Act 1999* (NSW) removed further discrimination of a number of laws at a state level. The federal government also removed any discriminatory pieces of law for same-sex couples at federal level and improved access to the law with the *Family Law Amendment (De Facto Financial Matters and Other Measures) Act 2009* (Cth) in matters where relationships are in the process of dissolving.

Irrespective of the reference to the issue faced, the remedies available and the types of access to the law faced in each situation must be continually addressed throughout.

Question 3
Refer to Question 2.
Some of the areas highlighted above illustrate where family law outlines the rights and responsibilities of people when there are problems within relationships. A judgement needs to be made on the extent to which the law has provided just outcomes to family members in these situations. However, it should be remembered that not all families are the same and the law at times struggles to balance competing rights in relationships.

Question 4
The majority of society accepts and believes in the law and therefore complies with it. Family law is more controversial in that it inevitably involves greater emotional turmoil. People who normally comply with all other laws may find compliance with family law more difficult. Justice Alastair Nicholson, the former Chief Justice of the Family Court, states:

> 'Family law is an area where unrealistic expectations of what a legal system can achieve sometimes results in disenchantment and anger. It is an area where human nature and black letter law do not necessarily combine to create harmonious outcomes.'

However, it should be remembered that compliance is much greater than non-compliance in the majority of family law disputes, and this is essential in order to achieve justice for all.

The following are some areas where the law strives to improve compliance.

Domestic violence: How does the law ensure offenders of domestic violence comply with the law? Examine the processes with respect to ADVOs and breaches of these. The law has developed to give victims greater immediate protection through these processes, but has also reformed bail laws and laws with respect to firearms. Statistics show that ADVOs have ensured a greater compliance because they make public the violent behaviour, and because breaching an ADVO is a criminal offence.

However, some people still do not comply with the law because of deeply held prejudices and beliefs that the law is not able to change. The deaths of Andrea Patrick in 1983, Jean Lennon in 1996 and Irene Davis in 1997, all by men who had ADVOs issued against them, are often used to show that laws are ineffective if certain people choose not to comply.

In March 1996, Jean Lennon (maiden name) was shot and killed by her estranged husband Mr Majdalawi outside the Parramatta Family Court. She was waiting for a custody hearing. He had threatened to kill her many times in the past, and Ms Lennon had used every avenue available to protect herself and her children. An ADVO had been issued against her husband and consequently his gun licence had been revoked, but he still possessed a gun. She had been on the run, living in refuges and changing accommodation each time he found her. She had changed her name to stop him tracing her, and was known by her maiden name when killed. The police and courts knew of her plight but, despite their attempts at protection, she was murdered. Her murder was used to encourage the state government to review the laws on domestic violence with the aim of providing effective protection.

Counselling and mediation processes are used frequently throughout the family law system. They aim to ensure a greater compliance with the law by encouraging the parties to arrive at their own solutions to their issues. Up to 95% of all parties to dissolution do not proceed to the adversarial aspect of the dispute through the family law court; they come to an agreement and file this at the Family Law Court. New laws mandate attendance at a Family Relationship Centre before a parenting order is finalised. This measure is to ensure a greater compliance in the use of the counselling and mediation services provided. As attendance is compulsory, it also ensures that there is greater compliance with the rights of the child in these matters, as the focus of these sessions firmly puts the rights of the child ahead of the parents' rights in these matters.

Enforcement of parenting plans: The *Family Law Reform Act 1995* (Cth) increased the focus on children's rights to have greater contact with both parents. This Act seeks to create greater compliance with parenting plans and the respective parenting orders that can be made. As stated earlier, the *Family Law Amendment Act 2000* (Cth) strengthened the enforcement of parenting plans and parenting orders via a three-tier approach. The new shared parental responsibility laws aim to ensure that parents comply with their responsibilities to care for and maintain their children, irrespective of a breakdown of the relationship.

However, it has also been suggested that the presumption of shared parental responsibility will encourage more parents to abduct their children and flee overseas, which has become a more common phenomenon in recent years.

Maintenance responsibilities: It is important for parents to adequately maintain their children, where they have the means to do so; otherwise this burden falls upon the whole community via welfare payments.

The creation of the Child Support Agency in 1989 significantly improved the enforcement of the payment of child maintenance. In 2006 several 'lone fathers' support groups criticised the current system, saying it unfairly placed substantial financial burdens on many fathers who do not enjoy permanent or regular time with their children. At present the government has resisted changing the system.

Self-employed persons or people whose annual incomes fluctuate make it difficult for the Agency to accurately assess the degree of maintenance they should be paying.

Your notes should address and outline those areas where people comply with the law and those where they fail to comply. Why is this so, and to what extent can the law provide justice for all? Examples such as more people paying maintenance, and more parents being involved with children post-separation because of an emphasis on parenting plans, could be highlighted as areas where family law is dynamic and ever-changing in order to promote greater compliance and more just outcomes for family members.

Question 5
This is a broad question that can be addressed via a number of areas where the law addresses conflict within families and attempts to reduce this conflict. A specific discussion of the dissolution of marriage must also be addressed. The response notes of Questions 1–4 in this section (family law) can be cited for specific legal and non-legal responses in some of the following areas.

Domestic violence costs the Australian community in excess of $8 billion dollars per year. It is an area of conflict that has warranted significant law reform over the years in order to better protect the victims and reduce conflict.

ADVOs have made domestic violence more visible to the community and provided more immediate protection to victims (primary and secondary). This has reduced conflict to some extent, but ADVOs deal with conflict at a stage where it has already become damaging. Some high-profile education/media campaigns (non-legal responses) have highlighted the issues surrounding domestic violence and have been aimed at encouraging cooperation, to the extent that perpetrators can obtain some assistance with their anger management issues.

More needs to be done at the preventative stage, where the causes of violence can be dealt with in a better resourced and more intensive manner once it has been identified. At the same time, domestic violence is also a product of some of the ways women are viewed in our society; until those change, the response to domestic violence will always be reactive.

Child protection: Conflict in this area stems from the needs of the state to protect children from abuse or neglect. At the state level, legislation provides for mandatory reporting to **Community Services NSW** (CSN, formerly known as DOCS) of children considered to be 'at risk'. The failings of this system, over the last five years especially, need to be highlighted as a product of a lack of resources in the face of increased reporting, as well as ineffectual systems of investigation and follow-up by CSN.

The NSW Ombudsman's annual report of 'reviewable deaths of children' in NSW each year highlights cases of children known to CSN who have died as a result of abuse or neglect. The NSW Government has increased the resources allocated, and a 2009 review by Justice Wood recommended a need to streamline reporting so that only more serious cases are referred on; others should be dealt with in a more localised area, e.g. schools.

Child protection is an area that should be coordinated at a federal level, and laws should be consistent across the nation. Reducing conflict in the area of child protection will continue to be problematic and, as mentioned above, constitutional constraints continue to hamper a better resourced and coordinated national response. There have been calls for the appointment of a National Child Commissioner to oversee such an area.

Federally, the recognition of child neglect and abuse during the dissolution stage of a relationship, especially since 1995, has been a significant development. Non-legal responses, such as media campaigns to highlight the need for reporting of neglect/abuse, have been successful in raising awareness of this as a serious area where conflict can be life-changing and very damaging. As discussed above with respect to domestic violence, prevention is much more cost-effective in the long run, but generally the law is reactive. Preventative measures that identify risk factors while enhancing protective factors would seem to be extremely important.

Dissolution: Since its inception in 1975, the Family Law Act has encouraged cooperation between separating couples in a bid to reduce potentially harmful conflict. This went a step further in 2006 with the introduction of Family Relationship Centres and mandated attendance at counselling sessions. Approximately 5% of matters are resolved adversarially in the Family Law Court, but these matters are usually very costly and time-consuming, with parties usually unhappy with the result.

In the midst of this conflict the needs of the child can become secondary. The introduction of the Children's Cases Program where one judge will deal with the matter from beginning to end, the streamlining of proceedings to reduce delays and putting the child at the centre of dissolution cases are all attempts to reduce conflict, especially in the eyes of the child. This has been a positive development.

Many separating couples file their own agreements, but there can still be residual conflict even after an agreement has been reached on the following:
- Guardianship – Shared parental guardianship is the starting point, but there is no evidence that this has reduced conflict. Parenting orders are still problematic and a significant number of parents ignore these orders.
- Maintenance – The payment of this has improved, but too many parents still fail to meet their obligations.
- Property – The move to recognise non-financial contributions, the fact that there is no set rule and the inclusion of superannuation in the calculation of family assets have provided more just outcomes, but has not necessarily reduced conflict.

There are other areas within the family law topic that could be discussed, as long as they are examined within the context of the degree of conflict and the extent to which the law has reduced this conflict through the proactive encouragement of cooperation.

NB: It should be noted that de facto couples (including same-sex couples) can now be included in this discussion of how the Family Law Court deals with the three issues above for separating couples.

Question 6

State and federal courts need to be examined in this question to address the extent to which they are able to balance the rights of family members in crisis. Two major areas could be examined in this question: the role of the federal court system in dealing with separating couples, and 'care applications' in the Children's Court dealing with incidences of children alleged to be at risk of harm.

The Family Court of Australia was introduced in 1975 by the Family Law Act as a specialised court, and it acts apart from other courts in the judicial hierarchy. The Family Court deals with the problems of separation and other disputes evolving out of relationships. It is made up of two main sections:
- The counsellors that couples can make use of via a Family Relationship Centre
- The judges and the registrars.

The Family Law Act encourages separating couples to attend counselling sessions in a bid to resolve their differences and file their own agreement with the Family Court registrar.

Traditionally, the court's jurisdiction was constrained by the Constitution under Section 51, which only allowed the federal government to regulate 'marriage and divorce'. But due to cross-vesting laws between four of the states and the federal government, all matters pertaining to separating couples are now heard in the Family Court. (De facto couples are recognised as couples in law under the *Property Relationships Act 1984* (NSW).) This means that these matters will be heard by a specialist court. A concern is that the additional workload of the court will require greater resources, as it already experiences delays in some matters coming to trial. At the time of writing, there was no indication that these resources would be forthcoming.

The court decides matters pertaining to guardianship, maintenance and property. It also decides ongoing issues, such as varying orders as a result of changes in family circumstances or ongoing incidences of family violence or child protection matters. *(Reference to these is made in the response notes for Questions 4 and 5 in this section.)*

Issues to be explored with the Family Court are delays and costs. Some matters can take two or three years to resolve, due to the workload of the court and (in some cases) the behaviour of the parties failing to agree on matters. At times the court may make interim orders, but because the matter is delayed so long those orders may need to be examined again before resolution because the children involved have matured and their needs are different.

The Children's Cases Program (CCP) was introduced for cases where children are involved to try to counter the intransigence of the parents and place the rights of the child at the forefront of proceedings. Formal evaluation of the program has found that it 'allowed those who had already experienced damaged relationships to resolve the important issues surrounding their children without the further potential damage an adversarial process could create'. It was also suggested that the CCP program had the potential to assist divorcing parents to parent more cooperatively. *(See the response notes for Question 5 in this section.)*

A significant percentage of women represent themselves in divorce proceedings, which again raises the issues of cost and access. A high percentage of separating couples do file their own agreement, but enforcement of the court's orders has become so problematic that it has to take a more punitive approach in ensuring that the rights of family members recognised in those orders are upheld.

The Children's Court is the arbiter of care applications made by CSN in matters pertaining to children deemed to be 'at risk' of harm. Under the *Children and Young Person's (Care and Protection) Act 1998* (NSW) Sections 71 and 72, the court may make care orders if it is satisfied on the 'balance of probabilities' that the child or young person is in need of care or protection. The principles that guide the court under the Act are those that are least intrusive in the life of the young person and his/her family, consistent with the paramount concern of protecting the child or young person from harm and promoting their development. The proceedings are conducted with as little formality and legal technicality as the case permits and not in an adversarial manner.

An order to relocate parental responsibility is the most drastic measure available, and must not be made unless the court is satisfied that no other order would be sufficient to meet the needs of the child or young person.

Figures tend to indicate that child neglect is on the rise, more so than any other form of abuse that a child may experience. By the time a matter gets to the court, the extent of the damage done to a child may be too great to rectify. Community Services NSW has failed to cope with a number of cases where children were at genuine risk of harm and the state government had failed to identify and proactively address the numerous causes of abuse. *(These issues can be explored further.)*

In addition, the court reassessing parental responsibility may be a necessary step and can be the circuit breaker that the child and parents need to reassess the family circumstances. Some adults are not fit to be parents, and the court can be the only step where the child's rights are recognised and protected.

Question 7
This question puts a different spin on things by asking for two areas to be compared and contrasted. This is a more content-driven question, as opposed to a broad question, with greater opportunity for higher-order analysis and evaluation.

The following are the legal requirements and responsibilities of a marriage. This can then be compared and contrasted with one alternative type of family arrangement, such as de facto relationships.

The requirements of a valid marriage
As well as the requirements mentioned in the definition of marriage, there are other requirements needed to ensure a marriage is valid.

Section 11 of the Marriage Act provides that a person cannot marry unless he/she is of marriageable age. Men and women are of marriageable age at 18. People can seek special permission from a court to marry at the age of 16.

Section 12 of the Act allows people to marry under the marriageable age. There are legislative controls in relation to this. These are:

- The person whom the applicant wants to marry must be of marriageable age.
- The magistrate or judge must be satisfied that the 'circumstances of the case are so exceptional and unusual as to justify making the order'. The Marriage Act does not say what constitutes 'exceptional and unusual circumstances'. It is for the judge or magistrate to decide on the facts before them. Some examples have included pregnancy, financial independence and parental consent. (See *Re Kay (an Infant)* (1964).)
- If the judge or magistrate makes an order authorising an applicant to marry, they must do so within three months, or the order will cease to exist.
- In the usual situation where both of the minor's parents are alive, he or she is not an adopted child, the parents are not living separately and apart, and the parents have not been deprived of the custody of the minor by a court order, the consent of both parents is required. If a judge or magistrate is satisfied that consent was refused unreasonably, he or she may give the necessary consent.
- This is not the case for de facto couples; recognition of their relationship does not require a formalised ceremony. It does require a combination of factors, such as a two-year period of the relationship (or thereabouts if other factors are present), common property, children and a public aspect to the relationship. Unlike in a marriage, a court must determine if de facto relationships exist, which usually only occurs when couples are in the process of separating.

Since the commencement of the Family Law Act the prohibited degrees of relationship were narrowed to the following categories:

- A man cannot marry a woman if she had been or was his ancestress, sister, or descendant. A woman cannot marry a man if he was her ancestor, brother, or descendant.
- Thus, a man cannot marry his grandmother, mother, sister, daughter or granddaughter. Likewise, a woman cannot marry her grandfather, father, brother, son or grandson.
- De facto relationships cannot be recognised in these instances either.

Section 42 of the Marriage Act provides that, as a general rule, a marriage cannot be solemnised unless the couple provide the celebrant with a 'Notice of Intended Marriage', not earlier than six months and no later than one month before the date of the marriage. In the notice, the intended bride and bridegroom are required to answer 12 questions, which must be signed by themselves and a witness. Two witnesses must be present at the ceremony, and they must be over the age of 18. As long as the parties believe the two witnesses to be 18 or over, the marriage is still valid.

An authorised celebrant must perform the ceremony. This can be a religious or a civil celebrant. If one of the parties honestly and reasonably believes the celebrant is authorised, then the marriage is valid.

A marriage certificate is issued by the celebrant after the ceremony is completed. This is signed by the celebrant, the bride and bridegroom, and the witnesses. This is proof that the ceremony was conducted according to law.

None of the above requirements are applicable for de facto couples.

Under Section 23 of the *Marriage Act 1961* (Cth) a marriage is made void where:
- Either of the parties is lawfully married at the time of marriage – de facto relationships are also monogamous.
- Consent was obtained by duress or fraud, mistaken identity, or one of the parties was incapable mentally of understanding the nature and effect of the ceremony.
- Either of the parties is not of marriageable age.

The last two points are not applicable to de facto couples.

When two people marry they assume certain legal consequences and responsibilities. Marriage confers a *duty of exclusive consortium*; it is a union of two only. Spiritually, morally, emotionally and practically, wives and husbands have many duties towards, and responsibilities for, each other. In legal terms, however, the only duties that are enforceable are those concerned with property, personal safety and children. These become easier to enforce when the marriage is in crisis or is over, rather than when it exists without legal intervention.

Generally speaking there is a duty of each spouse to provide '*consortium vitae*' (companionship, love, affection, comfort, mutual services and sexual intercourse) and to co-habit together. This is the same for de facto couples.

A husband is not allowed to force his wife to have sexual intercourse against her will, and vice versa. The NSW Crimes Act was amended in 1981 with the passing of the *Crimes (Sexual Assault) Amendment Act 1981* (NSW) to remove this common law barrier. It was also amended to protect the spouse from domestic violence. This applies to all relationships.

In addition to the above, the rights and responsibilities of married couples include **maintenance**. This is the payment by one spouse to help contribute to the care and welfare of the other spouse and any children of the marriage. In the past, it was the husband's duty to maintain his wife and children. If one spouse is incapacitated by a mental or physical illness and unable to work, it is the other's responsibility to earn an income not merely sufficient to meet his/her costs of living but the day-to-day expenses, especially necessities, of both. The same responsibility for maintenance also applies to de facto couples.

The level of maintenance is based on providing the necessaries of life such as food, clothing and shelter, education, etc. Since the passing of the Family Law Act in 1976, it is possible for a husband to seek maintenance from his wife. A formula is used to determine this when a marriage has broken down. This is outlined under the *Child Support (Assessment) Act 1989* (Cth) which also facilitated the establishment of the Child Support Agency (CSA). The CSA is responsible for ensuring maintenance payments are made by deducting payments from the liable parent's salary/wages.

Under the Family Law Act, a husband or wife may sue each other in contract or tort and cannot be held liable for each other's debts. A woman now has the same rights as a man to enter into contracts, whether she is married or not. This is also applicable to de facto couples.

As a general rule, the law regards communications between husbands and wives as confidential and treats them as privileged. In criminal trials spouses are able, but not compellable, to bear witness against each other. In civil cases, spouses are both able and compellable to give such evidence. Under Section 18 of the *Evidence Act 1995* (Cth) and Section 18 of the NSW and Victorian Evidence Acts modelled on that Act (the Uniform Evidence Acts), a de facto partner in either a same-sex or opposite-sex relationship cannot be compelled to give evidence against his or her partner in certain criminal proceedings. Not all states have such provisions in their Evidence Acts, however.

A person who dies without leaving a will is referred to as 'intestate' or 'partially intestate' if his or her will does not effectively dispose of all of his or her property. State laws governing intestacy determine how the property of the deceased is divided. Generally, with the exception of some monies that will be deducted for probate, the entire property will go to the surviving spouse, or the spouse and any children of the marriage. Other family members can also inherit. The parents and siblings of the deceased may all inherit if no valid will exists. In NSW, the property is distributed to certain family members according to a pre-determined formula under the *Succession Act 2006* (NSW), as amended in 2009 by the *Succession Amendment (Intestacy) Act 2009* (NSW).
The Succession Act was also amended by the *Succession Amendment (Family Provision) Act 2008* (NSW). While a person can leave his or her property to anyone he or she chooses, Section 58 of the *Succession Act 2006* (NSW) now allows certain family members to apply for a family provision order. A spouse or de facto spouse, child, grandchild, former spouse, or another person who was in a close personal relationship with the deceased can apply to the court for such an order.

Marriage automatically cancels any pre-existing will unless the person made the will in anticipation of marriage (*Succession Act 2006* (NSW) s 12). Divorce or annulment cancels any provision in an existing will that favours the divorced spouse under the *Succession Act 2006* (NSW). This is not the case for de facto couples, as there is a time lag before the law recognises the relationship to exist.

All women (regardless if they are single, married or in a relationship with another person) are permitted **access** to IVF treatment in New South Wales under the *Assisted Reproductive Technology Act 2007*. The *Miscellaneous Acts Amendment (Same Sex Relationships) Act 2008* (NSW) recognises co-mothers as legal parents of children born through donor insemination and provides birth certificates allowing both mums to be recognised. The *Surrogacy Act 2010* does not impose conditions about the gender of the parents and therefore altruistic surrogacy is now available to married or same-sex couples living in a de facto relationship.

Due to the changes in the way the law treats de facto couples since 2009, there is now little difference between the two types of relationships with respect to legal consequences and responsibilities for these types of family arrangements. It is fair to say that some people living in de facto relationships are unaware of the permanency of their relationship in law.

Question 8
This question relates strongly to the theme and challenge identified on page 26 of the syllabus, 'the role of law reform in achieving just outcomes for family members and society'.

Again, this is a broad question. Relevant changes to family law that could be discussed include:

- The evolution of domestic violence laws
- Changes to the law of divorce in 1975
- Recognition of de facto and same-sex couples
- Proposed changes in the Federal Parliament, with respect to the definition of marriage recognising same-sex relationships, continuing to be debated in 2012.

Question 9
The changing nature of parental responsibility

Family law, possibly more than any other area of law, is filled with issues that reflect community values and ethics. As these values and ethics change, so does the law. Changes have been made to existing legislation, new legislation has emerged, changes to court procedures have occurred and demands upon legal practitioners have been increased. This is essential if the law is to be truly reflective of the public morality (community values) of the time in order to ensure the rights of people are protected and they receive just outcomes usually when their relationships are in crisis.

The extent to which the law is reflective of changing community values and ethics in its attempt to deliver just outcomes to family members can be illustrated in the area of parents and children. The extent to which the law has improved the rights of children at the expense of parents is difficult to quantify. However, there has been an increased focus on attempting to ensure the 'best interests' of the child are the centrepiece of most family disputes.

Some areas that could be addressed and critiqued as a result of evolving community values in this question include:

- The passing of **the Family Law Act**, which embedded the principal of the 'best interests' of the child, has continued to develop the rights of children in family disputes and to ensure parents meet their responsibility, especially during and after the process of **dissolution**. The **Children's Cases Program** has put the rights of children before the rights of parents in a small percentage of drawn out and protracted adversarial trials.
- **The Family Law Reform Act 1995 (Cth)** changed the essential terminology around the guardianship of children and further developed the concept of parenting plans. It promoted the right of children to be able to spend as much time with each parent as is practicably possible and to be safe from violent family environments.
- The **Family Law Amendment (Shared Parental Responsibility) Act 2006 (Cth)**, which introduced shared parental responsibility as a starting point in deciding the primary residence of children, has generally improved the right of children to spend significant time with both parents, especially that of the secondary carer (generally the father). This act has come under criticism, especially the 'hostile parent' provision, because it stopped some parents raising issues of abuse that may have been difficult to prove. The federal government is in the process of removing this provision.
- The **Surrogacy Act 2010** recognised 'altruistic surrogacy' and allowed for commissioning parents to apply for a parentage order. It also outlawed commercial surrogacy and makes it an offence for people within NSW to enter into a commercial

arrangement with a surrogacy agency overseas. This Act has improved the rights of commissioning parents and streamlined the adoption process. Gay and lesbian couples, however, argue that outlawing overseas commercial surrogacy arrangements diminished their opportunities to become parents.

- The legal status of children born out of wedlock or as a result of birth technology methods is reaffirmed by the **Status of Children Act 1996 (NSW).** This has clarified parental responsibilities and issues around maintenance and inheritance. All women (regardless if they are single, married or in a relationship with another person) are permitted **access** to IVF treatment in New South Wales under the **Assisted Reproductive Technology Act 2007 (NSW).**

- The **Miscellaneous Acts Amendment (Same Sex Relationships) Act 2008 (NSW)** recognises co-mothers as legal parents of children born through donor insemination and provides birth certificates allowing both mums to be recognised. The latter has improved the rights of same-sex couples in these situations and the children born of these family arrangements.

- In the area of child protection the rights of children are still being neglected with inadequate resources and poor processes in the investigation and following up reports of children at risk of harm.

Question 10
The effectiveness of the law in achieving justice for parties involved in relationship breakdown remains a challenging undertaking. The law continues to evolve and keep pace with societal trends that impact guardianship of children and ensuring maintenance and property settlements are resolved in a just and equitable manner. (Refer to Questions 1 and 2: Chapter 7.)

Question 11
The law continues to evolve with respect to the rights and responsibilities of family members in the area of birth technologies and surrogacy. Protection for family members in both of these areas has improved historically, especially for same-sex couples. However, the evolution of technology, in particular stem cell research, and the prohibitive provisions with respect to sourcing overseas commercial surrogacy, should be evaluated.

Non-legal groups such as the Christian Lobby and gay and lesbian advocacy groups have criticisms of the current legislation regulating birth technologies and surrogacy. Reference to these opposing viewpoints will give some insight as to the extent to which the law has adequately protected family members, in particular children.

Reference should be made to the answers to Questions 1, 6 and 11 above.

Option 4 – Workplace

Question 1
This question is directly related to the theme and challenge, 'laws relating to the workplace as a reflection of changing values and ethical standards'.

Community values and ethics with respect to the workplace can be examined historically and into the present day. Legislative change and precedent decisions through the courts have reflected the shift from the master-servant relationship and the exploitation of workers, through the onset of 'high capitalism' to the growth of unionism and the benefits to workers of collective bargaining.

The appalling state of workplace conditions evident in the Industrial Revolution led to agitation for justice for individuals in the workplace. Improved rates of pay, better safety and the elimination of child labour were all areas where community values shifted to denounce criminal exploitation of workers.

Areas that could be explored to illustrate changing public morality with respect to greater justice in the workplace for workers include some of the following:

- The move by courts to regulate workplace agreements and imply terms into these contracts. Aspects of this include the **mutual duties** of employers and employees.
- The development of **industrial awards** that outlined working conditions across industries, ensuring greater justice for workers in the same work but in different workplaces. Historical decisions, such as the *Harvester* case decided by Justice Higgins, paved the way for the concept of a 'just wage' – minimum wage.
- **Agreements** (such as enterprise agreements) allow greater flexibility and are aimed at improved benefits for both employees and employers. The introduction of **individual workplace contracts** certainly improves justice for individuals in the workplace, so long as employees have some bargaining power to negotiate with.
- The **modern regulatory framework** is the culmination of generational conflict between employers, employees and government attempting to reach consensus about what is just and fair with respect to respective working conditions. Currently, the *Fair Work Act 2009* (Cth) has established 10 National Employment Standards (NES) and has redesigned all federal awards into a smaller set of modern awards. It also reintroduced a safety net and unfair dismissal laws for employers with 15 or more employees. All of these are examples of reaffirming community values in the workplace. The *Industrial Relations Act 1996* (NSW) is the main legislation in NSW that outlines the rights and obligations of employers and employees working under the state system.
- **Courts and tribunals** are a reflection of an agreed consensus that impartial adjudicating mechanisms should ensure justice for individuals in the workplace. Analysis of the jurisdiction of **Fair Work Australia (now the Fair Work Commission), the Fair Work Ombudsman** and the **Federal Court/Federal Magistrates Court** will provide examples of individuals seeking justice on matters pertaining to employment. The **Industrial Relations Commission** is the industrial umpire in NSW. Industrial courts and tribunals that exist at a state and federal level are examples of the community's need to ensure appropriate redress is available to individuals in the workplace.
- The **contemporary issues** outlined in the syllabus on page 33 lend themselves naturally to this question. Discrimination legislation has been in place for 30 years, both federally and in NSW, and they outlaw a range of discriminatory practices in the workplace. Examples include the *Anti-discrimination Act 1977* (NSW) and the *Sex Discrimination Act 1984* (Cth) as well as the *Race Discrimination Act 1975* (Cth). These Acts have their own adjudication mechanisms and reflect the community's attitude that there is no place for discrimination in the workplace. Other forms of discrimination still exist but the legislation has removed many forms of direct discrimination. Indirect discrimination has been harder to detect and purge, and sexual harassment still remains a major issue in the workplace.

- **Safety** has taken much more prominence in the last 20 years, due to a better understanding of the extent of workplace injuries, that they are preventable in many cases, and that the cost to the community is significant. There are significant measures now in place to ensure that employees and employers comply with their obligation under OHS legislations. The *Occupational Health and Safety Act 2000* (NSW) and cases such as *Briggs v James Hardie & Co. Pty Ltd (1989)* 16 NSWLR 549 can be discussed as a reflection of the community's commitment to a safer workplace. At a federal level the work of **Safe Work Australia**, which is an independent statutory body established in 2009, seeks to improve occupational health and safety and workers' compensation throughout Australia.
- Every year there are a number of cases of **unfair dismissal**, where individuals claim they were wrongfully dismissed from their employment. The *Fair Work Act 2009* (Cth) prohibits wrongful dismissal on several grounds and provides redress for individuals in this situation. The community condones the dismissal of employees who do not fulfil their obligations lawfully to their employers.
- **Leave** is seen as essential for employees to assist them to balance work and life. Various occupations have different leave provisions, depending on the ability of those groups to individually or collectively bargain for them. **Paid maternity leave** came about in 2010 after a long campaign by unions and other interested groups over a period of 20 years.

Question 2
This question is related to the key theme and challenge, 'the role of law reform in recognising rights and enforcing responsibilities in the workplace'. This is a broad question examining change in laws that have created rights for employees and employers' rights, along with ensuring corresponding responsibilities. Any development of legislation and any precedent decision can be considered law reform.

This question can also be discussed from a historical point of view, as outlined in the earlier part of Question 1. Attitudes to industrial relations can and do change depending on the government of the day, as can legislation and policing. For example, certain unfair dismissal laws were removed under the Howard Government, but were reinstated under the Rudd Government. Therefore, when discussing the current legislative regime, it should be remembered that this is a product of the evolving nature of workplace law.

Reference to the content in Question 1 and subsequent questions should be made as examples of law reform in the workplace. The contemporary issues section of the syllabus is also an excellent example of the development of the law in this area.

Question 3
It is in the national interest, as well as the interest of individuals and groups within the workplace, to ensure greater compliance with the regulatory framework that exists at a state and federal level. The modern industrial landscape seems to be characterised by greater compliance, most likely due to the process of workplace negotiation of working conditions. Industrial action tends to cause much less disruption than was previously seen in the 1970s and 1980s. Generally speaking, action can be taken during the negotiation period of an enterprise agreement; any action taken outside this period may be deemed to be illegal. This has given greater certainty to employers and employees. At times, though, disagreement is inevitable, and compliance with the law will vary depending on the government of the day and its policies.

Discussion of the following is one way of approaching this question, by examining the framework in place to encourage compliance and reduce non-compliance:

- Examination of the regulatory framework at a federal and state level under the *Industrial Relations Act 1996* (NSW) through the Industrial Relations Commission in NSW and the *Fair Work Act 2009* (Cth) through Fair Work Australia (now the Fair Work Commission).
- The process of **negotiation** between employees and employers has generally improved compliance with working conditions once they have been negotiated for a nominated period of time. This provides greater certainty, especially when enterprise agreements are finalised. Individual workplace contracts cannot offer conditions that would put employees in a worse position than the appropriate award imposes.
- Both the *Industrial Relations Act 1996* (NSW) and the *Fair Work Act 2009* (Cth) aim to increase compliance through a focus on negotiation and mediation. Both Acts promote a consensus-orientated approach to dispute resolution. **Arbitration**, which pits both parties in an adversarial situation, is usually seen as the last resort.
- Compliance is also encouraged and enforced through the role of **courts and tribunals**. In NSW the Industrial Relations Commission, which refers matters to the NSW Industrial Relations Tribunal, investigates alleged breaches of state industrial legislation, awards and enterprise agreements. It will first order a compulsory conference between the parties, then conciliation; it only employs arbitration to deal with an industrial dispute if conciliation is unsuccessful. Its orders are binding.
  At a federal level, Fair Work Australia (now the FWC) is the industrial relations tribunal. It can arbitrate matters and make rulings on unfair dismissal and other matters emanating from industrial disputes. The *Fair Work Act 2009* (Cth) created a Fair Work Division of the Federal Magistrates Court, which can hear small claims matters under the value of $200 000. It also created a Fair Work Division of the Federal Court.

Greater compliance in the workplace can also achieve justice in addressing the issues of **discrimination, safety, leave** and the manner in which **termination of employment** is decided. These areas from the 'contemporary issues' section would be a good way to look at the development of relevant law and cases, as outlined earlier in the summary overview section. It is in these areas that non-compliance is an issue, one where the law can find it hard to ensure compliance. For example, **enforceability** is a problem in achieving justice for people experiencing discrimination. **Protection of individual rights** and **resource efficiency** were two factors exposed in the Hardies asbestos case. Unfair dismissal can result in a lack of accessibility if the matter is to be decided adversarially in the courts.

Question 4

'Encouraging cooperation and resolving conflict' is a key theme and issue in this topic. The industrial relations model of negotiation is fundamentally aimed at encouraging both parties to resolve their issues at the bargaining table, not in the courts and tribunals. This is usually possible, so long as workplace laws are a fair balance between the aspirations of employees and employers. This question also asks for a discussion of negotiations between employers and employees.

Negotiations about the type of work and working conditions that take place between employees and employers are known as **workplace bargaining**. When all employees within the workplace are united on a series of workplace issues, they can negotiate with their employer from a position of strength and are better able to achieve their desired results. **Enterprise agreements** reached through collective bargaining by the employees, or their union representatives, often contain conditions that are more generous than those contained in awards.

When an individual employee is hired, the employer will usually present a contract of employment specifying working hours, pay rates, leave entitlements and so on. The terms of the contract cannot be less favourable than the wage rates or conditions set out in the modern award for that occupation (or the workplace's applicable enterprise agreement). The employer should tell the employee which award or agreement he or she will be working under. Most but not all employees are covered by a modern award, if not by an enterprise agreement. However, no employment contract can provide for entitlements less favourable than the National Employment Standards (NES).

'**Award/agreement-free employees**' (those not covered by either a modern award or an enterprise agreement) may make agreements that vary the operation of the NES about a limited number of matters such as:
- averaging of hours of work
- cashing out of paid annual leave
- substitution of other days for public holidays
- extra annual leave in exchange for not taking an equivalent amount of pay
- extra personal or carer's leave in exchange for not taking an equivalent amount of pay.

Fair Work Australia (now the Fair Work Commission) sets minimum wage levels for employees who are not covered by a modern award. In reality, there are still a number of low-skilled/trained workers who have little bargaining and negotiation power. It is these workers who are more vulnerable in the negotiation process. Some employers may cooperate less in negotiation because the employees' lack of knowledge about their rights makes them more vulnerable.

Question 5

Reference to the response notes for previous questions can be made in answering this question. Discussion of these questions has addressed the following issues, highlighting the historical changes to which workplace law has responded:
- The nature of the workplace has changed, with the development of collective bargaining alongside the rise of trade unionism and greater legislative protection of workers.
- The introduction of Australian Workplace Agreements (AWAs) reflected the reality of a new aspirational workplace that compulsory unionism did not suit. These were replaced with (for want of a better name) 'common law contracts' in 2009.
- The regulatory framework that exists today is a product of change globally and within Australia. The deregulation of the workplace, with minimum safety nets in place for less skilled and educated workers, attempts to balance the need for some government intervention into workplace law. This area can be explored further.
- The laws related to the contemporary issues section of the syllabus also reflect changes in the public morality in these areas. The thinking around these issues has developed over time, and hence the law has responded to this.

Again, this is a broad question that is similar in some ways to Question 6 on law reform. Reference to the response notes for this question will also provide examples of content that can be discussed in the context of the changing Australian workplace.

Question 6
At the heart of all workplace laws is the tension that exists between employees (and their representatives) and employers (and their stakeholders). Workplace law has developed over the years in response to developments in society.

The casualisation of the workforce is a major cause for concern from a societal perspective; employers always seek to reduce their operating costs, of which labour is usually the largest. In this context it has always been hard to balance competing interests, and especially to adjudicate on what can be considered fair pay and conditions from industry to industry.

The law has attempted to achieve justice through some of the following:
• Awards and agreements
• Other statutory conditions which outline the rights and responsibilities of employees and employers
• The industrial relations framework that allows for the negotiation of workplace conditions and pay as well as the dispute resolution processes that exist.

Some of these can be examined in the context of the question. It should be noted that there is less industrial disruption to the workplace than ever before, so to this extent the law has proactively sought a balance in the conflicting rights and responsibilities of all stakeholders. At the same time, this is because workers have fewer rights to flex their industrial strength in order to pursue matters important to them.

Question 7
It is in the national interest, as well as the interest of individuals and groups within the workplace, to ensure that the regulatory framework that exists at a state and federal level fairly balances the rights and responsibilities of employers and employees.

The modern industrial landscape seems to be characterised by greater compliance, most likely due to the process of workplace negotiation of working conditions. Industrial action tends to cause much less disruption than was previously seen in the 1970s and 1980s. Generally speaking, action can be taken during the negotiation period of an enterprise agreement; any action taken outside this period may be deemed to be illegal. This has given greater certainty to employers and employees.

At times, though, disagreement is inevitable and achieving a balance between the rights and responsibilities of employers and employees is problematic.

This is a broad question that essentially requires a discussion on section 2 – 'Regulation of the Workplace'. The contemporary issues section could also be referred to as examples of employee and employer rights and responsibilities.

(Reference to the response notes for previous questions in this section, 'Workplace', should be used for further elaboration on some of this content.)

Question 8
Refer to Question 2 Chapter 8 which overviews this question. Reference can then be made to a selection of the questions from Chapter 8 and solutions as provided above.

Question 9
This is a wide-ranging question that ultimately is asking for clarity on the role that government should play in regulating workplaces and the limitations that should be placed on government in this role. This is reflected in the state and federal industrial framework that regulates contracts and awards and agreements. It is also reflected in statutory bodies that have been established to adjudicate disputes between employers and employees, and by clarifying the rights and responsibilities of employees and employers.

It is also evident in the role of government in the 'Contemporary issues concerning the workplace' section of the syllabus on page 33, specifically in the areas of discrimination, safety, termination of employment and leave, which is addressed in part A. There is only so much that can be covered so the range and depth of discussion can vary but the role of government must be assessed to the extent that it balances the rights and obligations of employees and employers.

Reference should be made to the answers to the questions 1, 3, 4 and 8 above.

Option 5 – World Order

Question 1
The legal system in this question primarily refers to the international legal system and how it responds to changing (international) community values and ethics in achieving world order. International values and ethics continue to evolve, so the law must respond if it is to play a part in helping build consensus between nation states. This question also relates to the theme and challenge of changing values and ethical standards.

Values and ethics, with respect to world order, refer to a consensus between nation states on issues related to regional and global security and crimes against humanity. Morality and ethics on these issues are also driven by economic and political will, which at times will decide how nation states react to regional and global security issues, or to crimes against humanity being committed on a civilian population.

The growing **interdependence** of nation states makes consensus even more necessary today than in the past. This interdependence can assist nation states to find common ground on issues that reflect an agreement on values and ethics. It can also contrast the very different viewpoints held by different states, which may increase tension and put up obstacles to regional and global security.

Sovereignty must also be addressed; under the UN Charter, all nation states are equal and have the power to determine their own affairs. Again, this can be an obstacle to world order or it can promote order, depending on the values and ethics of each nation state with respect to world order issues.

The need for world order became even more apparent after World War II. Conflict arises when countries have differing morals and ethics. Increased interest in limiting war, and the development of **rules regarding the conduct of hostilities**, can be cited as common ideals (values) shared by most nation states in the world. The fact that armed conflict has erupted in many parts of the world since the inception of the UN suggests that the world community has many issues where there is no consensus.

Some examples of how the law has responded to the changing values and ethics of the international community include the following:

- **International treaties and conventions:** Give examples of these and how they demonstrate shared values and ethics between the nation states involved. You should also include examples where nation states ignore their obligations under international instruments to deal with regional and global security and crimes against humanity. Use multilateral and bilateral examples, and refer to the concept of *jus cogens* ('compelling law'). An example is the recognition of the increased stockpiling of nuclear weapons and the signing of the **Nuclear Non-Proliferation Treaty (NPT)** 1966, which reduced the stocks of nuclear weapons held by nuclear nations. The more recent **Comprehensive Nuclear Test Ban Treaty (CNTBT)** was another step in this direction, but it has been limited because only nine of the 43 signatories have ratified it. This indicates a lack of political will to comply.
  ANZUS is a more immediate example of an international treaty in our own region, which seeks to promote stability and good relations because of a common set of goals and values.
- **The Lombok Treaty:** Indonesia and Australia signed a new security treaty in 2006, aimed at smoothing ties through greater security cooperation and underlining support for Jakarta's sovereignty over restive provinces. The signing of the treaty enhances anti-terrorism cooperation and joint naval border patrols, as well as formalises military exchanges and training. This is also indicative of increasing consensus on regional issues affecting both nations.
- Other world order instruments that could be referred to include the **South Pacific Nuclear Free Zone Treaty (1986)**, the **Sea-Bed Treaty (1971)** and the **Geneva Protocol**. These are all examples of common values and ethics for the signatory nations to these instruments.
- **The United Nations:** You need to critique the UN as a representative of the moral and ethical stance of nation states around the world. All have signed off on the UN charter and in principle agree to the articles in the charter, but many ignore or question articles at times in order to promote their own agendas. How representative is the UN Security Council of the nation states of the world today? Does it truly reflect the common values of the international community? What are its successes and its failings? Use case studies such as Rwanda and Darfur to highlight the inadequacy of the veto power of the five permanent members; there are major issues on which they fail to act decisively because of a lack of common values and ethics.
- How are **bodies and tribunals** reflective of the morals and ethics of the world community? Examine the strengths and weaknesses of the ICJ, the ICC and other bodies. For example, the creation of an International Criminal Court reflects that a large section of the international community agree that despotic leaders should not be able to hide behind their own sovereignty. These nation states also agree that if particular nations will not prosecute crimes against humanity in their own jurisdiction, it is appropriate for the international community to attempt to do so.
- To what extent do **IGOs** (intergovernmental bodies) reflect the values and ethics of particular regions of the world? Use examples such as NATO's intervention in

Kosovo, the EU, or the African Union's desire to regulate the peace in Darfur. The development of the International Crisis Group could also be highlighted.

- **NGOs** are also a reflection of common values, especially with respect to humanitarian law. Some of these could be mentioned, such as the Red Cross and the work they do within the legal framework to provide humanitarian intervention in areas of conflict, hopefully contributing to greater cooperation and compliance.

Case studies should be used throughout. Be critical either way. Address the question periodically through your response.

Question 2

This question from 2002 can be related directly to the theme and challenge 'the role of law reform in promoting and maintaining world order'. Law reform in this case primarily relates to international law reform, although nation states can ratify treaties that help contribute to regional and global peace and security.

With respect to world order, any change to the way the international community deals with issues concerning regional/global security and crimes against humanity can be considered law reform. These can be recent changes, such as the Lombok Treaty, or more historical changes, such as the Geneva Conventions and conventions on the regulation of nuclear weapons. Changes that occurred in the past can still be considered law reform in the context of their time.

Some possible aspects to discuss in the role of law reform in promoting and maintaining world order are:

- The **sovereignty** of nation states has encouraged law reform, but at the same time it has impeded law because of economic and political self-interest.
- The need for world order arises, in part, because of the enormous costs of historical conflict. The interest in **limiting conflict** and **regulating the conduct of hostilities** are examples of a shift in thinking by the international community on these issues. Refer to the **Geneva Convention** and its protocols, and how it has evolved and will continue to do so.
- The **interdependence** of nation states has resulted in a move towards law reform and the formation of closer ties. Interregional organisations developing multilateral and bilateral agreements to promote peace and reduce conflict can be examples of this.
- The **United Nations** and its agencies are an example of historical law reform after World War II. (Refer to the UN articles that guide the conduct of nation states and reaffirm their rights to sovereignty.) Highlight the ability and inability of the Security Council in bringing about law reform (give examples). It generally fails in this regard, so major law reform may therefore be required for the UN to be better able to respond to regional and global issues and nation states. In particular, the permanent members of the Security Council have been reluctant to commit to any possible changes to the UN Charter.
- **International instruments** are all examples of law reform, as is international customary law, although this reform may occur over time. The principle of *jus cogens* promotes law reform when it is recognised. The world community has shown fundamental shifts in morality and ethics in thinking about many world order issues, often through the influence of international instruments. *(Refer to Question 1 for examples of international treaties that can be used as examples of law reform.)*

- The **media** can be a powerful advocate for law reform through the reporting of regional and global security issues, especially crimes against humanity. This was the case in Darfur.
- **International tribunals** such as the IJC and the ICC may affirm what the law is or clarify an aspect of law. The transition from ad-hoc tribunals to the ICC is a classic example of law reform, especially in the area of crimes against humanity.
- **Australia's federal structure** enables it to be a player on the world stage and therefore contribute to (or impede) law reform initiatives. It played a significant role in the emergence of East Timor as a new sovereign state. Australia has been a key player in the Asia-Pacific region, such as in the signing of the Lombok Treaty.
- The recent development of the doctrine of the **Responsibility to Protect (R2P)** is an evolution on the concept of sovereignty. Some believe that the UNSC can use its Chapter VII powers to intervene where a nation is failing to protect its citizens. Others hold the view that the principle of state sovereignty, upheld by Article 2.7 of the UN Charter, does not permit humanitarian intervention on these grounds. R2P is aimed at bridging the gap between these two views of state sovereignty.
- **Non-legal remedies** can also bring about law reform where the formal mechanisms have failed. Force, persuasion and political negotiation all have strengths and weaknesses in this regard. Explore this further with appropriate examples, such as the situations in Darfur and Kosovo.

Use of case studies is needed, and an evaluation of the effectiveness of law in promoting and maintaining world order is required.

Question 3
This question can be derived from the themes and challenges of the topic 'issues of compliance and non-compliance'. It is necessary to examine why nation states comply with the law, as opposed to reasons they put themselves outside the law, and the extent to which this can lead to injustices. The extent to which the law can promote the compliance of nation states is also an issue inherent in this question.

Aspects of the coursework that could be discussed with respect to compliance with the law include the following:
- The **interdependence** of nation states encourages greater compliance because of closer relationships and common ground, especially on a regional level. It may also highlight different views and approaches to certain world order issues, and may contribute to non-compliance.
- **Sovereignty** is often an impediment to compliance, but also may encourage compliance, especially when two or more nation states agree on world order issues.
- Moves toward a **world or regional government** would override issues around sovereignty and could promote compliance, but may not cater for cultural uniqueness and differences as nation states do now.
- **Regulation of the conduct of hostilities** and the desire to limit war (via the Geneva Conventions and other non-legal measures) encourage compliance when nation states are in conflict with each other. Conversely, various forms of conflict are evidence of non-compliance, as under international law nations states can only use force in self-defence. The catastrophic potential of nuclear conflict has generally ensured compliance, especially around nuclear non-proliferation and test bans; however, North Korea did not comply when it tested a nuclear device.

- **International treaties** are the main instrument used to attempt to get nation states to comply with the law. Give examples of international treaties and evaluate how well they do this. North Korea's testing of nuclear devices in 2006 and 2009 is an issue to be explored with respect to non-compliance.
- **International customary law** can also be evaluated in the extent that it encourages compliance, and to the extent that it can be ignored. An example of a case can be cited.
- **The UN and the Security Council** need to be evaluated to the extent that they ensure compliance with the law by nation states. Use your case studies here. Weaknesses in the structure of the UN undermine compliance and encourage non-compliance. Reference to Rwanda, Darfur or other events can be made.
- **Intergovernmental organisations** (IGOs) promote compliance on a regional level, but at times this can be at the expense of the interests of other regions in the world.
- **International tribunals** such as the ICJ, the ICC and ad-hoc tribunals are seen as enforcement mechanisms, and can be evaluated on their successes and failures in ensuring compliance with the law. To what extent do these tribunals deliver justice? The ad-hoc tribunals in the former Yugoslavia and Rwanda will never be able to bring to justice all the perpetrators of the genocide in those countries. Resources are such that only the main perpetrators of such mass atrocities may be brought to justice. The extent to which the ICC will be able to deliver justice and promote compliance with the law is yet to be seen.
- **Australia's federal structure** can be examined in relation to its role in the Asia-Pacific region. Refer to the 'arc of instability', the group of politically unstable nation states in the Asia-Pacific region, such as Fiji and East Timor. The Australian Government has concerns over these countries becoming failed states and hence promoting non-compliance with the law.
- **Regional and global situations** that threaten peace and security can be referenced. Examples include nuclear threats and regions where crimes against humanity are being perpetrated. What injustices are occurring, and to what extent can the international community put an end to these?
- **Non-legal remedies** such as force, persuasion and political negotiation are generally used when nation states are not complying with law. They can be used to encourage compliance. Force is generally ineffective in producing long-term compliance with the law.

Case studies and media reports should be used throughout this response where possible.

Question 4
The law referred to in this question is mainly international law. Again, this question is derived from the themes and challenges of the topic. Most of the content for this response can be sourced from part two of the topic 'Responses to world order' on page 34 of the syllabus. In particular, this question asks for a discussion of the implementation of international agreements. *(See Question 1 for some examples of a number of world order international instruments and examine the extent to which they have encouraged cooperation and helped to reduce or even resolve conflict.)*

Additional discussion of the following factors is warranted, along with the role they play in encouraging cooperation and resolving conflict:
- The United Nations/Security Council

- Courts and tribunals
- IGOs
- Non-government organisations
- The Australian Government.

Non-legal responses are usually utilised when legal measures fail or have limited success. The strengths and weaknesses of some of the legal measures to address regional and global world order issues have been elaborated on in the response notes for Questions 1–3 in this section.

Question 5
With respect to the relationship of culture and values to world order, refer to the response notes for Question 1 in this section.

Even in a world order that seeks regional and global peace and security, conflicts appear to be inevitable. The remedies to these conflicts depend on the nature of each conflict and its resolution. Conflict can be characterised as either interstate (between different nation states) or intrastate (within a single nation state).

There are many forms of interstate conflict:
- **Conventional war** involves the use of large, well-organised military forces. During such a war, soldiers wear clearly identified uniforms and there is a clear command structure. The majority of wars in history have been conventional, although these may become a thing of the past due to technological advances.
- The development of **nuclear weapons** at the end of World War II saw the emergence of weapons of mass destruction and the possibility of a nuclear war. The trend today is for nations to reduce their nuclear stockpiles, hence creating an environment where the likelihood of a nuclear conflict is minimised. This is contrasted by some nations agitating for the right to develop nuclear technology, including Iran and North Korea.
- Another form of conflict that has emerged (especially over the last 10–15 years) is the possibility of so-called **'cyber warfare'**. Due to the interconnectedness of the world through the internet, the potential to disrupt important infrastructure and defence systems is very real.

Intrastate conflict comprises the main form of conflict in the world today. Forms of intrastate conflict include the following:
- **Guerrilla warfare** is an unconventional warfare where a small group of combatants use mobile tactics (ambushes, raids, etc.) to combat a larger and less mobile formal army. The Taliban uses these types of tactics against coalition forces in Afghanistan, where they face a superior force with technologically better weapons.
- **Civil war** is a conflict between two or more sides within one country. There are many examples throughout history of conflict within a nation state.
- There continue to be many conflicts where governments wage war against their own people. At times this results in crimes against humanity as a result of mass atrocities. These types of genocide have been newly termed **'democide'**.

A further cause of conflict is access to resources. As the world comes under increased pressure for resources, it may be inevitable that conflict will eventuate over the ownership or the right to access resources. Oil reserves continue to diminish and access to fresh water is becoming increasingly scarce for some nations.

The remedies to these legal issues can be discussed through examining the legal and non-legal measures as outlined in previous questions. A particular focus on the role of international tribunals is also required.

Question 6
The law is fundamental to achieving world order as it provides the framework for the relationships between modern nation states. Historically, nations developed their own agreements with other nation states over a period of time based on agreed practice. This developed into international customary law for many nations. The legal framework that facilitates relationships between nations can be found within international instruments, as outlined in the response notes for Questions 1 and 5 in this section.

As outlined in previous questions, there are many examples where the law has failed to deliver peace and security on a regional or global level. As such, non-legal measures such as the media play an important role in maintaining world order, as the work of journalists in the media highlights and puts the spotlight on many conflict situations and instances of crimes against humanity that many parts of the world, the developed world in particular, can at times be unaware of or simply lack the political will to leverage aspects of sovereignty to improve such situations. Media exposure can also set in train other non-legal measures such as negotiation and persuasion to improve or resolve a world order situation. *(Refer to the response notes for Questions 1–4 in this section.)*

The law is fundamental for world order because it builds consensus on matters related to world order issues. Further development of the law (law reform) is also important as the international community continues to evolve.

Cases need to be cited to illustrate how the law has helped bring about world order. Cases also need to be cited to illustrate how at times it fails to resolve conflict and encourage cooperation.

Question 7
The world has strived for peace and security for centuries, but conflict has proven impossible to prevent. Human beings strive to compete for resources, highlighting the social, moral and religious differences that create a constant tension between nation states. Therefore, the central aim of world order is to promote international peace and harmony and reduce conflict. The main obstacles to achieving this are sovereignty and the differing moral and ethical standards evident in different nation states.

A **world order issue** is anything that threatens peace and security on a regional or global level. It also includes any incidences of 'crimes against humanity', as these are mass atrocities that in most cases cannot be confined to one nation state. For example, crime against humanity in the Darfur region of Sudan saw many flee to neighbouring Chad, escalating the conflict to a regional level and making it a world order issue. The world today is interdependent; communities around the world interact with each other on a scale never before witnessed. As such, the regional/global impact of conflict has enormous implications for all nation states that act out of economic and political self-interest first and foremost.

Being a state brings with it fundamental rights and responsibilities. First, once a nation is recognised as a state, it becomes an international 'person', empowered to enter into a relationship with other states and to act in world affairs. Many issues confronting the world today are therefore dealt with in a multilateral manner, based on relationships and agreements between states.

Sovereignty is the second consequence of statehood. A state has a right to be autonomous, and as such has the exclusive right to control its own society and territory through domestic legislation and government policies. Sovereignty allows a state to act independently, reflecting its own unique culture.

Once initial discussion has orientated the idea of world order issues and the notion of the state, the rest of the essay can be used to discuss the legal and non-legal means of achieving world order, and the role a state may play in assisting this or impeding it.

For example, states can decide what legal instruments they want to be a part of, if they will respect the decisions of international tribunals, or become a member of specific intergovernmental organisations. States make up the permanent members of the UN Security Council; the role they have played through various crises such as Rwanda, Kosovo and Darfur could all be examined. Australia's role in the emergence of East Timor as an independent state, and in managing those neighbours that make up the 'arc of instability', are examples of a proactive state contributing to regional security.

Reference to the response notes for previous questions in this section on world order should be used for further elaboration on some of this content.

Question 8
This question is drawn from section 3 of the topic 'Issues that must be studied'. A number of situations can be discussed, or (with respect to this question) a single situation can be addressed. Whatever the approach, the case study of a situation or situations should be used to apply aspects of sections 1 and 2 of the topic. Critical analysis must be demonstrated with respect to the effectiveness of the legal and non-legal measures used to respond to the conflict/s discussed.

An example of a conflict where peace and security is threatened is Darfur in Sudan. While this conflict began in 2003, and a peace accord has been entered into, it still has the potential to continue to threaten peace and security in the region. The following is an overview of this conflict.

It is believed that approximately 300 000 people are dead and up to 2.7 million people have been displaced in the Darfur region of Sudan. The current crisis began in February 2003, when a rebel uprising was brutally suppressed by Arab militias. The militias have been accused of carrying out mass killing and rape. The UN has described Darfur as the world's worst humanitarian crisis. On July 2005 the US Congress described it as genocide, and the British Government considered sending 5000 troops.

The conflict began when two rebel groups, the Sudan Liberation Army (SLA) and the Justice and Equality Movement (JEM), began attacks on government targets. The SLA claims that the government had been oppressing black Africans, neglecting their region and supporting Arab ethnic groups. In response, the government mobilised, armed and directed mainly Arab Janjaweed ('rabble' or 'outlaws' in local dialect) militia groups using scorched earth tactics, massacre and starvation as cheap counter-insurgency weapons.

In terms of ethnicity, Darfur Arabs are indigenous Africans, as are Darfur's non-Arabs. Darfurians used the term 'Arab' in its ancient sense of 'Bedouin'. These Arabic-speaking nomads are distinct from the inheritors of the Arab culture of the Nile and the Fertile Crescent. Many of the Janjaweed come from Arab groups in Chad, mobilised in the days when Libya tried to invade Chad. Most of the Darfurian Arabs are not involved in the conflict.

International pressure has forced the government in Khartoum to give permits for UN relief agencies, aid workers and journalists to work in what was previously a closed region. Huge numbers of displaced people have managed to get to camps inside Sudan or across the border in Chad. The UN Commissioner for Refugees moved 170 000 refugees away from the insecure Chad–Sudan border region into camps in Eastern Chad.

It has also been reported that Janjaweed camp police offered bribes to refugees who agreed to return to their homes in the danger zones. By returning to their homes the refugees could hold back a looming agricultural problem, as the Janjaweed are nomadic Arab tribes that herd and graze animals. The Africans who have been forced from their homes are farmers whose work provides the cereals and sorghum that feed the region. The war has won the Arabs control of this fertile land, but they have little idea of how to make use of it.

There is some speculation that the Janjaweed want the Africans to return to work the land that was stolen from them, on behalf of the Janjaweed.
The UN Security Council has identified 51 people thought to be behind the killing and rape as a deliberate weapon of war. The names have been referred to the International Criminal Court on a sealed list after the USA, which refuses to work with the ICC, agreed not to veto the move. The ICC will take time to prepare the case, but by lifting the sense of impunity its intervention should help deter new crimes.

The African Union sent 2000 troops in as peacekeepers to monitor the situation, but it is argued that a new mandate is needed so that these troops can confront the gunmen rather than merely make reports. This initial response was inadequate, as the African Union was not equipped adequately for this role. Both America and Britain were reluctant to become embroiled in a conflict with another Arab state.

Two years of internationally mediated efforts to resolve the conflict in Darfur through a new peace agreement with the armed movements have failed, dashing hopes for a period of stability in western Sudan as the South prepares to form an independent state. With Sudan embarking on a period of extreme uncertainty, efforts to end the conflict in Darfur are failing as the peace process has been unproductive.

Ultimately, the main responsibility rests with the government of Sudan. The people of Darfur are its citizens. Unless Khartoum wants another 20 years of civil war, the Sudanese Government must rein in the Janjaweed and work hard to make the latest peace accord a success.

The reason it took so long for the crisis to be put firmly on the top of the Security Council's agenda is probably due to a lack of economic interest and/or political will. China and Russia both have oil interests in Sudan and did not want to jeopardise this. It was only when the situation became truly appalling that the world sat up and took notice. Non-legal measures, such as media attention and a series of protest concerts around the world, forced China into agreeing finally to Security Council sanctions, especially as the Beijing Olympic Games were approaching.

This case study again shows the limited ability of the Security Council to take decisive action, even when crimes against humanity are unfolding. It also highlights the need for reform of this institution, and how the recently developed doctrine of Responsibility to Protect (R2P) may be seen as a positive development as can be seen by the quick response to initiate air strikes in Libya in 2011 to protect community members that were part of the uprising against authoritarian rule in that country.

The role of the ICC will also be further judged on the outcome of possible prosecutions of those people responsible for mass atrocities.

Question 9
World order is hard to achieve because many nation states exercise their sovereign right to self-determine their own course of action pertaining to matters of self-interest.

Many nation states have differing values and ethics on a number of areas that concern world order. This question can be critiqued by examining the need for world order and the major causes that disrupt world order.

There have been many attempts to bring peace and security to the world community through the use of treaties, the United Nations, courts and tribunals, IGOs and at times NGOs. This continues to be a struggle today, which can be illustrated with reference to nation states that refuse to live up to their treaty obligations, or where crimes against humanity are being perpetrated.

Question 10
This question focuses on the role of the nation state in bringing about peace and security at a regional and global level and essentially is derived from the principal focus of the topic.

The UN Charter recognises and upholds the sovereignty of all nation states. Hence an introduction to the question must address a definition of world order, highlight the issue of sovereignty and the interdependence of the global community, which is a feature of the world today, and explain with examples how nation states promote world order or work to impede it.

Sovereignty means that a state has a right to be autonomous and in so doing has the exclusive right to control its own people and territory through domestic legislation and government policies. Sovereignty allows a state to act independently, reflecting its own unique culture. Predominantly nation states act in their own self-interest, usually about whichever issue of the day that is driving political or economic will. The following areas that may be discussed in this question should be considered in this context.

- The development of international treaties – signed by nation states to promote regional and global security. The failure of some states to live up to their treaty obligations – refer to North Korea detonation of a test nuclear device in 2006 and 2009.
- The role of the UN Security Council – the Permanent 5 Veto power and its failures and successes. Refer to Rwanda, Kosovo and Darfur. A success could be viewed as the NATO intervention in Libya under the auspices of R2P in 2011.
- The ability of nation states as members of Intergovernmental Organisations to intervene in areas of conflict – refer to NATO in Kosovo and the African Union in Darfur.
- The ability of nation states to support or undermine international courts and tribunals. The ICC – lack of support from China and the US. The limitations of the ICJ as a result of state sovereignty.
- The role of the Australian state in working towards greater regional stability in light of the concerns about the 'arc of instability'.
- The importance of non-legal measures to pressure nation states to improve their responses to issues around the world, especially crimes against humanity.
  (Refer to Questions 1–3 in Chapter 9: solutions in Chapter 10.)

Question 11
This question is taken from the contemporary issues section of the topic and again requires a broad-based response that can utilise many areas of the content in critiquing the ability of global cooperation to achieve regional and global peace and security.

Global cooperation can take many forms. Reference the role played by international instruments, the ability of the United Nations and in particular the Security Council to resolve situations around the world in particular crimes against the international community.
Explicit reference to state sovereignty and a number of case studies would be required to effectively critique the successes and failures of the international community to achieve global cooperation.

(Reference to the response notes for previous questions in this section on World Order should be used for further elaboration on some of this content.)

Question 12
The response of the legal system to various forms of conflict requires a variety of legal and non-legal approaches, which predominantly fail to adequately resolve differences between nation states and between groups within nation states due to state sovereignty and the inability of the international community to arrive at a consensus on a way forward.

There are many forms of interstate conflict. Some of these are:

- **Conventional war** involves the use of large, well-organised military forces. During such a war, soldiers wear clearly identified uniforms and there is a clear command structure. The majority of wars in history have been conventional, although these may become a thing of the past due to technological advances. Reference can be made to the UN Charter that allows the use of force in self-defence and limited circumstances on humanitarian grounds. Assessment of the inability of conventional conflict to provide peace and security, which is highly dubious, is needed.

- The development of **nuclear weapons** at the end of World War II saw the emergence of weapons of mass destruction and the possibility of a nuclear war. The trend today is for nations to reduce their nuclear stockpiles, hence creating an environment where the likelihood of a nuclear conflict is minimised. This is contrasted by some nations agitating for the right to develop nuclear technology, including Iran and North Korea. Reference should be made to multi-lateral treaties concerning bans on testing and non-proliferation of weapons stockpiles in the context of the danger the existence of nuclear stockpiles poses to world order.
- Another form of conflict that has emerged (especially over the past 10–15 years) is the possibility of so-called **'cyber warfare'**. Due to the interconnectedness of the world through the internet, the potential to disrupt important infrastructure and defence systems is very real.

Intrastate conflict comprises the main form of conflict in the world today. Some of these develop into crimes against humanity due to the escalation of the conflict. Methods of addressing such crimes and bringing offenders to justice have been attempted by ad hoc war crimes tribunals and the International Criminal Court. Reference to these should be made and an evaluation of their effectiveness addressed in their ability to promote regional peace and security. Also the inability of the Security Council to provide decisive action should also be addressed, in particular the problematic nature of the veto power to get sanctions passed. Forms of intrastate conflict include:

- **Guerrilla warfare** is an unconventional warfare where a small group of combatants use mobile tactics (ambushes, raids, etc.) to combat a larger and less mobile formal army. The Taliban uses these types of tactics against coalition forces in Afghanistan, where they face a superior force with technologically better weapons.
- **Civil war** is a conflict between two or more sides within one country. There are many examples throughout history of conflict within a nation state.
- There continue to be many conflicts where governments wage war against their own people. At times this results in crimes against humanity as a result of mass atrocities. These types of genocide have been newly termed **'democide'**.

A further cause of conflict is access to resources. As the world comes under increased pressure for resources, it may be inevitable that conflict will eventuate over the ownership or the right to access resources. Oil reserves continue to diminish and access to fresh water is becoming increasingly scarce for some nations.

The challenges that these types of conflicts pose for the international community are many and its ability to adequately deal with these can be discussed through examining the legal and non-legal measures, as outlined in previous questions. Case studies should be used to highlight the various types of conflict and the difficulty in bringing these to resolution. Examples could include Darfur and of recent times Syria and Libya as examples of intrastate conflict.

Reference should be made to the answer to Question 3 under World Order above.

The development of the **Doctrine of Responsibility to Protect (R2P)** can also be examined in light of increasing intrastate conflicts. A particular focus on the role of international tribunals is also required, specifically their ability to bring justice to victims of these conflicts, in particular victims of crimes against humanity. There is potential for the international community to intervene under R2P to minimise the disruption to regional order in areas of ongoing intrastate conflict as evident in Syria in 2012.

Reference should also be made to the answers to Question 1 and 3 under World Order above.

Chapter 11

2014 Examination

Total marks – 100

(Section I)
20 marks
- Attempt Questions 1–20
- Allow about 30 minutes for this section

(Section II)
30 marks
This section has two parts. Part A and Part B
- Allow about 1 hour for this section

Part A – 15 marks
- Attempt Questions 21–23

Part B – 15 marks
- Attempt Question 24

(Section III)
50 marks
- Attempt TWO questions from Questions 25–31 each from a different Option
- Allow about 1 hour and 30 minutes for this sectio

General Instructions
- Reading time – 5 minutes
- Working time – 3 hours
- Write using black or blue pen
  Black pen is preferred

Section I

20 marks

Attempt Questions 1–20

Allow about 30 minutes for this section

---

1   What is self-determination?

(A) The right to vote

(B) The right to a jury trial

(C) The right to legal representation

(D) The right of a group to make decisions for itself

2   Which court would hear the offence of speeding in a school zone when it first becomes a court matter?

(A) Drug Court

(B) Local Court

(C) District Court

(D) Supreme Court

Use the following information to answer Question 3 and 4.

> Andrew illegally downloaded music from the internet.

3   What role did Andrew play in committing this offense?

(A) Accessory after the fact

(B) Accessory before the fact

(C) Principal in the first degree

(D) Principal in the second degree

4   Which category of crime does Andrew's behaviour fall under?

(A) Conspiracy

(B) Preliminary crime

(C) Economic offence

(D) Offence against the person

5   Which of the following can be a member of the United Nations?

(A) A head of state

(B) A sovereign state

(C) A state government

(D) A minister for foreign affairs

6   Who determines if the standard of proof has been met in a criminal case?

(A) The jury

(B) The police

(C) The defendant

(D) The prosecution

7   Which of the following is an example of an intergovernmental organisation?

(A) Federal Parliament

(B) Amnesty International

(C) Commonwealth of Nations

(D) Australian Human Rights Commission

8   The Supreme Court is hearing a criminal case. At the conclusion of the third day, two jurors visit the crime scene. They discuss the defendant's evidence and then encourage other jurors to find the defendant guilty.

What is this an example of?

(A) A role of the jury

(B) A denial of justice

(C) An aggravating factor

(D) A peremptory challenge

9   A magistrate orders an offender to serve six months in gaol, to be served only if the offender is not of good behaviour during this time.

This is an example of

(A) probation.

(B) imprisonment.

(C) a suspended sentence.

(D) a diversionary program.

10 Peter, while under the influence of drugs, has caused the death of another person. He is charged with murder.

Which court will be the first to hear the charge against Peter?

(A) Drug Court

(B) Local Court

(C) Supreme Court

(D) Coroner's Court

11 How are international human rights protected under Australian law?

(A) Treaties are enacted by a federal statute.

(B) Covenants are ratified by the Governor-General.

(C) Declarations are incorporated into the Australian Constitution.

(D) Conventions are enforced by the Australian Human Rights Commission

12 How is the right to legal representation best described?

(A) It is a right limited under common law.

(B) It is a right protected under the Australian Constitution.

(C) It is a right to free legal aid provided in most criminal cases.

(D) It is a right protected under the Universal Declaration of Human Rights.

13 The purpose of specific deterrence in sentencing is to

(A) direct the offender to undertake education and training.

(B) direct the offender to complete a community service order.

(C) discourage the offender from committing the offence again.

(D) discourage others who may consider committing a similar offense.

14 The police hold Susan in custody because they believe she may commit a serious crime.

What is this an example of?

(A) Remand

(B) Recidivism

(C) Protective custody

(D) Preventative detention

15 Which of the following is a feature of statutory protection of human rights in Australia?

(A) Parliament cannot change human rights legislation.

(B) Judges interpret and apply human rights legislation.

(C) A referendum is required to amend human rights legislation.

(D) Human rights treaties are enshrined in the Australian Constitution.

16 Which of the following is true of the International Criminal Court?

(A) It is an ad hoc tribunal.

(B) It is established by a treaty.

(C) It deals with transnational crimes.

(D) It is the judicial arm of the United Nations.

17 Which of the following is true of a victim impact statement?

(A) It allows a victim to recommend a punishment.

(B) It provides evidence for the prosecution in the trial.

(C) It must be given by a person against whom the offence was committed.

(D) It must be received by the court in writing after the conviction of the defendant.

18 Kim is 12 years old. She has been accused of shoplifting from a major retail store. The matter has proceeded to court.

Which of the following applies to Kim?

(A) She will have a criminal record.

(B) Her case will be heard in the Local Court.

(C) She is presumed to be incapable of committing the offence.

(D) She is below the age of criminal responsibility and will be acquitted.

Use the following information to answer Questions 19 and 20.

Judy was charged with murder. Her defence of substantial impairment by abnormality of the mind was accepted. Judy was then convicted of manslaughter in a judge-only trial. She had prior serious criminal convictions and was sentenced to three years imprisonment.

19 For Judy's defence, it was necessary for her to show evidence of

(A) provocation.

(B) remorse for her actions.

(C) her innocence beyond reasonable doubt.

(D) her limited ability to understand events.

20 In this case an appeal is most likely to be made by

(A) Judy, against her conviction for manslaughter.

(B) Judy, as the sentencing judge did not consider aggravating factors.

(C) the Director of Public Prosecutions, as the sentence was inadequate.

(D) the director of Public Prosecutions, as the case was not heard by a jury.

Section II

30 marks

Allow about 1 hour for this section

Part A – Human Rights

15 marks

Attempt Questions 21–23

Question 21 (3 marks)

Outline how ONE international human rights document contributes to the development of human rights.

Question 22 (5 marks)

How are human rights protected by the Australian Constitution?

Question 23 (7 marks)

Compare the roles of international and domestic courts in protecting human rights.

Part B – Crime

15 marks

Attempt Question 24

In your answer you will be assessed on how well you:
• Demonstrate knowledge and understanding of legal issues relevant to the question
• Communicate using relevant legal terminology and concepts
• Refer to relevant examples such as legislation, cases, media, international instruments and documents
• Present a sustained, logical and cohesive response

Question 24 (15 marks)

LAW ENFORCEMENT (POWERS AND RESPONSIBILITIES) BILL

Page: 4846

Bill introduced and read a first time.

Second Reading

Mr DEBUS (Blue Mountains-Attorney General, Minister for the Environment, Minister for Emergency Services, and Minister Assisting the Premier on the Arts) [7.30 p.m.]: I move:

That this bill be now read a second time.

The Government is pleased to introduce the Law Enforcement (Powers and Responsibilities) Bill. The bill represents the outcome of the consolidation process envisaged by the Royal Commission into the New South Wales Police Service to help strike a proper balance between the need for effective law enforcement and the protection of individual rights. This bill constitutes significant law reform. It radically simplifies the law in relation to law enforcement powers, setting out in one document the most commonly used criminal law enforcement powers and their safeguards. Previously complex and diverse law enforcement powers and responsibilities once buried in numerous statutes and casebooks have been consolidated into the bill so that the law is now easily accessible to all members of the community.

Matters included in the bill represent a codification of the common law, a consolidation of existing statute law, a clarification of police powers, or a combination of these. In acknowledgement of the significance of this legislation the Government has consulted widely in the preparation of the bill. Stakeholders and other potentially interested parties were afforded an opportunity to comment on an exposure draft of the bill. The majority of amendments to the exposure draft were made in response to the 29 submissions received. While generally the bill simply re-enacts existing legislation, it does in some circumstances make amendments intended to more accurately reflect areas of the common law or to address areas in the existing law where gaps have been identified. Unless expressly stated, the bill is not intended to change the common law.

I do not propose to address each clause of the bill separately. Unless otherwise stated, the effect of the provisions is intended to reflect the current meaning already provided in the statute books. I will, however, address the areas where there has been substantive reform, in particular: revised powers of entry, simplification of personal search powers and related safeguards, new provisions regarding notices to produce, new provisions regarding crime scenes, revised powers of arrest, revised powers relating to property in police custody, and new general safeguards that apply broadly to the exercise of all police powers.

I turn first to powers of entry. Part 2 of the bill codifies the existing common law powers of entry. Clause 9 provides that a police officer may enter premises if the police officer believes on reasonable grounds that a person has suffered significant physical injury or that there is imminent danger of significant injury to a person. This power to enter premises to prevent death or significant injury represents a clarification of police powers at common law and reflects legitimate community expectations of the role of police. Clause 9 also enacts the common law power of police to enter premises where a breach of the peace is being or is likely to be committed and it is necessary to enter immediately to prevent the breach of peace. The bill deliberately does not define the term "breach of the peace"; this is a well-established concept at common law, and will remain so. A police officer who enters a premises by virtue of the powers in clause 9 may remain on the property only as long as is reasonably necessary in the circumstances.

Clause 10 codifies the existing powers of police to arrest a person, to detain a person under another Act, or to arrest a person named in a warrant where the officer believes on reasonable grounds that the person is in the premises. I turn to the question of search and seizure without warrant. Part 4 of the bill details the powers of search and seizure without warrant. Police powers to conduct personal searches have been significantly simplified without reducing or increasing existing powers, so that police are able to readily understand the types of search that they may undertake, and the community can understand more readily the powers that police have in this respect. A regime of three tiers of searches has been adopted, and safeguards have been introduced to ensure that civil liberties are upheld and that the integrity of the police process is not compromised. I will address the new regime and safeguards in greater detail shortly.

Clause 23 (2) addresses a gap in the law identified in the course of consolidation: While at common law police have the power to search a person who has been arrested on suspicion of committing an offence, it is not clear whether police have the power to search a person arrested otherwise than for an offence. Clause 23 (2) provides that police will have the power to search a person arrested other than for an offence in limited circumstances, that is, where the arresting police officer has a reasonable suspicion that the arrested person who is being taken into custody is carrying something which she or he may use in a way that could endanger a person, or assist a person to escape from custody.

This provision addresses concerns about safety of police and others in custody and is a justifiable law enforcement power. The search powers set out in clause 23 are powers that may be exercised at or after the time of arrest. These powers should be distinguished from those set out in clause 24, which sets out the search powers that may be exercised by a police officer after a person has been arrested and taken into custody, for example, at a police station. Division 3 of this part consolidates the existing police power to search for knives and other dangerous implements. The existing provisions have been substantially redrafted to ensure that the applicable powers and safeguards are consistent with the three-tiered search regime detailed in division 4 of this part, which I shall come to shortly.

The redrafted provisions do not extend or restrict the powers police currently have to search for a knife or other dangerous implement in a public place or school. The existing safeguards have either been incorporated into the safeguard provisions which apply generally to all personal searches conducted under the bill, or have been incorporated within the new definitions of the searches. Division 4 of part 4 details provisions that apply to all personal searches conducted under the bill. In order to provide greater regulation of police search powers, the bill substantially adopts the three-tiered personal search model contained in the Commonwealth Crimes Act 1914, which in turn is based on the Model Criminal Code.

The bill introduces a regime of frisk, ordinary and strip searches in respect of all personal searches conducted under the bill. The bill details the circumstances in which each of the three levels of search may be warranted and provides safeguards to protect the privacy and dignity of persons being searched. The bill provides specific safeguards for any person subjected to a strip search and specific safeguards for children and persons with impaired intellectual functioning who are subjected to a strip search. A frisk search is defined as a search of a person conducted by quickly running the hands over the person's outer clothing or by passing an electronic metal detection device over or in close proximity to the person's outer clothing and an examination of anything worn or carried by the person that is conveniently and voluntarily removed by the person.

An ordinary search is defined as a search of a person or articles in the possession of a person that may include requiring the removal and examination of specified items of outer clothing. A strip search is defined as a search of a person or of articles in the possession of the person that may include requiring the person to remove all of his or her clothes, but only those clothes necessary to fulfil the purpose of the search, and a visual examination of the person's body and a search of those clothes. A strip search may be carried out only where the police officer suspects on reasonable grounds that it is necessary for the purposes of the search and that the seriousness and urgency of the circumstances require a strip search. The bill requires that the least invasive kind of search practicable in the circumstances should be used.

The bill introduces safeguards intended to preserve the privacy and dignity of all persons subjected to personal searches under the bill. Clause 32 incorporates a number of safeguards intended to ensure that a police officer conducting any search has regard to the searched person's right to privacy and maintenance of dignity throughout a search. The police officer must comply with the safeguards set out in section 32, unless it is not reasonably practicable in the circumstances to do so. What is reasonably practicable in the circumstances will, of course, be dependent on the individual circumstances. These safeguards require the officer to inform the person of the nature of the search, request their co-operation, conduct the search out of
public view and as quickly as possible, and not to question the person searched at that time in relation to a suspected offence.

Clause 33 provides specific safeguards for a person subjected to a strip search. The safeguards in subclauses (1) to (3) of clause 33, which relate to privacy, the absence of people not necessary for the purpose of the search and the presence of support persons, must be complied with unless it is not reasonably practicable in the circumstances. Clause 33 (3) provides for the presence of a support person for children aged between 10 and 18, and persons who have impaired intellectual functioning who are subjected to strip searches. This provision has been included to protect the interests of those who may not be able to protect their own interests, and may also assist police in the conduct of the strip search. The safeguards in subclauses (4) to (6) of clause 33 are, without exception, mandatory and clarify that a strip search is, in fact, a visual search and not an examination of the body by touch. Clause 34 provides that a child under 10 may not be strip searched. The safeguards in division 4 are in addition to safeguards in part 15 that apply generally across the bill. The safeguards better define what a police officer can do when conducting a search, and ensure the integrity of the criminal justice processes.

I turn now to search and seizure with warrant or other authority. Part 5 repeals and re-enacts existing powers set out in the Search Warrants Act 1985 and sections 357EA and 578D of the Crimes Act 1900. The provisions in this part regarding notices to produce clarify and provide a legislative basis for the practice of obtaining documents held by financial institutions. Search warrants, in this context, are considered a blunt instrument: a search warrant may authorise police to search the entire premises for documents held by the financial institution, when only a specific customer's records are sought. In practice, banks produce the documents sought when presented with a search warrant, rather than have police search through all of their records.

The bill will allow a police officer who believes on reasonable grounds that an authorised deposit-taking institution holds documents that may be connected with an offence-such as fraud or money laundering-committed by someone else to apply to an authorised officer for a notice to produce the relevant documents. The notice to produce provisions in the bill do not replace search warrants. The intention of the provision is that police may apply for either a notice to produce or a search warrant, depending on the circumstances. Although the new power imposes a duty on financial institutions to produce particular documents which does not now exist, the change is largely one of process. The provision will not alter the type of documents that can be obtained-a document, for example, can include a document in electronic format-but merely the process in which the documents are obtained. Consistent with the existing Search Warrants Act 1985, the bill provides that the penalty for failure to comply with a notice to produce, without reasonable excuse, is the same as the penalty for obstructing or hindering a search warrant.

I turn now to crime scenes. It is important that the community has confidence that evidence at a crime scene will not be interfered with, contaminated, lost or destroyed. This bill takes the opportunity to unequivocally clarify the powers that police currently exercise when establishing and undertaking certain actions at crime scenes. Part 7 of the bill outlines when police may establish a crime scene and the powers that may be exercised at a crime scene. The bill creates a two-tiered approach for crime scenes. If police are lawfully on the premises and establish a crime scene, certain basic powers to preserve evidence may be exercised in the first three hours without a crime scene warrant. The powers that may be exercised in the first three hours are aimed primarily at the preservation of evidence and include directing people to leave a crime scene and preventing persons entering a crime scene.

The remaining crime scene powers are investigatory, and search and seizure powers. These powers may generally be exercised only once a crime scene warrant has been obtained. The application procedures for, and safeguards relating to, crime scene warrants are the same as those for a search warrant. The authorised officer may issue a crime scene warrant authorising a police officer to exercise all reasonably necessary crime scene powers at, or in relation to, a specified crime scene. However, police may exercise any of the crime scene powers in the first three hours-that is, without a warrant-if the officer or another officer applies for a crime scene warrant and the officer suspects on reasonable grounds that it is necessary to immediately exercise the power to preserve evidence.

The exception to the requirement for a warrant before the exercise of certain powers is vital. For example, police may need to immediately take a photograph if a crime scene is being flooded, or gain access to a room that is on fire and which police suspect contains evidence of an offence. In these circumstances, waiting for a crime scene warrant to be issued would not be practicable, as the evidence would be destroyed. The bill provides for a number of safeguards for the use of crime scene powers, such as providing time limits on the establishment of a crime scene and specified powers available to use at a crime scene. The bill does not interfere with the ability to establish a crime scene in a public place. The bill does not prevent an officer from exercising a crime scene power or doing any other thing if the occupier consents. Nor does the bill provide police with a new power of entry. Police will only be able to exercise crime scene powers if they are already lawfully on premises or have been granted a crime scene warrant.

The range of offences for which crime scenes may be established is limited to serious indictable offences and where there is an offence committed in connection with a traffic accident causing death or serious injury to a person. The officer must be of the opinion that it is reasonably necessary to establish a crime scene to preserve or search for or gather evidence of such offences. As with notices to produce, these powers are not intended to detract from the search warrants powers. Consistent with the existing Search Warrants Act 1985, the bill provides a penalty for obstructing or hindering a police officer exercising crime scene powers, without reasonable excuse.

I turn now to powers relating to arrest. Part 8 of the bill substantially re-enacts arrest provisions of the Crimes Act 1900 and codifies the common law. The provisions of part 8 reflect that arrest is a measure that is to be exercised only when necessary. An arrest should only be used as a last resort as it is the strongest measure that may be taken to secure an accused person's attendance at court. Clause 99, for example, clarifies that a police officer should not make an arrest unless it achieves the specified purposes, such as preventing the continuance of the offence. Failure to comply with this clause would not, of itself, invalidate the charge. Clauses 107 and 108 make it clear that nothing in the part affects the power of a police officer to exercise the discretion to commence proceedings for an offence other than by arresting the person, for example, by way of caution or summons or another alternative to arrest. Arrest is a measure of last resort. The part clarifies that police have the power to discontinue arrest at any time.

The application of the safeguards contained in part 15 of the bill represents the classification of the common law requirement that persons must be told of the real reason for their arrest and a clarification of the additional requirements that officers must provide their name, place of duty and a warning. I turn now to powers to give directions. Part 14 repeals and re-enacts without amendment legislative provisions in relation to police powers to give reasonable directions. It is intended under clause 197, which sets out the power of police officers to give directions in public places, that a police officer may be "a person affected by the relevant conduct" for the purposes of issuing a direction.

I will now deal with property in police custody. While substantively re-enacting the relevant provisions of the Criminal Procedure Act 1986 and the Police Service Regulation 1990, the bill makes a number of minor amendments to address concerns raised by operational police concerning the disposal of property lawfully in police custody. I turn to the question of overarching safeguards. Part 15 of the bill incorporates generic safeguards applicable to the majority of powers exercisable under the Act. When, for example, police exercise powers of entry, search and arrest, they must, before exercising the power, provide a person subject to the exercise of the power with evidence that the officer is a police officer, his or her name and place of duty; provide the reason for the exercise of the power; and warn that failure or refusal to comply with a request of the police officer in the exercise of the power may be an offence.

The bill recognises, however, that police may not always reasonably be able to comply with the safeguards prior to using their powers, such as in an emergency situation. Accordingly, the clause requires in such circumstances that the safeguards should be exercised as soon as reasonably practicable after the power has been exercised. Even in emergency situations, however, police should strive to comply with all safeguards set out in the bill. The existing law has been preserved in the case of a power to request disclosure of identity, give a direction, or request a person to produce a dangerous implement.

These requirements must be met before the power is exercised. The bill provides that the Ombudsman will monitor for two years from the commencement of the proposed Act the newly enacted provisions of the bill, including the personal search provisions, the safeguards, crime scenes, notices to produce and other minor changes to police powers. The Minister for Police and I will undertake a review of the proposed Act three years after its assent. With power comes responsibility. The bill represents ideals of transparency, accountability and legitimacy.

Over time this Parliament, as the representative of the community, and the courts have given police certain powers required to effectively fulfil their role in law enforcement. In return for these powers, however, police are required to exercise their power responsibly, particularly when these powers affect the civil liberties of members of the community whom the police serve. The Law Enforcement (Powers and Responsibilities) Bill balances these two ideals admirably and I commend it to the House.

Debate adjourned on motion by Ms Hodgkinson.

THE HONOURABLE ROBERT DEBUS, ATTORNEY-GENERAL,
Second Reading Speech
Law Enforcement (Powers and Responsibilities) Bill 2002 **(NSW)**
17 September 2002

To what extent does the criminal investigation process balance the rights of victims, suspects and society?

In your answer, refer to the above statement.

Section III

50 marks

Attempt TWO questions from Questions 25–31, each from a different Option

Allow about 1 hour and 30 minutes for this section

In your answers you will be assessed on how well you:

- Demonstrate knowledge and understanding of legal issues relevant to the question
- Communicate using relevant legal terminology and concepts
- Refer to relevant examples such as legislation, cases, media, international instruments and documents
- Present a sustained, logical and cohesive response

Question 25 – Consumers (25 marks)

(a) To what extent does consumer law reflect changes in values and ethical standards?

OR

(b) Assess the roles of organisations, tribunals and courts in resolving consumer law issues.

Question 26 – Global Environmental Protection (25 marks)

(a) Compare the effectiveness of legal and non-legal responses in addressing global environmental issues.

OR

(b) Discuss the role of state sovereignty in promoting and achieving global environmental protection.

Question 27 – Family (25 marks)

(a) To what extent has law reform achieved just outcomes for those in same sex relationships?

OR

(b) Evaluate the roles of the law and the media in responding to issues affecting family members.

Question 28 – Indigenous Peoples (25 marks)

(a) Explain why the right to self-determination is important in achieving justice for Indigenous peoples.

OR

(b) Compare the effectiveness of legal and non-legal measures in achieving recognition of land rights for Indigenous peoples.

Question 29 – Shelter (25 marks)

(a) Compare the effectiveness of legal and non-legal measures in responding to homelessness and issues of discrimination relating to shelter.

OR

(b) Discuss how compliance with the law promotes justice both for those seeking and those providing shelter.

Question 30 – Workplace (25 marks)

(a) To what extent have dispute resolution mechanisms been effective in achieving justice in the workplace?

OR

(b) Assess the role of law reform in balancing the rights and responsibilities of employers and employees in the workplace.

Question 31 – World Order (25 marks)

(a) Evaluate the effectiveness of legal and non-legal measures in encouraging cooperation between nation states to achieve world order.

OR

(b) Discuss how state sovereignty can assist or impede the resolution of world order issues.

Chapter 12

2014 Examination suggested solutions

Section I – Multiple choice

1	D	5	B	9	C	13	C	17	D
2	B	6	A	10	B	14	D	18	C
3	C	7	C	11	A	15	B	19	D
4	C	8	B	12	A	16	B	20	C

Section II

Part A – Human Rights

Question 21

Reference could be made to any of the documents that comprise the 'international bill of rights such as the Universal Declaration of Human Rights or the twin treaties that developed from this document such as the International Covenant on Civil and Political Rights (ICCPR) and the International Covenant on Economic, Social and Cultural Rights.

The contributions these documents have made to the development of human rights have been significant. They have had an educative effect on the international community, have set a benchmark of the standards expected and have encouraged the development of numerous human rights NGOs which have promoted the protection of human rights around the world.

Question 22

There are very few direct protections for human rights contained in the constitution as it does not contain a 'charter of human rights' entrenched in it. There are however structural indirect protections contained in the constitution and historically these have protected Human Rights to some extent in the past. For example it sets up the institutions of government (House of Representation and the Senate as well as embedding the separation of powers and processes for responsible government responsible to the people through the election cycle. S71 also establishes the High Court which acts as a check on government power. S51 the Division of powers has ensured that no level of government can become too powerful by placing limits on its jurisdictional authority.

The constitution contains very few explicit entrenched human rights.
There are 5 express rights (entrenched) – s80 right to a trial by jury, s116 right to freedom of religion, s41 right to vote in Commonwealth elections. Implied rights also exist derived from judicial interpretation of the constitution in relation to matters before them such the right to political freedom of speech.

Question 23

Courts either at an international or domestic level can provide significant human rights protections, however they are ad hoc and reactive and generally provide a narrow definition of a human rights issue. Courts at an international level combat the issue of sovereignty which can render providing just outcomes difficult to achieve. At a domestic level courts are usually confined to the rules of precedent or the legislative framework from which they are asked to interpret.

At a domestic level an example of this is the limited right to legal representation created in *Dietrich v The Queen*. This approach can be effective at times but it is sporadic and haphazard if one is looking to the courts to ensure our rights are safeguarded. It should be noted though that the courts will look to our international human rights treaty obligations and may incorporate these into their decision, as seen in the Teoh High Court case which used the Convention of the Rights of the Child (CROC) to override a ruling by the immigration department to have Teoh deported as he had children in Australia.

Internationally, the ICC seeks to prosecute individuals who commit crimes against humanity even though it is burdened by state sovereignty and the problematic nature of gathering evidence and prosecuting, in particular mass atrocities associated with such crimes. However prosecution in the Lubanga case in 2012 and the Katanga case in 2014 demonstrate that it is possible to secure convictions and how important, if somewhat symbolic, such prosecutions are. Such trials are not resource-efficient but are important to illustrate that enforcement of human rights is important even though it is restricted by state sovereignty.

Part B – Crime

Question 24

The criminal investigation process is fundamental to the protection of justice within society. It allows the rights of the community to be protected however this is sometimes at the expense of the rights of the individual. Various facets of the criminal investigative system have eroded some fundamental civil rights and thus challenge the ability of the criminal justice system to find a proportional balance between police powers of investigation and the protection of the rights of the accused, victims and protection of the community. Expanding police powers, flaws within the system of investigation of serious indictable offences, the presumption of bail and changes to rules surrounding detention and interrogation have proven to be problematic in maintaining this balance. *(Sample introduction)*

The NSW Police force is the main investigative and enforcement body of Australian law, and as a result is given special 'powers' that cannot be afforded to the general community. The problem therefore lies with the extent in which these powers are used and expanded. The Law Enforcement (Powers and Responsibilities) Act 2002 (NSW) (LEPRA) is the most significant piece of legislation pertaining to police powers and outlines the boundaries of their investigative methods in order to better protect the rights of the individual. The act outlines powers such as interrogation, reasonable suspicion, search and seizure, influence in the granting of bail and use of reasonable force. The introduction of LEPRA consolidated a number of pieces of legislation outlining police powers into one act and was a positive development in providing better transparency regarding the limits of on these powers. The purpose of the legislation at the time of introduction was to simplify police powers, without extending or limiting existing powers, so that those powers will be better understood not only by police but also by members of the community and to protect civil liberties while balancing the interests of the community in law enforcement. However, oversight of the use of police powers in ensuring this balance will always be a challenge to government and its agencies such as the Police Integrity Commission (PIC).

There are a number of considerations in approaching this question but the following would need to be included in such a discussion.

- Police must follow their own code of practice and behaviour known as CRIME, and may be subject to investigation by the NSW Ombudsman's Office or the Police Integrity Commission. Codes of practice do not necessarily reflect all legislative obligations and even with the clarification of police powers within LEPRA checks on corruption of the police force are a constant battle for all governments, due to the secretive nature of various arms of the police force and the difficulty of the crimes to detect. However, the ambiguous nature of some powers, for example reasonable suspicion and search and seizure, means that the individual's rights are sometimes sacrificed in order to protect the rights of the community.
- The Patrick Waring Case of 2006 highlighted serious flaws within the Criminal Investigative Processes which caused severe injustices for the accused in an attempt to 'protect' the community. Waring was 15 years old when he was accused of a violent rape and put on trial. The case upon which the prosecution intended to gain a conviction contained inadequacies both in DNA/forensic evidence and other evidence collected by police. The outcome of this case brought into question police procedures on the gathering of evidence and the use of DNA, in particular the use of DNA evidence without need for corroborating evidence during a trial.
- There is discussion on the need to ensure that forensic experts/scientists (as in the UK) gain access to a crime scene before the police force as this ensures that experts are able to assess the evidence's reliability and whether it may be considered relevant to the case. It also ensures that evidence is collected and tested with due process to ensure its credibility and decreasing its likelihood of contamination, which if not correctly handled may lead to false convictions. Matters can still be taken to trial on DNA evidence alone and this at times seriously challenges some convictions due to a lack of corroborating evidence.
- DNA evidence has been a significant development in the prosecution of crime and hence protection of the community but it is not without its flaws. It is not an 'exact science' and has, at times produced false interpretations, resulting in the denial of human and civil liberties of an individual through false incarceration. An example of this is the Gilham case of 2008 in which a man was falsely convicted of killing his parents and brother before setting his house alight to burn the evidence. Its confusing nature in presenting evidence against an individual has also been a contentious issue within the legal circle, especially when involving a jury as it increases the vulnerability of the accused for false conviction and imprisonment.
- Police powers with regards to search and seizure have proven to be problematic in attempts to balance the rights of the community with the rights of the individual. Amendments to LEPRA have given police greater powers of search and seizure, such as using sniffer dogs to search without founded 'reasonable suspicion' and the

powers to search anyone they believe to be committing an offence. The use of 'reasonable suspicion' has been considered highly contentious as it does not provide objective criteria and therefore may be easily abused, thus eroding an individual of their civil liberties and fundamental freedoms.

- The use of search warrants has been made mandatory in some circumstances. The rights and privacy of the accused could be further improved by increasing the difficulty in obtaining a search warrant; however this would make the investigation and conviction of various crimes increasingly difficult for police and would have an overall negative effect on society. In the 2015 NSW Parliamentary Enquiry into the police bugging of up to 100 police officers it was found that a number of the warrants were fabricated to ensure the courts would allow electronic surveillance to go ahead. Oversight at the command level was clearly lacking as police investigated police.

- It is also argued that the use of the nominative system of criminal investigation, rather than an eliminative system, in NSW can produce serious miscarriages of justice. Under a nominative system of law enforcement the focus generally is centred on the suspect/s and a case is built around them, as opposed to the use of evidence to eliminate certain people as used in the UK. This can at times erode the presumption of innocence, as an individual is believed to be guilty and therefore evidence may be viewed through this paradigm.

- Arrest should be seen as a last resort, and police must have a valid reason to do so. LEPRA contains the conditions upon which an individual may lawfully be arrested and detained including reasonable grounds to believe that an individual has committed an offence, possessing a warrant for an individual's arrest or catching a suspect in the act of committing an offence. Most arrests are made without warrants and reasonable force may be used in order to detain the accused. The use of reasonable force to arrest individuals is a fine line and can easily be crossed, thus eroding the rights of an individual; it may become particularly problematic because the system generally favours the police officer in cases of excessive force. This is particularly noticeable in the arrests of young offenders.

- New legislation in response to various terrorist attacks around the globe has widened powers of detention and interrogation if it is believed that the individual is involved in terrorist acts. Laws such as the *Anti-Terrorism Act (No. 2) 2005 (Cth)* mandate that the accused may be held in preventative detention for up to 14 days in order to prevent an imminent attack on the country. This is a radical diversion from general laws regarding charge and release outlined in the *Law Enforcement (Powers and Responsibilities) Act 2002 (NSW)*. These acts have the potential to cause gross violations to civil rights and are seen as a dramatic diversion from accepted international safeguards that exist for the protection of the accused. Mohamed Haneef was the first person to be held under preventative detention in Australia. He was denied the right to a bail hearing and various other safeguards for the protection of individuals and thus undermining the doctrine of the presumption of innocence. Recent developments such as 'data retention' laws have the potential to seriously erode privacy in the quest to detect radicalisation within Australian communities. The extent of the threat of such attacks can be questionable as the public is not privy to what governments know.

- The right to a bail hearing is a fundamental liberty for individuals accused of an indictable offence. Those that are released on bail awaiting trial will often have to pay a large sum of money and/or have to report to a bail officer or police station regularly to ensure that they are not a flight risk. Wrist and ankle monitoring devices may also be used as part of a bail agreement. However, the accused may be denied bail if they are considered a danger to the community or a flight risk. Under section 29 of the Bail Act 1978 (NSW) once a bail application is denied the individual cannot apply again. This has created serious concern within many legal avenues as it can be seen to erode the 'presumption of innocence' that is afforded to the accused, as it is up to the individual to convince the court that they should maintain their freedoms and liberties until trial. This is especially evident in matters pertaining to juveniles. The notion of the 'presumption of innocence' is a cornerstone for the Australian justice system and the denial of a right to a bail hearing is a clear miscarriage of justice as an individual may, in fact, be found innocent.

The gathering of evidence, increased police powers, development of technology, and the notions of arrest, interrogation and bail/remand are central to the protection of the rights of the community. However, balancing these rights with the rights of the accused has proven to be difficult with the rights of the individual often eroded. Broadening police powers with regard to search and seizure, interrogation regulations and bail hearings has been balanced with restrictions of the investigative processes (e.g. warrants) which has, in turn made investigating and prosecuting crime harder but has ensured that the rights of the individual are protected. This has improved the potential for the criminal investigative processes to provide justice for both the individual and wider community. There will always be an ongoing tension between the rights of the individual and the rights of the accused which has led to gross injustice and more needs to be done in order to address this.

Section III – Options

Question 25 – Consumers

(a) This question is addressed in Question 1 Chapter 5. References should be made to answer to Question 1 under Consumer Law in Chapter 10.

(b) There are numerous organisations, courts and tribunals that have been established to resolve consumer issues. Effectively delivering just outcomes to all parties in consumer disputes is difficult given the rapidly changing commercial world in which consumers and sellers operate.

There will always be ongoing challenges to protect consumers and the onset of the global marketplaces has seen consumers expose themselves to suppliers outside state and federal jurisdictions. Hence the ability of consumer institutions to resolve consumer issues continues to be challenged.

- There are a number of **state and federal government organisations** that provide education, advice, investigative procedures and mediation and adjudicating mechanisms. These need to be discussed in respect to their jurisdiction and with examples of the types of matters they may assist in. The **Office of Fair Trading** in NSW is one such organisation. It also is the place where small businesses register the owner of their organisations.
Federal government organisations include the **Australian Competition and Consumer Commission (ACCC)**. The ACCC is an independent statutory body that administers the *Competition and Consumer Act 2010* (Cth) and other Commonwealth Acts. Its role is to promote competition and fair trade in the

marketplace. The **Australian Securities and Investments Commission (ASIC)** is an independent statutory body which regulates Australia's corporate, markets and financial services sectors and ensures that Australia's financial markets are fair and transparent.

All of these bodies attempt to ensure greater compliance with the law through effectively addressing the rights of vendors and consumers and the complaints and issues that confront them. They have at times been criticised because the Corporations Law they work under does not have enough 'clout' to punish corporate offenders heavily enough. Gathering sufficient evidence that will hold up in court can also be problematic for these bodies.

- Some industries have developed their own style of **ombudsman**. This office acts on behalf of the whole industry and consumer complaints can be dealt with at this level. Examples include the **banking ombudsman** and the **Energy and Water Ombudsman NSW**. These types of industry initiatives attempt to ensure greater compliance with industry standards, but some critics question the extent to which they are independent. They have no statutory authority to punish offenders.

- There are particular **courts and tribunals** that adjudicate on consumer conflict. The ***Consumer, Trader and Tenancy Tribunal Act 2001* (NSW)** established the Consumer, Trader and Tenancy Tribunal. The Act outlines the operation of the tribunal. The role of this tribunal is to resolve disputes between entities involved in consumer relationships. Some of these are tenants, landlords, traders and consumers. Like most tribunals they are a relatively cheap and fast way to resolve disputes, making the law more accessible to consumers for matters not involving large sums of money and providing a much needed avenue of justice.

- There are a number of non-government organisations that exist to represent the interests of consumers by raising concerns with governments, educating the public about specific issues or supporting consumers in advocacy matters. Some examples of consumer non-government organisations include Choice, Consumer Credit Legal Centre (NSW) and Incorporated and Consumers' Federation of Australia. A number of these pressure government to act on areas that may pose problems for consumers.

- **The media** is another important non-legal measure for raising awareness of consumer issues in society. All media is biased to some extent, but can still provide an invaluable service in putting pressure on governments and informing consumers of recent developments that may put consumers at risk financially or physically. It can at times call for redress of problems, and exposure may spark a more immediate response. (A media case that centres on any of the contemporary issues raised on p23 of the syllabus.)

Question 26 – Global Environmental Protection

(a) Non-legal measures continue to be imperative to highlight issues, pressure governments as they build a coalition 'of the willing' to persist in demanding greater global environmental protection.

Refer to previous questions to highlight such international instruments, conferences and non-legal measures and the extent to which they have fulfilled their potential for global environmental protection. Reference should be made to the answers to questions 2, 4, 5, 6, 7 and 10 under Global Environmental Protection in Chapter 10.

(b) A recurring theme when dealing with international law is the ability of sovereign nation states to promote or impede the effectiveness of the implementation of legal measures. This is especially the case in respect to global environmental protection. Many nation states are at different stages of development in respect to economic prosperity and growth, and culturally they view environmental issues through differing paradigms.

Discussion of this question is broad but ultimately would assess the ability of international legal measures to advance the protection to the global community in the face of many significant environmental challenges. Discussion on international conferences and instruments would centre on the extent to which they have progressed legal protection.

International courts and tribunals as well as the ability of intergovernmental organisations to progress consensus must also be examined in the light sovereignty as promoting or impeding global environmental protection. Non-government organisations and non-legal measures should also be examined in the context of influencing the decisions of nation states – hence getting them to make sovereign decisions that advance global environmental protections.

Reference should be made to the answers to the questions under Global Environmental Protection in Chapter 10.

Question 27 – Family

(a) Family Law, like other areas of law, operates within a society that continues to evolve. The evolution of family law over the last 30 years has been quite dramatic. Significant shifts in the types of living arrangements and the ability of the law to deal with the conflicting rights and responsibilities of family members continues to challenge the laws ability to deliver just outcomes. The contemporary issues listed in the syllabus (page 27) are areas of Family law where the law is under pressure to adapt tho these circumstances. Between 1999 and 2009, various Australian states and territories introduced a number of legislative changes to provide more just outcomes for those Australians living in same-sex relationships. However, same-sex relationships are still not recognised as having the same status as a 'marriage' under federal laws.

Federal Initiatives

In 2008, following the Australian Human Rights Commission's report *Same-Sex: Same Entitlements*, the Australian government introduced reforms with the aim of removing discrimination and providing same-sex couples the same entitlements as those presently enjoyed by heterosexual de facto couples. Since 2008 under the Same-Sex Relationships (Equal Treatment in Commonwealth Laws – General Law Reform) Act, federal law reforms have removed areas of discrimination from a range of laws and programs by amending and/or extending definitions such as 'de facto partner', 'child', 'parent', 'couple' and 'family' to include same-sex relationships.

For example, the *Health Insurance Act 1973 (Cth)* now allows a same-sex couple and their children to register as a family for Medicare and receive the same entitlements as a heterosexual couple and their children. Additional areas amended have been tax, social security, family law, superannuation, workers' compensation and child support. Same-sex couples will be able to claim the same tax concession as those presently available to married or heterosexual de factos. They and their children will be able to claim superannuation benefits, and to receive the same social security and family assistance payments as heterosexual couples.

A major change in state laws concerns the recognition of a same-sex partner as the 'parent' of their partner's child. Male partners in a heterosexual marriage or de facto relationship have parental rights and responsibilities towards in child conceived during the relationship – that is, biological parents are regarded as having joint responsibility for the child. However, a partner of the same sex had no legal standing and could not make decisions about the day-to-day care of the child unless the Family Court had so ordered. Children conceived through donor insemination or assisted reproduction had only the mother listed on their birth certificates. The Miscellaneous Acts Amendment (Same-Sex Relationships) Act 2008 (NSW) granted equal parenting rights for the female partners of mothers, and both are listed as mothers on the child's birth certificate. This change gives children born into same-sex relationships equal rights to inheritance from both 'parents' and protects the rights of both mothers in matters involving the children if the relationship were to end.

Under the *Family Law Amendment (De Facto Financial Matters and Other Measures) Act 2008 (Cth)*, property and maintenance matters for separating homosexual couples are determined by the Family Court or the Federal Magistrates' Court. The act extends the definition of 'de facto' to include two people who are not married or related by blood who live together 'on a genuine basis'. The Act does not distinguish between a relationship between two people of the same or opposite sex.

State initiatives

The law has recognised relationships that exist outside the traditional concept of marriage. The De Facto Relationships Act 1984 (NSW) was amended by the Property (Relationships) Legislation Amendment Act 1999 (NSW) and renamed the Property (Relationships) Act 1984 (NSW). The Property (Relationships) Act 1984 (NSW) recognises same-sex relationships as having the same legal standing as heterosexual de facto relationships, and provides the same protection. Section 4 of this Act defines a de facto relationship as 'a relationship between two adult persons who live together as a couple, and who are not married to one another or related by family'. The Act provided protection to people in same-sex de facto relationships in property division, inheritance and decision-making in illness and after death.

The definition of 'de facto' in this Act also applies to persons making an application for family provision under the Succession Act 2008 (NSW), and to entitlements of the de facto partners of individuals who died intestate, under the laws amended by the Succession Amendment (Intestacy) Act 2009 (NSW). In other words, same-sex partners have the same entitlements under those laws as if they were married.

Section 4AA(5) of the *Family Law Act 1975 (Cth)* states that a de facto relationship can exist whether the persons are of the same sex or different sexes. Therefore, the Family Law Act governs property settlements between separating same-sex couples.

Same-sex couples may also adopt under reforms to the Adoption Act 2000 (NSW) but it has been argued that changes to the Surrogacy Act 2010 (NSW) preventing residents of NSW travelling overseas to engage in commercial surrogacy arrangements was aimed squarely at same-sex couples influenced by the Christian right lobby groups at the time of drafting.

Prior to legislative change as outlined above at a state and federal level the court increasingly recognised the rights of same-sex couples in an ad hoc manner which seemed to reflect the greater need to recognise these relationships in order to protect economic rights and to ensure children were provided for.
The *Hope and Brown v NIB Health Fund Ltd 1995* recognised the rights of families not to be discrimination against in seeking health policies for members of their families. NIB initially refused to recognise Hope's two-year-old son on a family policy with Brown and the Equal Opportunity Tribunal ruled that this was discriminatory.

The *Mum v Mum* case where the Supreme Court of NSW recognised the biological mother was owed maintenance for the child born through IVF that they had raised together. There is now a presumption of parentage for non-biological parents of same sex-couples for children born through birth technologies.

The Australian Human Rights Commission has held a number of inquiries into areas of discrimination and human rights violations. The Commission also makes recommendations to the government regarding the removal of institutionalised discrimination and legislation which does not comply with UN human rights treaties. In 2007, Commission's report *Same-Sex: Same Entitlements* (www.hreoc.gov.au/HUMAN_RIGHTS/samesex/report/index.html) recommended amending federal laws that discriminated against same-sex couples and their children in the area of financial and work-related entitlements and benefits.

Non-legal responses to the reforms have been varied, ranging from complete support to criticism of the various state and federal governments for not going far enough, to individuals and groups who are highly critical of any added protection of the rights of same-sex couples. Groups that actively lobby and campaign for the legal rights and social equality of gay and lesbian couples include Australian Marriage Equality (www.australianmarriageequality.com) and the Gay and Lesbian Rights Lobby (www.glrl.org.au). Australian Marriage Equality argues that the legally recognised institution of marriage should not exclude these couples. A different classification sends the message that their relationships are of a lesser standard or character and that the people are second-class citizens. Justice requires changing the law to make marriage is available to all Australians who choose it, not classifying same-sex couples as de factos or permitting them only to form 'civil unions'. The Gay and Lesbian Rights Lobby has a wide-ranging agenda, including advocacy, lobbying government and the media to address discrimination, hosting consultations, educating the gay and lesbian community on their rights and providing referrals to legal and welfare services.

Some sections of the media have been critical of these changes and have resorted to ridicule. For example, in 2003 two radio program hosts made comments 'capable of inciting severe ridicule of homosexual men' and therefore were held to have breached the vilification provisions of the Anti-Discrimination Act 1977 (NSW). In 2008 the hosts' appeal was settled, with a public apology on air and a written apology in the *Sydney Morning Herald*.

Most of the lobby groups that oppose equal rights for homosexual couples have a religious affiliation, such as the Australian Christian Lobby (www.acl.org.au). Under the current discrimination laws, religious groups continue to be able to discriminate on the basis of sex, sexuality, race, disability and age. This allows these organisations to withhold services to individuals.

The Anti-Discrimination Board of NSW is part of the NSW Department of Justice and Attorney General. It administers the anti-discrimination laws of New South Wales. It handles complaints of discrimination, and also informs the public of how individuals can prevent and deal with discrimination, through consultations, education programs, seminars, talks, community functions and publications. The Board's third function is to advise the government and make recommendations. It has made a number of submissions to both the state and federal governments concerning changes to current legislation that are necessary in order to provide same-sex couples the same legal rights and protections that are now enjoyed by married couples. However anti-discrimination legislation has been criticised in the past because not all complainants see the legislation as having significant coercive powers and the damages usually awarded under federal and state tribunals is very small.

However, arguments against the recognition of same-sex relationships continue to exert an influence in the public sphere. The legislative changes to de facto entitlements by the Rudd government in 2008, while welcomed, sat alongside a continuing refusal to amend the Marriage Act to permit same-sex marriage.

In his speech at the Conference on Legal Recognition of Same-Sex Partnerships in 1999, then High Court Justice Michael Kirby stated: 'As a people committed to equal justice for all under the law, I have confidence that the Australian legal system, and those who make laws in Australia, will, in due course, eradicate unfair discrimination on the basis of sexuality. The scales are dropping rapidly from our eyes. Injustice and irrational prejudice cannot survive the scrutiny of just men and women'.

Both the state and federal governments have legislated to predominantly end discrimination people living in same sex relationships. Recognition of same sex marriage seems to be the last bastion of social convention that will continue to be challenged as values and ethics surrounding this issue continue to evolve.

(b) This is a broad based question that specifically targets the legal response to issues affecting families (legal responses) and specifically the media (non-legal) response to the many issues that can be highlight in this question to evaluate legal and non-legal (media) responses to the issues affecting families. Reference to past responses in Chapter 10 (family law) should be used with a focus on the important role the media predominantly plays in highlighting issues that require greater legislative attention to reporting on cases or commissions such as Royal Commission into Institutional Responses to Child Sexual Abuse, which is still ongoing. The ability of the law to respond to a number of issues affecting families predominantly can ensure a degree of responsiveness to the needs of the community through greater media vigilance.

Please note that this book does not provide suggested examination answers for Questions 28 and 29, which relate to the Options Indigenous Peoples and Shelter.

Question 30 – Workplace

(a) Justice in the workplace is usually best achieved through negotiation and mediation requiring specialist courts and tribunals to resolve matters as a last resort. Modern awards and protections within 'contracts of employment' attempt to provide greater certainty regarding negotiating periods and minimum conditions of work but disputes are inevitable. As such specialist courts and tribunals have been set up to deal with workplace disputes.

In NSW the **Industrial Relations Commission**, which refers matters to the **NSW Industrial Relations Tribunal**, investigates alleged breaches of state industrial legislation, awards and enterprise agreements. It will first order a compulsory conference between the parties, then conciliation. It will only employ arbitration to deal with an industrial dispute if conciliation is unsuccessful. Its orders are binding.

At the federal level, **Fair Work Australia** (now the FWC) is the industrial relations **tribunal**. It can arbitrate matters and also make rulings on unfair dismissal and other matters emanating from industrial disputes. The *Fair Work Act 2009 (Cth)* created a **Fair Work Division** of the **Federal Magistrates Court,** which can hear small claims matters under the value of $200 000. It also created a **Fair Work Division** of the **Federal Court**.

There are a number of **governmental organisations** at the state and federal levels that also support various courts and tribunals and to undertake other specific roles with respect to industrial relations. The **NSW Industrial Relations Commission (IRC)**, apart from the adjudicating role mentioned earlier, also engages in the formulation of awards and approving enterprise agreements for workers operating under the state system. The commission can also regulate and register employer associations. This work is an important proactive view that attempts to ensure that workplace justice is well negotiated with all parties having input into the development of agreed workplace condition.

Fair Work Australia (now the FWC), in addition to being an industrial tribunal, also oversees the federal industrial relations system. It can modify awards, provide advice about the industrial framework to businesses and workers, make decisions concerning minimum wages and review and approve enterprise agreements.

The **Fair Work Ombudsman**, as outlined in Section 68 of the *Fair Work Act 2009* (Cth), is to advance 'harmonious, productive and cooperative workplace relations and to ensure the provisions of the Act are complied with'. It does this by providing education and advice in addition to investigating and enforcing breeches of the Act, awards and agreements.

Industrial disputes tend to disrupt the workplace less than ever before. It could be argued that processes have improved the ability of competing parties to input into workplace agreements. However such courts and tribunals are necessary to ensure the most vulnerable members of the workplace have some 'safety nets' and protections to ensure fairer outcomes are a possibility for all working people.

(b) Reference should be made to answers to Question 2 and 8 under Workplace in Chapter 10.

Question 31 – World Order

(a) The international community continues to be challenged to achieve world order through a range of legal and non-legal responses which attempt to reduce conflict promote peace within nation states. However it can be seen that the effectiveness of legal and non-legal measures in promoting and maintaining world order is questionable due to obstacles such as interdependence of nation states and state sovereignty.

Legal Responses

The concept of **state sovereignty** was enshrined in Article 2.7 of the UN Charter and can be seen simultaneously to assist in attaining world order, while acting as an impediment to the concept. Statehood empowers nations by providing a legal status to act in world affairs. All international treaties and declarations are based upon nations working together and exercising their sovereignty. However states can also impede the influence of international law by using their sovereignty as a shield against outside interference in their domestic affairs. For instance, sovereignty has been a great hindrance in ridding the world of nuclear weapons. If a nation believes it is in their own national interest to acquire nuclear weapons there is very little the international community can do to stop them which was clearly demonstrated by North Korea detonating a nuclear weapon in 2006 in contravention of the Nuclear Non-Proliferation Treaty 1966. The success of world order is thus reliant on compliance and cooperation of nation states; however nation states will only act if it is in their own political and economic interests.

The **United Nations** has as its primary aim to promote international peace and harmony and reduce conflict (Article 1 UN Charter). The laying down of international guidelines was significant as it attempted to set an international standard by promoting cooperation between nations to prevent war and maintain peace. However today it can be seen that the United Nations is severely under-resourced, with the total system running on less than $15 billion a year. Thus, it must be seen that the UN does significant work in peacekeeping and humanitarian legislation considering its inadequate budget.

However, the UN's failure to achieve just outcomes can also be seen to derive from its inflexible structure and the dominance of the five permanent members of the **United Nations Security Council (UNSC)**. The United Nations charter has been criticised for representing an out-dated world order, yet it is very difficult to change.

The UNSC has primary responsibility for maintaining international peace and includes 15 non-permanent members and five permanent members consisting of the United States, France, United Kingdom, China and Russia – the victors of World War II and thus very Eurocentric in its views. There is criticism that the permanent members need to be more inclusive and representative of the world as a whole, for instance to include a Muslim nation. If any one of the permanent members of the UNSC disagrees with a proposal they may halt any proposed action by exercising its power of veto.

This is problematic in halting many substantive actions and hampering any significant reform. This was seen in the Kosovo conflict in which very little action was taken by the UN as permanent members of the UNSC, Russia and China, had political and economic interests in Yugoslavia and thus opposed any intervention. The veto power has thus seen many crises unresolved and resulted in humanitarian crisis such as Kosovo and Rwanda in which the world was paralysed to act and the UN did not intervene in time. However the United Nations has also had many successes including the Responsibility to Protect doctrine which strengthens global intervention in international crises by providing more legal force. Military strikes by the UN against Libya and the Ivory Coast have been justified by the R2P doctrine. This represents a pivotal moment in which the UN, generally unwilling to intervene forcefully in international affairs, has taken forward action against forces that threaten world order.

Treaties refer to 'binding agreements voluntarily entered into by states' and are the foremost source of international law. Treaties provide a standard for world order within the international community. Treaties can refer to multi-lateral (between many nations) or bi-lateral agreements between two nations such as the Lombok Treaty between Indonesia and Australia signed in 2006. The Lombok treaty aims to diminish tension between these states through greater security cooperation. The signing of this treaty ensured anti-terrorism cooperation, joint naval border control and is indicative of increasing consensus on regional issues affection both nations. The United Nations Charter was perhaps the most significant treaty signed as it set up the mechanism of the United Nations and the machinery for legitimising international treaties. Article 1 of the UN charter states that its primary aim is 'to promote peace and security throughout the world' thus sanctifying the importance of this treaty to world order. The Nuclear Non-Proliferation Treaty of 1968 was an agreement for nations possessing nuclear weapons to continue reducing their stock hold if nations lacking nuclear weapons ensured they wouldn't develop them. However, the sovereign right of a nation has seen North Korea and Iran acting contrary to this treaty by trying to develop nuclear capability thus demonstrating the lack of enforcement of international instruments. The more recent comprehensive Test Ban Treaty 1966 was a further step in this direction, in which signatory states agreed not to undertake any nuclear weapon test explosion at any place under its jurisdiction. However this is limited due to the fact that only 9 of the 43 signatories have ratified the agreement, indicating a lack of political will to comply. There is also lack of political will to comply demonstrated by North Korea's weapon testing in October 2009.

Treaties are guided by the principal of *jus cogens* ('compelling law') which ensures nations cannot sign a treaty that is contrary to international global public morality.

For instance, a treaty signed by nation states to regulate slavery would not adhere to the principle of *jus cogens* and thus would not be recognised. It must be seen that treaties set an international benchmark and afford a collective morality on significant issues in respect to regional and global peace and security.

The Responsibility to Protect Doctrine is a new doctrine of international approach and evolution on the concept of Sovereignty in order to respond to the failure of the international community to respond to world order issues. It can be seen that some people believe the UNSC can use its Chapter VII powers to intervene where a nation is failing to protect its citizens. Others hold the view that the principle of state sovereignty, upheld by article 2.7 of the UN charter does not permit humanitarian intervention on these grounds. Therefore the R2P is aimed at bridging the gap between these two views of sovereignty. According to the doctrine if a state is unable or unwilling to protect its citizens it becomes the international community's responsibility to do so. For example, intervention in the Libya crisis was directly attributed to R2P. The UNSC explicitly recalled 'the Libyan authorities' responsibility to protect its population' and with failure to do so NATO (North Atlantic Treaty Organization) justified military actions against Libya by reference to the R2P Doctrine. Promoting action on the basis of R2P is still reliant however on agreement by the Permanent Members of the Security Council and faces the same obstacles as resolutions to be passed.

International courts and tribunals can be seen to be indispensable in achieving world order. The International Court of Justice (ICJ) hears and deals with disputes between nation states as well as offering advisory opinions on contentious issues of international law. However, the effectiveness of the ICJ is hindered by nation states ability to refuse the ICJs jurisdiction, the lack of enforceability and impotency of its actions. The ICJs recognition of state sovereignty therefore limits the means of enforcing the courts verdict as state governments may 'consider the recognition of the jurisdiction of the court as infringing on their sovereignty'. An example of this can be seen in Nicaragua v United States in which the ICJ ruled the United States' actions against Nicaragua was in violation of their obligation not to use force against another nation and thus ordered them to stop and pay reparations to Nicaragua. The United States however ignored this decision. Despite this the ICJ has issued important judgements that carry the weight of international law and act as a significant guide to future action.

Prior to the ICC, serious international crime was usually prosecuted domestically or by specialised ad hoc tribunals such as the International Criminal Tribunal (ICTY) for the former Yugoslavia in 1993, as well as the International Criminal Tribunal for Rwanda in 1994. These were important symbolic actions demonstrating that the international community would take forward action to deliver justice to the victims of these horrendous crimes. However the tribunals were unwieldy due to the vast amount of evidence and resources required in order to find the 'smoking gun'. For example, the International Criminal Tribunal for the Former Yugoslavia had difficulty in finding proof that Milosevic issued the orders for the ethnic cleansing in Kosovo. There were also difficulties with cooperation from the nations involved which led them to being largely ineffective in bringing the criminals to justice. There is also a serious resource efficiency issue due to the enormous costs of investigating and prosecuting these crimes against humanity. For example, the Slobodan Milosevic trial was estimated costing $600 million dollars only to see him die before the completion of his trial. As such, prosecuting international crime is limited by the lack of funding and will thus never be able to prosecute all international crimes. The NSW Solicitor-General, Michael Sexton wrote in 2002 that 'a new form of trial is needed for those in the category of Saddam and Milosevic, whether it is carried out in an international tribunal or at the domestic level.' Therefore there were calls within the international community to replace ad hoc tribunals with an international criminal court – a permanent judicial body.

The creation of a permanent **International Criminal Court** in 2002 by the 1998 Rome Conference has been extremely significant to achieving world order. It is a permanent and independent entity which was formed to prosecute the international crimes of genocide, crimes against humanity and war crimes, as well as the crime of aggression. This permanent international court is symbolically very powerful. It sends a message to the individual that they may no longer rely on state sovereignty as a shield when committing despicable acts against the community. The ICC encompasses the principle of complementary jurisdiction. This means that where nation states are unwilling or unable to investigate and prosecute serious abuse under their domestic law the ICC will assume responsibility for fulfilling that duty on behalf of the international community. This can at times create problems in achieving justice. For instance in Darfur the people identified for crimes against humanity are all high-ranking government officials. This may see Sudan implement the complementary jurisdiction provision of the Rome statute and thus could reduce the likelihood of the perpetrators being brought to justice. Therefore the ICC is only effective in addressing world order issues where the international community genuinely complies with its jurisdiction.

There are serious limitations that exist with the enforcement of the ICC. There is a limited scope and capacity to handle cases as it can only exercise jurisdiction on states that have signed the treaty. The treaty lacks membership of many world powers such as the United States, which limits the courts ability to achieve justice. This highlights how the effectiveness of the ICC is thus determined by the cooperation of nation states; the court can be seen to lack enforceability. It can also be said that the international criminal court is a reactive tool in responding to international crime after it has already happened. A more proactive approach would involve preventive techniques, such as investigation into the underlying causes of international crime. However it can be seen that the ICC have been significant in investigating the Darfur situation after being referred by the UNSC in 2005 and have since made three public arrest warrants against high-ranking officials. The ICC is a relatively new body and therefore its true effectiveness in achieving international peace and world order is yet to be completely determined however it is envisaged that the ICC will be symbolically powerful and thus essential in prosecuting international crimes.

Intergovernmental organisations play an integral role in encouraging world order, by advocating the welfare of their region; however they also have the ability to impede regional security. The North Atlantic Treaty Organization (NATO) is a regional defence pact established in 1949 which promotes the concept of collective security. In the past NATO has been successful in assisting the termination of conflicts in Kosovo by exercising the right of humanitarian intervention and commissioning a series of air fights against Serbian forces. The European Union can be seen as the most effective and significant Intergovernmental organisation, generating a quarter of the world's global wealth as well as providing security for its members and enhancing social cooperation making a war between any one of its 27 members virtually impossible. The EU holds a great deal of political persuasive power for nations seeking admission to the EU as well as providing peacekeeping troops around the world. A relatively new regional organisation is the African Union which intervened in the Darfur conflict in 2003. The African Union was severely inadequately equipped and ill-prepared and thus ineffective, demonstrating the reliance on sufficient resources in order to effect change. However as this IGO develops it may be able to increasingly help volatile African states with political, social and economic issues. Hence it can be established that IGOs act as a forum for political negotiations, conflict prevention and crisis management.

Non-legal Measures

There are numerous **non-government organisations (NGOs)** which have been important in promoting peace and security around the world such as the International Crisis group. This was formed in 1995 due to the lack of response from the international community to the genocide that occurred in Rwanda and Bosnia. The ICG is gaining a lot of prominence around the world as an accurate source of information for bodies that are working to respond directly to conflict situations as well as promoting responsibility to protect doctrine on the national agenda. Other NGOs that specialise in promoting peace and security include the Global Police Forum, which monitors international policy making and the Campaign for Nuclear Disarmament. The International Committee of the Red Cross has been important in promoting the concept of humanitarian law and also limiting the methods of warfare. It can be seen that NGOs play a vital role in researching, reporting and informing the global community on breaches of International law. NGOs also expose violations by governments and thus provide a check and balance on government power to ensure power is not too centralised. It must therefore be seen that NGOs are vital to World Order.

The **media** plays a crucial non-legal role in highlighting world order issues, influencing public opinions and thus consequently pressuring governments for the need for world order and dealing with world order issues. It was the media pressurising the Security Council during the Darfur crisis that eventually resulted in some sanctions against Sudanese government for crimes against humanity. For instance the *Sydney Morning Herald* article of May 2006 titled 'Genocide by famine: Darfur aid halved' questions 'How bad does it have to get before the international community acts?', thus demonstrating how the media is a powerful advocate to evoke change. However, media outlets tend to be dominated by a small number of powerful transnational corporations and are influenced by the cultures and values of the society they exist within and thus can be subject to bias.

Political negotiation is the most straightforward and typically used means of resolving disputes between nations and it can be fast and extremely effective. However it can also be ignored as seen in Darfur where former British Prime Minister Tony Blair attempted to intervene by meeting with the Sudanese president and writing an open letter to the members of the European Union calling for a unified response to the crisis. He stated 'we should strongly call upon government of Sudan and non-signatories alike to stop immediately the violence in Northern Sudan' however this had very little effect.

If political negotiation fails the next option is the use of **persuasion** as an alternative method by pressuring nations through world public opinion. This is done by 'naming and shaming' as well as threatening political and economic sanctions if nation states do not comply. Persuasion can at times be highly effective for instance China has had to raise its trade standards in order to be a member of the World Trade Organization. However, persuasion can as well be ineffective and considered a soft option, such as the world putting pressure on China to support a Security Council resolution against the Sudanese government in Darfur which has so far been unsuccessful.

When political negotiation and persuasion have no impact **force** may be employed. This can be problematic as there are many issues surrounding the legality of the use of force and it may lead to retaliation and intensification of hostilities. Legally force can only be employed under Article 51 of the UN charter in a manner of self-defence or as stated in Chapter 7, on the grounds of humanitarian intervention. For example, the United States argued that its invasion of Afghanistan was legal on the grounds of self-defence in response to the September 11 terrorist attacks. This is further demonstrated in the crisis of Kosovo where the UNSC voted against action; however NATO exercised the right of humanitarian intervention and thus commissioned a series of airstrikes against Serbian forces.

It must therefore be seen that the attainment of world order is idealistic and made difficult by the obstacle of state sovereignty which is driven by political and economic will.

However there exists a multitude of legal and non-legal mechanisms. These mechanisms are however undoubtedly hampered by the concept of state sovereignty which ensures there must be sufficient political and economic will on behalf of sovereign states in order to achieve compliance. The international community must therefore encourage cooperation between nation states and legal and non-legal bodies in order to achieve world order.

(b) This is broad question that questions the underlying key problem for achieving world order – reduction of conflict and the promotion of peace and security. State sovereignty can promote or impeded world order and many examples can be cited in responding to this question. The concept of **state sovereignty** was enshrined in Article 2.7 of the UN Charter and can be seen simultaneously to assist in attaining world order, while acting as an impediment to the concept. Statehood empowers nations by providing a legal status to act in world affairs. All international treaties and declarations are based upon nations working together and exercising their sovereignty. However states can also impede the influence of international law by using their sovereignty as a shield against outside interference in their domestic affairs.

Reference to many of legal measures referred to in 31 (a) and responses in Chapter 10 (World Order) can be discussed in respect to their effectiveness based on state sovereignty. Non-legal measures can also be highlighted in their attempt to influence state sovereignty by encouraging state to act in manner that promotes peace and security within their region and/or globally as in the case of nuclear arms.

1. Criminal law – The nature of crime

- A crime is an act or omission of duty against society at large that is punishable by the state.
- For most crimes, two elements must be present at the time the crime is committed: (1) the physical act of the crime, called the *actus reus* (Latin for 'guilty act'); and (2) the mental element referring to the offender's state of mind or intention to commit the act, called the *mens rea* (Latin for 'guilty mind').
- Crimes can be widely categorised into: **indictable offences,** which are more serious offences triable before a judge and jury, and **summary offences,** which are less serious offences tried before a magistrate.
- There can be different **parties to a crime,** depending on the role or level of involvement of a person in committing the crime. These can include: principal in the first degree, principal in the second degree, accessory before the fact and accessory after the fact.
- Crime prevention strategies are used to reduce the likelihood of crime being committed in the first place, and may be more resource efficient in the long term. The two main approaches are **situational crime prevention and social crime prevention.**

2. Criminal law – The criminal investigation process

Police are responsible for investigating crimes and gathering evidence against individuals suspected of committing a crime. The police are given special statutory powers to carry out these duties. These include certain powers of **search and seizure,** powers of **detention, arrest and interrogation,** and the power to use **reasonable force.** Sometimes police will need a court-approved **warrant** before they can exercise a particular power.

Police powers are contained in legislation at the state and federal level. The main piece of legislation in NSW is the *Law Enforcement (Powers and Responsibilities) Act 2002 (NSW).*

Tension sometimes arises between police powers, with their potential for misuse, and the rights of the community and the individual. For this reason limits are imposed on the extent of police powers and how they are used, for example by requiring a court warrant. In recent years there has been an increase in police powers in NSW, especially in respect to search and seizure.

3. Criminal law – The criminal trial process

Once a formal **charge** is laid against an accused, the case against them will be heard or tried in an appropriate court. The process will differ depending on many factors, such as the type or seriousness of the crime, the plea entered, the stage in the court process or the accused's age. These considerations will determine where in the **court hierarchy** the case will be heard.

The trial process begins with the **plea,** where the accused will elect to plead guilty or not guilty. A plea of guilty will proceed to trial and a determination of guilt, whereas a plea of guilty can proceed to sentencing. At trial, the prosecution has the **burden of proof,** and must prove the case **beyond reasonable doubt.**

In Australia, the criminal trial process is based on an **adversary system** of justice. This means two opponent sides (**prosecution** and **defence**) control and present their cases before an impartial judge and jury. The **judge's role** is similar to an umpire in enforcing the court **rules of procedure and evidence.** If the case is heard by a **magistrate** alone, the magistrate will determine the verdict. In a jury trial, a **jury** of randomly selected citizens determines the verdict based only on the evidence presented. Unanimous verdicts are usually required, but **majority verdicts** can now apply in some circumstances.

4. Criminal law – Sentencing and punishment

If an accused is found guilty in court of committing a crime, the court will hold a **sentencing hearing** to determine and impose the most appropriate sentence. The *Crimes (Sentencing Procedure) Act 1999* (NSW) is the primary source of sentencing law in NSW.

A judge or magistrate will use **judicial discretion** to determine the most appropriate penalty, taking into account many different factors, including the **maximum penalty,** the **nature of the offence,** the **nature of the offender** and any **aggravating factors** or **mitigating factors.** The judicial officer will also consider the **purposes of punishment** when determining the sentence.

There are many possible penalties that can be applied, ranging from **no conviction** or a **fine,** to court-imposed conditions like a **bond,** to custodial sentences like **imprisonment.** There are also **alternative methods** of sentencing available in some circumstances.

After sentencing is concluded, **post-sentencing** considerations will also be relevant, such as security classification, parole, continued detention, sexual offenders registration or deportation.

5. Criminal law – Young offenders

The criminal justice system recognises different levels of **vulnerability** and **responsibility** of children for young people compared to adults.

Doli incapax is the legal presumption that a child cannot be convicted of a criminal offence because they are incapable of forming the requisite *mens rea.* In NSW, the **minimum age of criminal responsibility** is 10 years old. For children aged 10–13 years, the prosecution may **rebut** *doli incapax* in some circumstances. From 14–17 years of age, a young person can be fully criminally responsible, but different processes will apply.

When dealing with police, young people have different rights that recognise their greater vulnerability, including the right to an **interview friend.** Proceedings involving minors are heard before a magistrate in the **Children's Court,** and special procedures apply. In NSW, the *Young Offenders Act 1997* (NSW) provides for diversionary methods in some circumstances for young offenders, as an alternative to the court process. These methods include: police **warnings, cautions** and **youth justice conferences.**

6. Criminal law – International crime

International crime can include any crime with international origin or consequences, or recognised as punishable by the international community. There are two broad categories:

- **crimes against the international community,** which are very serious crimes punishable internationally; examples include genocide, crimes against humanity and war crimes
- **transnational crimes,** which are crimes that occur across international borders, in origin or effect; examples include trafficking illegal goods or substances, human trafficking, international fraud or transnational internet crimes.

Coordination of **regional and international agencies** and sharing of **resources** is essential in combating transnational crimes. There has also been a growth in Australian **federal and state agencies** responding to the threat of transnational crime.

The main development in dealing with crimes against the international community has been the establishment of the **International Criminal Court** (ICC). However, issues of jurisdiction, cooperation, resources and political will have made the **prosecution of individuals** responsible for such crimes problematic.

7. Human rights – The nature and development of human rights

Human rights refer to basic rights and freedoms believed to belong justifiably to all human beings. They differ from ordinary rights as they are considered to be **universal**, **inalienable** and **inherent** in all people. They are a collection of fundamental standards for the treatment of individuals in a fair, just and free society.

Various movements throughout history have fought for the recognition of particular human rights, including the abolition of **slavery**, the campaign for **universal suffrage**, the trade union movement and **labour rights**, the campaign for **universal education**, the right to **self-determination**, attempts to establish a **right to peace** or, more recently, **environmental rights**.

The main international human rights document is the *Universal Declaration of Human Rights*, adopted by the United Nations in 1948. Although a 'soft law' document, it has been highly influential worldwide. It has been followed by various 'hard law' treaties with concrete obligations on states to respect more specific rights, including the *International Covenant on Civil and Political Rights* and the *International Covenant on Economic, Social and Cultural Rights*.

© Cambridge University Press

8. Human rights – Promoting and enforcing human rights

Human rights are advanced on two broad levels: internationally and domestically. **State sovereignty** refers to a state's freedom from external influence over its own affairs. Without international enforcement mechanisms, some states may use sovereignty as a shield allowing them to continue violating the human rights of their citizens. The UN, **intergovernmental organisations**, **regional organisations** and **international courts** have all played an integral role in promoting and enforcing human rights around the world. **NGOs** and the **media** also play a crucial role in promoting recognition and enforcement of human rights locally and internationally.

Australia is a **dualist system** under international law – once a treaty is **ratified**, it must be **incorporated** into Australian law before it is effective domestically. In Australia, human rights arise from various sources. The **Australian Constitution** contains only a few limited rights, including **express rights** and **implied rights**. Instead, most rights are found in **statute**, like anti-discrimination legislation. The **courts** also enforce rights and in some cases help develop rights. Recently, Australia has been debating whether a national **charter of rights** should be introduced to entrench human rights for the future.

© Cambridge University Press

9. Consumer law – The nature of consumer law

The **objective of consumer law** is to protect the welfare of consumers by regulating the relationship between consumers, suppliers and manufacturers of goods, and the government. Consumer law arises from both the **common law**, particularly contract law, and statute law, particularly the *Competition and Consumer Act 2010* (Cth) and *Fair Trading Act 1987* (NSW).

A **contract** is an agreement between two or more parties recognised by the courts as legally binding. Contracts can be **oral**, **in writing** or **both**, and contain both **express terms and implied terms**. The elements required for a contract to exist include: **intention to create legal relations**, **offer**, **acceptance** and **consideration**.

Some contracts and contract terms are considered unjust or unfair. A party may be able to **rescind** a contract if they are a victim of **duress**, **undue influence** or **unconscionable dealing**. Goods must be **fit for purpose** and of **merchantable quality**, and sellers must not engage in **misleading or deceptive conduct**, or make **false representations**. If a manufacturer or supplier fails to take reasonable care in providing goods or services, and causes harm or injury to a consumer, they may be liable under the law of **negligence**.

© Cambridge University Press

10. Consumer law – Consumer redress and remedies

Self-help avenues, particularly complaining directly to suppliers or manufactures, can be the most efficient and effective way to resolve consumer complaints.

Various state and federal **government organisations** provide educational, advisory and investigative services for consumers, and in some cases mediation or adjudication. The main bodies are the **NSW Office of Fair Trading** and the **Australian Competition and Consumer Commission**. Particular **industry organisations** can also assist with regulation, complaints and remedies, for example industry associations or an **industry ombudsman**.

Litigation in court, seeking legal relief through common law or statutory provisions, is usually a last resort for dispute resolution. The **NSW Consumer, Trader and Tenancy Tribunal** (CTTT) is the main forum for hearing consumer disputes. **Alternative dispute resolution** methods, such as conciliation and mediation, are strongly encouraged.

Other avenues include: **non-government organisations** that can assist consumers directly or help raise concerns with government or industry, or the **media**, which can help raise awareness of consumer issues.

© Cambridge University Press

11. Consumer law – Contemporary issues

- **Credit** can take many different forms, and refers to a financial loan where goods or services are purchased in advance of payment at a later date. Most consumer credit issues arise where a person is **unable to repay**, where it is **made available to** individuals who are unlikely to be able to repay, or where **insufficient information** is supplied by the credit provider.
- To help ensure the safety, standard and reliability of goods sold to consumers, various systems of **product certification** are in place. These ensure goods are tested and accredited and meet the applicable minimum standards.
- **Marketing** is the process by which a business makes consumers aware of its product or services. Consumer laws helps protect against misleading, aggressive or fraudulent marketing practices designed to exploit consumers.
- **Technology** has broadened the consumer marketplace and created new forms of transacting for consumers and suppliers. Some of the issues that have arisen include **privacy** issues of invasive technology, technology **fraud** (particularly over the internet), and issues of **jurisdiction** where goods and services are provided across international borders.

© Cambridge University Press

12. Global environment – The nature of global environmental protection

Environmental protection law attempts to regulate competing interests in the use and management of the environment. This area of the law has largely developed only in recent decades.

The main Australian statute on environmental protection is the *Environment Protection and Biodiversity Conservation Act 1999* (Cth). It contains a broad **definition of 'environment'**, including **ecosystems** and their constituent parts, **natural and physical resources**, **qualities and heritage values** of places, and **social, economic and cultural aspects** of these things.

Ecologically sustainable development (ESD) refers to 'development that meets the needs of the present without compromising the ability of future generations to meet their own needs' (*Brundtland Report*, 1987). Obligations regarding ESD were central to the Rio Conference in 1992, which elaborated upon the principle to include four pillars: **biodiversity**, **intergenerational equity**, **intragenerational equity** and the **precautionary principle**.

© Cambridge University Press

13. Global environment – Responses to global environmental protection

The development of **international conferences** on the environment, particularly the regular **mega conferences** or summits that commenced in Stockholm in 1972, together with the negotiation of numerous **multilateral treaties** on environmental issues, reflects the growing recognition of governments of the **need for global environmental protection**.

Increasing consumption and development worldwide, due partially to the effects of **globalisation**, has also increased the impact on the environment. One of the difficulties is in convincing governments that the long-term needs of the environment may outweigh individual countries' short-term economic and political interests.

The UN has established several programs and specialised agencies to deal with environmental issues, such as the Food and Agriculture Organization, the **UN Development Programme** and the **UN Environment Programme (UNEP)**. The UN also oversees the **International Panel on Climate Change (IPCC)**, which reviews and assesses the most recent scientific information relating to climate change.

14. Global environment – Responses to global environmental protection (cont.)

International instruments have been central to the development of global environmental protection. There are two main types: '**soft law**', which includes international **declarations** that apply only moral or political pressure on governments, and '**hard law**', which includes international agreements like treaties and conventions that apply legally binding obligations on states.

The **International Court of Justice (ICJ)** has heard some environmental cases, such as the **nuclear test cases** of 1974 to 1975 involving Australia and New Zealand against France. However, some argue that a more powerful international forum is needed.

Some **intergovernmental organisations**, like the Organisation for Economic Co-operation and Development (OECD), monitor and advise on environmental issues. Numerous **non-government organisations (NGOs)** also work on environmental issues and help to research, educate, investigate and put pressure on governments to act. The **media** is also a powerful tool for informing debate about global environmental issues.

15. Global environment – Contemporary issues concerning global environmental protection

At the core of global environmental protection is the need to resolve conflict between the immediate need for and use of resources, and ecologically sustainable development. An effective resolution to global environment issues requires cooperation to resolve these conflicts, but **state sovereignty** ultimately allows each state to decide which obligations it will adopt according to its own best interests or economic and political will.

Australia's response to international initiatives for global environmental protection has been mixed, partially due to restrictions imposed by the Australian Constitution, but Australia has now ratified most of the major international agreements.

An **international, cohesive, coordinated, global and holistic approach** based on ESD principles is the most effective way to achieve global environmental protection. Such a large-scale international response is the ideal, but the barriers limiting a coordinated international response mean that what is attainable may be a different matter.

16. Family law – The nature of family law

The social and legal concepts of '**family**' have continued to evolve over time. The main **function of family** is the care and protection of its members. As society has changed, so too has the structure and recognition of families. Family law now extends protection to a much **broader range of domestic relationships** between partners and children than the confines of traditional marriage. It aims to ensure that the various parties to a family are provided adequate rights and protection and that justice can be achieved if a dispute arises.

Marriage is a major area of family law. Under the Australian Constitution, marriage is a **Commonwealth responsibility**. The *Marriage Act 1961* (Cth) defines marriage as 'the union of a man and a woman to the exclusion of all others, voluntarily entered into for life'. There are other requirements relating to **gender, marriageable age**, certain **prohibited relationships** and **notice of marriage**. Marriages that do not meet these requirements may be declared invalid.

The law also recognises relationships of **de facto or same-sex couples** who are 'living together on a genuine domestic basis'. It now imposes many of the same rights, responsibilities, entitlements and protections as for married couples.

17. Family law – The nature of family law (cont.)

Separation is another major area of family law, particularly regarding the **division of property** and **children** of the relationship. The legal principles applied are similar whether or not the couple was married.

For married couples to legally separate, however, they must **divorce**. In Australia, divorce is a **no-fault** approach: the only ground that needs to be shown is the **irretrievable breakdown** of the marriage. Couples must have been living '**separately and apart**' for a period of 12 months. The parties are only officially divorced once a '**decree absolute**' is issued.

Family law also defines the responsibilities of parents toward their **children**. The primary focus of family law is on the '**best interests of the child**', rather than on the rights of the parents. Examples of parental responsibilities include providing food, shelter and access to education, consenting to medical treatment, or protecting the child from harm and others from harm by the child.

Adoption is the process of transferring legal rights and responsibilities from the biological parents to the adoptive parents. The aim of adoption law is to ensure that the best and most appropriate parents are found for the child. The needs of the adults are secondary to the needs of the child.

18. Family law – Response to problems in family relationships

Under the Australian Constitution, different aspects of family law are shared between the Commonwealth and the states. The main Commonwealth statute governing family law is the *Family Law Act 1975* (Cth).

If a dispute between family members arises, '**family dispute resolution**' is encouraged. Where **adjudication** is necessary, particularly regarding issues of property division or the care of children, the main federal courts with jurisdiction to hear family law matters are the **Family Court** and the **Federal Magistrates' Court**.

These courts hear most matters relating to **division of property, parenting arrangements** and **divorce**. The Commonwealth and the states recently agreed to refer powers relating to separation of de facto couples (including same-sex de facto) to the Commonwealth, so that they can be dealt with by the federal courts with expertise in family law matters. Matters relating to adoption, however, still fall under the jurisdiction of the states.

- Recent changes to state and federal laws mean that legal **rights**, **responsibilities and entitlements** of **same-sex couples** are now largely the same as for de facto couples. However, the *Marriage Act 1961* (Cth) still excludes same-sex couples from the **right to marry** or, for overseas couples, have their marriage recognised.
- The law's focus has changed from parental rights to **parental responsibility**. The 'primary' consideration is for the child to have a relationship with both parents, before other 'additional' considerations apply. If **equal time** is not in the child's best interests, then 'substantial and significant time' may be applied.
- The parentage status of parents who attempt to have children through surrogacy arrangements poses unique issues for family law. While '**altruistic surrogacy**' is permissible in NSW, '**commercial surrogacy**' is prohibited. NSW has recently legislated to streamline adoption procedures in these cases.
- **Domestic violence** can be any act, verbal or physical, of a violent or abusive nature within a domestic relationship. NSW legislation provides for the use of ADVOs as an initial response to this type of violence. The NSW **Children's Court** also has jurisdiction to determine **care applications** for children deemed to be '**at risk**'.

© Cambridge University Press

Modern workplace laws have developed gradually over many centuries. Under the **feudal system** in England (800–1400 CE), most people worked on the land in farming, producing food and goods for their own use, with little choice but to work for their landlord in exchange for the right to live on the land.

Society was transformed during the **Industrial Revolution** in the 18th and 19th centuries, as production changed and large populations moved to factories and cities where they could find paid work. With the economy based on a *laissez-faire* approach, **working conditions** were severe and unregulated, with extremely long hours, and substandard, unsafe and unhealthy working environments. Employer–employee relationships were based on the legal principle of **freedom of contract**, where parties were free to negotiate the terms of their contract. This encouraged the exploitation of employees by wealthy and powerful employers.

Workers began to organise into groups called **trade unions** to increase their **bargaining power** against employers and to convince employers to improve wages and working conditions. At first, trade unions were frequently opposed or outlawed, but eventually governments and employers were forced to recognise the need to improve workers' rights.

© Cambridge University Press

There are two different types of workplace contracts: contracts of service and contracts for services. A **contract of service** is a contract of employment between an **employee** and **employer** that imposes specific rights and duties on both parties in a relationship of employment. A **contract for services** is an agreement by an independent **contractor** to do one or more specific tasks for an agreed fee, and does not give rise to a relationship of employment.

Contracts of employment contain both **express terms** (like a position description, hours, location or pay) and **implied terms** (like the duty of an employer to provide a safe working environment).

Industries may be governed by an **industrial award**, which sets out the minimum wages and working conditions for workers in the industry. **Enterprise agreements** can also be made by collective bargaining, which can negotiate specific terms and conditions suited to the workplace, higher than the applicable industrial award. There is also a set of minimum **National Employment Standards**, which set out certain 'safety net' terms below which a contract cannot be made.

© Cambridge University Press

'**Industrial relations**' refers to the relationship between employers, employees, the government and trade unions. Each of these groups is considered a stakeholder in the process of negotiating what is in the best interests of each in terms of awards, enterprise agreements and individual workplace arrangements.

The *Fair Work Act 2009* (Cth) is the main piece of legislation that governs Australian workplace law and industrial relations. Under the **Constitution**, the **federal parliament** had only limited power to legislate on workplace issues. However, after state governments recently **referred** most of their industrial relations powers to the Commonwealth, most workplaces, including federal government employees and private industry, are now covered by the national legislation.

State governments are still responsible for laws relating to state government employees, like state-employed teachers or police officers.

© Cambridge University Press

The industrial relations system emphasises **consensual** forms of **dispute resolution**, such as mediation. If disputes cannot be resolved, the matter will usually move to arbitration. There are specialist courts and tribunals established to deal with workplace disputes.

The main body responsible for settling workplace disputes is the federal body **Fair Work Australia** (now the Fair Work Commission), which can hear disputes arising out of workplace agreements or out of the provisions of the *Fair Work Act 2009* (Cth). If the matter remains unresolved, it may be taken to the **Federal Court** for determination. The **Fair Work Ombudsman** can also deal with some disputes about pay, entitlements or breaches of workplace laws. The state body responsible for determining state-related workplace disputes is the **NSW Industrial Relations Commission.**

Industry groups, trade unions or employer associations can also assist employees in resolving workplace disputes, and may provide information, negotiate or advocate on their behalf. Non-government organisations may also provide useful assistance.

© Cambridge University Press

- **Discrimination** is the unfavourable treatment of a person or group relative to how others are treated, and can be either **direct** or **indirect**. Workplace discrimination is prohibited in most cases by federal and state legislation, for example on the basis of sex, race, age, national origin or sexual orientation.
- **Workplace safety** is variable depending on the workplace and includes safe equipment, safe work systems and appropriate training procedures. The workplace safety regime is broad and includes **workers' compensation schemes**, **statutory duties** or **negligence** law, but compliance continues to be a challenge.
- **Termination** of employment can occur in different ways and is a common area of dispute. **Resignation** occurs when an employee voluntarily decides to terminate their employment, or **retirement** usually occurs when a person voluntarily leaves due to age or health issues. Employers may also **dismiss** an employee **with notice** if it is not harsh or unjust, or **without notice** in limited circumstances like serious misconduct.
- **Leave** is a fundamental right of employees and is protected by international treaties. Minimum leave rights are included in all modern awards and enterprise agreements and protected under both state and federal legislation.

© Cambridge University Press

25. World order – The nature of world order

'World order' refers to the activities and relationships between major world actors, including **states** and significant **non-state actors**. It relates to the **legal and political framework** in which they occur, how these actors influence global events, and the arrangements between them for **promoting global stability and resolving conflicts**.

Central to world order are the principles of:

- **state sovereignty** – a state's authority and independence from external control within its own territory
- **multilateralism** – cooperation between states for mutual benefit or protection from common threats.

State sovereignty can act as an impediment to close cooperation where states act only in their own political and economic interests. However, states today are increasingly **interdependent** – economically, politically and legally – and cooperation on many world order issues has become essential.

Conflicts, often influenced by **access to resources**, still occur today and can have serious global effects. They may be either **interstate** (between two or more states) or **intrastate** (within a state). Intrastate conflict is the main form of conflict today.

26. World order – Responses to world order

The **United Nations Charter** was signed in 1945 after the end of World War II. The UN was established as an international organisation open to membership of all '**peace-loving**' states willing to accept the obligations of the UN Charter. Through cooperation and **collective security**, it aimed to maintain international peace and security, develop friendly relations between states, cooperate in solving international problems and promote respect for human rights.

International instruments, which include **bilateral and multilateral treaties**, are today the main source of international law and the means to achieve international cooperation. Some of the most significant treaties for world order have been the UN Charter, the Geneva Conventions and the Nuclear Non-Proliferation Treaty.

International courts, such as the **International Court of Justice**, or regional courts, like the **European Court of Justice**, assist in resolving disputes between states. The newly established **International Criminal Court** can help to bring individuals responsible for mass atrocities to justice.

27. World order – Responses to world order (cont.)

Intergovernmental organisations (IGOs) are bodies established between states to assist cooperation in an area of mutual interest. Some of the most important include the UN, the European Union, the Commonwealth of States and the North Atlantic Treaty Organization.

Non-government organisations (NGOs) have multiplied in the past century and are increasingly important global actors. NGOs usually work in a specific area of interest, and may conduct important groundwork, investigative work, reporting, education or lobbying governments for change. Some important NGOs include the International Committee of the Red Cross, Amnesty International and Oxfam.

Australia continues to play an important role in global affairs, providing valuable contributions to international agreements and assisting in global peacekeeping missions. Under the Australian **Constitution**, the federal government has responsibility for Australia's external affairs.

28. World order – Contemporary issues

- '**Responsibility to protect**' is a new international doctrine to encourage the international community to prevent and react to grave humanitarian crises in other states. It commits states to assist one another in **preventing** serious crises, and allows the UN Security Council to **intervene** if they do occur.
- **Nuclear weapons** are one of the greatest threats to global security. The **Nuclear Non-Proliferation Treaty** signed in 1968, and numerous bilateral treaties between individual states, have hugely reduced the threat of nuclear weapons. However, some states have continued to pursue their own nuclear agenda.
- The UN intervention in **East Timor** is one example of successful global cooperation in resolving conflict. The UN provided essential resources and peacekeeping troops to assist East Timor on its path to independence. Australia also played a crucial role in resolving the conflict.
- **International humanitarian law** involves the regulation of armed conflict and the conduct of hostilities. The *Geneva Conventions*, originating in 1863, form the basis of this law. Today, the **International Criminal Court** is a permanent court with jurisdiction to prosecute war crimes.

Notes

Notes

Notes

Notes

Notes

Notes

Notes

Notes